THE INEVITABLE BATTLE

From the Bay of Pigs to Playa Girón

THE INEVITABLE BATTLE

From the Bay of Pigs to Playa Girón

JUAN CARLOS RODRÍGUEZ

Editorial Capitán San Luis
Havana, Cuba, 2009

Translation: Rose Ana Berbeo
Design: Eugenio Sagués Díaz
Cover design: Toni Gorton
Desktop publishing: Luisa María González Carballo
Original title in spanish: Girón, la batalla inevitable

© Juan Carlos Rodríguez, 2009
© About the present edition: Editorial Capitán San Luis, 2009

ISBN: 978-959-211-337-4

Editorial Capitán San Luis
Calle 38 no. 4717 entre 40 y 47, Playa, Ciudad de La Habana, Cuba.
Email: sanluis@mn.mn.co.cu

*To Fidel, architect of the victory at Playa Girón,
who made the Cuban Revolution an integral part of
the history of the Americas, and who, 45 years later,
continues to be its principal safeguard.*

*To José Ramón Fernández,
Hero of the Republic of Cuba,
who encouraged the writing of this book,
removed obstacles, and supported it
to the end.*

*One's capacity for being a hero is measured
by the respect paid to those who came before.*

JOSÉ MARTÍ

*1959 is a new opportunity offered to you by
life; it is as if we were providing a blank sheet of paper
upon which you will write, with your actions,
the course of your lives.*[1]

[1] Horoscope published in *Bohemia* magazine in December 1958, just one week
before the victory of the Revolution.

Contents

Preface

Bay of Pigs: The Inevitable Battle *is testimony exploring the origins, development, and climax of one stage of the U.S. effort to destroy the Cuban Revolution—a stage that ended in the defeat of Assault Brigade 2506 on the sands of Playa Girón.*

Based on thorough research, the book highlights previously unpublished and little-known aspects. Most striking, perhaps, is the magnitude of the CIA's plan, told in all its military, economic, and political detail: the preparation for and launching of an insurgent war in the mountains; the subversive destabilization of the country, including, in its worst form, terrorism; the creation of a psychological climate. The plan included the setting up of recruitment and training centers, and giving top-quality training to the counterrevolutionary forces for conventional clashes of a limited scope. It included details as sophisticated as providing mosquito hats for protection against irritating insect bites, and placing technical resources at the disposal of these forces. It included assembling and structuring these forces, and the ideological work done toward them. In all of this, U.S. military leaders and politicians played a manipulative and dominant role.

The Playa Girón disaster is one of the events that generated the greatest number of analyses, reports, articles, and books in the United States. It produced profound bitterness in political circles and in the agencies of the administration, which were forced to explain what had failed in the almost-always perfect U.S. military apparatus. With very few exceptions, it is hard to find an explanation today in U.S. literature for what happened on those beaches that is not loaded with preconceived notions and assumptions. Not enough air raids;

difficulties with supplies; perhaps the invasion should have been at Trinidad or somewhere else; and so on. Most U.S. analyses do not mention the obvious factor—which turned out to be decisive and is completely valid forty-five years later. That is, the unquestionable fact that the Cuban population was living through a revolutionary apex, and was in full agreement with Fidel's political ideas. And at the same time we were expecting an invasion, including a direct U.S. invasion. For the Cuban people it was a question of confronting, repelling, and defeating a foreign invasion. And there is one force more powerful than steam, electricity, or atomic energy: the determination of man.

The author extensively describes the work carried out by the Revolution to confront and defeat the enemy's plans. He highlights the actions against banditry, the penetration of the CIA's center in Havana, and of its counterrevolutionary organizations in Cuba and the United States. He details the fight against sabotage, which reduced to ashes some of the country's most important commercial centers and various factories. He tells how plots were foiled to assassinate the Commander in Chief, plots that reached a record number in the period leading up to Girón. He highlights Fidel's work of education and clarification in face of the plans to intimidate the people through psychological operations. He lays bare the entire arsenal of resources, methods, and techniques used in the subversive war of propaganda, including its main weapons: Radio Swan, disinformation and rumor campaigns lacking a shred of ethics and displaying unprecedented cynicism, exemplified by the "parental custody" operation aimed at violating the purest values of the Cuban family.

From the standpoint of strategy and tactics, the operation as it was conceived cannot be faulted. They chose an area to land that had an airstrip and infrastructure but was separated from solid ground by a swamp crossed by only three access roads—and it was over these three roads that the paratroopers were dropped. They came well-organized, well-armed, and with good support. But the cause they were defending was neither right nor just. That's why they did not fight with the ardor, courage, firmness, valor, and spirit of victory shown by the revolutionary forces.

This explains the extraordinary scope of the Cuban people's victory, which must have come as a great surprise to the United

States government, which expected a different outcome. The outcome can only be explained by the courage of a people that saw in the triumph of January, 1, 1959, the real possibility of controlling their own destiny. That is why they proudly wore the blue denim shirt and olive-green beret, and were willing to fight with the certainty that "No pasarán"—the enemy shall not pass.

The men who cheered Fidel Castro as he traveled through almost the entire island in victory in those early days of January 1959 were the same ones, now convinced of their cause, rifle in hand, who on April 17, 1961, were determined to resist and defeat the U.S. aggression. In that short period of time, the work of the Revolution, and especially Fidel's words, took deep root in the feelings of the Cuban people. They took as their own the concepts of national sovereignty, social justice, equality, and dignity. The Revolution had solved the problem of the land. It was taking sure and tangible steps to eliminate racial discrimination and discrimination against women. It was ensuring the great masses access to jobs, education, public health, sports, and culture. Its effort to eradicate every type of corruption was becoming rooted in popular consciousness.

In addition to the esthetic and political merits of the author's narration, his account of the changes that began to take place in 1959 in the Zapata Swamp—the future theater of operations—is a concrete demonstration of the economic and social achievements the Revolution attained in that short period.

"The Cuban people were experiencing intense moments of patriotism and revolutionary fervor. Support for the Revolution and for its leader Fidel Castro had risen to a level never seen before for any other leader in the hemisphere," the author said, and that would be the main cause of the mercenaries' defeat.

"Get up, the invasion is here and the Americans are attacking! The Americans are in the swamp!" Those were the voices that ran from house to house in the town of Jagüey Grande, the closest to the landing site. They thought they were Yankee Marines, and began gathering at militia headquarters, the municipal government, and Rebel Army headquarters, asking for weapons and instructions.

The millions of Cubans who were preparing to resist, like the inhabitants of Jagüey, those who directly faced the invasion and gave their lives or were victorious, and those who neutralized the genuinely pro-annexation internal counterrevolution knew why they

XIII

were doing what they did. In contrast to the situation of other nations, ours was not unarmed or disorganized when the attack occurred.

Moreover, not even the necessity of defending the Revolution against such an enormous danger led Fidel to make concessions. Being a militia member was not easy. You had to win that right.

I was at the camp of the School of Cadets in Managua, at the mouth of the La Magdalena River on the southern side of the Sierra Maestra. From there we climbed Turquino Peak. The order was to climb to the top twenty times, and when we had completed half the mission, I received the order to appear before the Commander in Chief here in Havana. He told me to find a place to set up a school where we would give classes to a large group of selected workers, union leaders, and students who would, in turn, lead the militia battalions. I should mention that by the time I had contact with the first class, its members—following Fidel's instructions—had climbed the Turquino five times.

A few weeks after this class was held at the Militia Leadership School in Matanzas, the militia battalions began to be organized. Fidel sent for me to lead the training of battalions in the capital. That was when he asked us what test we would give to the volunteers in order to measure their determination, firmness, and drive to become militia members.

I remember that Fidel proposed that they go and return in a single day from Managua to Santa Cruz del Norte. We looked for the map and measured the distance. It was more than one hundred kilometers there and back. A man would have to be in exceptional physical condition and well-trained to do it in one day. It was almost impossible. Finally, the route chosen was through Managua, taking the highway that leads to Batabanó, continuing to San Antonio de las Vegas, and from there to Ruda, then taking the Central Highway to San José and Cuatro Caminos and returning to Managua. That was the start of the famous sixty-two-kilometer test.

The first battalion to pass the test and the school was the 111th. Each militia member was given a small card that was marked at different points to prove the course had been followed. That night, there was a tremendous rainstorm. Fidel joined in the march at one point as it was raining. The next morning, nobody had returned at the estimated hour. We assumed that they were going to start arriving a little after sunrise, but the sun rose and nobody came. At about 10 a.m., the first ones arrived, and then at 11 and 12 and 1, little by little, they began to show up, exhausted. Later, the ones who didn't pass the test began arriving in any vehicle they had managed to find. At about 4 p.m., we assembled the leadership cadres and I was there analyzing and reviewing our performance in a classroom when the door opened and Fidel came in. I explained to him what was going on. He ordered me to have the battalion form ranks. We organized those who were there, some more cheerful than others. Fidel spoke to the militia members. To those who didn't pass the sixty-two-kilometer test, he said they had to do so in order to be part of the battalion; but he noted that it was voluntary. He grouped together the ones who had arrived first and told them they were a "light combat company," which was a unit with a different purpose and weapons, a shock force. In his final comments, he said to those who hadn't passed but who wanted to leave that they could do so if they liked; those who decided to stay would have to do the march again. Nobody left. "When do we do it?" they asked. There are always those who get carried away and that day there were some. "Let's do it today!" many of them said passionately. It was decided to do it two days later. And everybody passed.

It's important to say that throughout the course, the militia members did not live or sleep indoors; it was the hammock, under the trees. They cooked outdoors with firewood; used rudimentary latrines dug in the ground, and lived without running water or showers. The only light they had was the moon and stars. When it rained, they lived in water and mud. They did military exercises all day and guard duty at night. It wasn't easy. And each battalion had 995 troops.

When the two-week course was over, each militia member was given the green beret that became an emblem. The presentation of the beret was cause for celebration. The militias became a giant school of revolutionaries. From the anonymity of their ranks came the leadership cadres; they did not come from castes. They were industrial and agricultural workers, intellectual workers, and students.

The soldiers and officers of the Rebel Army and the National Revolutionary Police were also subjected to very hard tests. They were knowledgeable about guerrilla warfare and were just beginning to learn about the new weaponry and the art of conventional warfare when the landing happened. The tank crewmen were learning how *to load the guns on the road as they headed for the battlefield. The few pilots we had took off in planes that they themselves described as "Homeland or Death"; the planes were not in or out of commission, they simply flew because of the inventiveness of their mechanics and the courage of their aviators. The soldiers in the main columns were constantly mobilized.*

All of those tests and Fidel's concepts—which were not new, they were from the Sierra—contributed much to the high morale of the militias and the Revolutionary Armed Forces, above all among men from the city who had never led such a rough life, day and night; so difficult, out in the open, under the rain, the night dew. These factors were decisive to the defeat of the armed bands and the mercenaries at Girón and were important during the October [Missile] Crisis. It is a requirement that has been repeated many times, and is now a popular tradition.

I should not fail to mention that the same spirit, the same revolutionary passion that Fidel implanted in the Sierra in the early days of the struggle are the same spirit and passion in which our Revolutionary Armed Forces continue today to be educated, under the leadership of Raúl. They are examples of austerity, honor, selflessness, and patriotism.

It is a passion like the one demonstrated in recent times, above all, in face of a real, imminent danger like Girón, a passion that produced a victory that surprised the world and preserved the Revolution, because Fidel had unleashed the strength of the people. That is the only way we can explain the defeat of an undertaking as enormous and aggressive as the one described in this book.

JOSÉ RAMÓN FERNÁNDEZ

H-hour

The rubber raft moved away from the speedboat, and its occupants —five frogmen and their commanding officer, Grayston Lynch (Gray)— silently headed for the coast. Their faces were painted black, like the swimming trunks, tank tops and flippers they were wearing.

They rowed toward the far right, where a high seawall would hide them from any furtive glances, although intelligence reports had informed them that the zone was practically uninhabited, and that the few Cubans around were construction workers building a tourist facility. Because it was Sunday, they would be in their homes, far away.

Their information was accurate.

A short while later, after verifying the depth as approximately two fathoms, the five swimmers dived into the water. Grayston remained on the raft, lying down, with the barrel of his automatic rifle pointing over the prow.

The frogmen spaced themselves apart and began swimming toward the beach, keeping an eye on the ocean bottom for obstacles.

Spaces between obstacles on the ocean's floor were marked with buoys, as were the most likely points for beaching the LCU [landing craft utility] and LCVP [landing craft, vehicle, personnel] naval vessels that would lead the armored vehicles, heavy weapons and troops, marked with position lights and visible only from the sea, where the fleet was waiting.

It was H-Hour of D-Day. Assault Brigade 2506 was preparing to carry out an amphibious and air landing, with the mission of capturing a beachhead on an inhospitable strip of the mainland covered with lush vegetation and isolated from the rest of the island of Cuba by a vast swamp. There they would establish a base from which they would carry out ground and air operations against the government of Fidel Castro, and between D+3 and D+5 days, they would constitute a provisional government and ask Western nations, particularly in Latin America, for official recognition and military aid for its consolidation. To that end, the formation of the Cuban Revolutionary Council (CRC) had been announced to the world a month earlier.

The man who emerged as its president was José Miró Cardona; he was not tied to any previous governments, and had been prime minister in the revolutionary Cabinet of January 1959. A half dozen other prominent individuals from Cuban political life were in this executive body, considered to be the nucleus of a provisional government.

The entire operation was being run by the U.S. government, but steps had been taken so that it would appear to the world to be an action by Cuban exiles who opposed Fidel Castro. That was the basic condition.

Before approving the plan, President John F. Kennedy had insisted on there being no overt participation by the armed forces of the United States. His decision was determined by the relationship of forces between the East and West at the time. The U.S. president knew that if he authorized intervention by the Navy or Air Force, defeat could not be contemplated, and that would most likely mean a massive attack against Cuba. That could lead the United States into a war with the USSR or the loss of Berlin, where the other superpower could take the initiative; this didn't rule out actions by it in any other part of the world. In addition, and no less importantly, an attack on Cuba would mean facing fierce resistance from the Revolution's supporters, and according to some intelligence estimates, they would be the overwhelming majority.

Taking the administration's decision into account, Operation Pluto had been prepared and approved by its organizers to be carried out successfully without massive help from the United States. The landing was inspired by the most complex amphibious operation of the entire war in the Pacific, the assault on Okinawa, and the invasion of Inchon, Korea. There, the Americans had had to face coasts with no ports, where the disembarkation points were beaches. It was no coincidence, then, that the man heading up Brigade 2506 was U.S. Marine Corps Colonel Jack Hawkins.

However, unlike the beaches of Okinawa, infested with machine-gun nests, the sands of Bahía de Cochinos [Cochinos Bay] were practically defenseless. Fidel Castro knew about the invasion preparations. It is impossible to hide preparations for a conventional, frontal and massive attack from the enemy; history attests to that. But the revolutionary leadership did not know where, when or how the invasion would take place, and so it was forced to scatter its forces along the island's 5,746 kilometers of coastline. There was another stroke of luck for the brigade: a few days earlier, Commander Fidel Castro had ordered a militia battalion to be placed in the disembarkation area, but difficulties and shortcomings in military organization at the time prevented the order from being carried out, and in the early morning hours of D-Day, "Blue Beach" (Playa Girón), the main beachhead, was defended by only a half dozen charcoal workers who were part of the local militia.

The only military forces of any considerable size that were close to the landing area were stationed at the Australia Sugar M ill, 30 km from "Red Beach" (Playa Larga) and 74 km from Blue Beach.

The information about the absence of any considerable enemy forces on the coasts had been provided to the brigade's general staff during its send-off briefing. That is why the military chiefs standing on the decks of the ships that had brought them from the Atlantic Coast in Nicaragua to southern Cuba were observing, with unusual anxiety, the signal lights marking the distance between the obstacles and their landing points. They appeared before their eyes in a straight line, parallel to the coast, as bright as stars.

The invaders felt confident and secure; they were not arriving in fragile boats or poorly armed. The flotilla that had brought them was comprised of five merchant ships carrying thirty-six 18-foot aluminum boats with outboard motors; two LCIs (landing craft, infantry) vessels refitted as escorts and with heavy artillery; three LCU multi-purpose landing craft and four LCVP (landing craft, vehicle personnel), carrying five tanks and other equipment, that had been moved toward the shore by the U.S. Navy landing ship dock U.S.S. San Marcos. The maneuver it had carried out two hours earlier was excellently performed.

"It was the landing ship dock (LSD) *San Marcos* moving up the column of invasion ships rapidly, exactly on time. By the time the ships stopped, the LSD already had 'ballast down': its crew had pumped in water to flood the well deck where all the LCVPs with their tanks, trucks and other equipment were waiting. As soon as the water was up to the level of the sea outside, the LSD opened its rear doors and the seven small vessels steamed out, manned by the CIA instructors who had trained its Cuban crews in Vieques [Puerto Rico].

"An eighth craft appeared on Gray's radar, also according to plan. It was a landing craft mechanized (LCM) with an American Navy crew. It headed for the *Caribe*, picked up Silvio Pérez and his forty-three Brigade men and then moved along the next column of LCUs and LCVPs. At each landing craft, the CIA crew got off and the Cuban crew and vehicle drivers got on.

"[...] Again the Cubans were impressed by the precision of American seamanship and the LSD's further visible demonstration of close Navy support. Most of the men had seen the San Marcos only as an enormous blacked-out shadow, but its size and distinctive sounds told them that it was an American mother ship. [...] Captain Tirado of the *Río Escondido*, who had been in radio contact with the LSD, felt good when an American voice wished him good luck."[1]

After receiving the order from Grayston Lynch, who was on the coast, Cuban-born commander José Pérez San Román instructed his subordinates to jump onto the boats that would take them to Playa Girón. Excited, he commented, "Like in the war movies."

He was far from imagining how, two weeks later, he would be seated on the floor of a cell, analyzing the tactical details of the battle together with Fidel Castro.

The first men began climbing down the ropes. Over the next hours, they were followed by: five M-42 Walter tanks; eleven 2.5-ton trucks fitted with 12.7-mm machine guns; thirty 81-mm and thirty 106.70-mm mortars; eighteen 57-mm and four 75-mm recoilless cannons; 50 bazookas; 9 flamethrowers; forty-six .50-caliber and .30-caliber machine guns; 3,000 M-1 and Garand semi-automatic rifles, Browning automatics, M-1 and M-2 carbines and M-3 submachine guns; eight

---

[1] Peter Wyden: Bay of Pigs. The Untold Story. A Touchstone book. Simon & Schuster, New York, 1979, p. 216 [All notes are author's]

tons of powerful explosives; communications equipment, field telephones and mobile switchboards; 38,000 gallons of fuel for vehicles and 17,000 for airplanes; 150 tons of munitions; 24,000 pounds of food and sufficient potable water; 1.5 tons of white phosphorus; 700 air-land missiles; 500 fragmentation bombs; 300 gallons of aviation oil; 20 tons of .50-caliber munitions; 10 quarter-ton jeeps; one 5-ton tanker truck; one tractor; one tractor-crane, and 13 trailers.

In addition, each soldier carried a load consisting of enough ammunition for three days of combat.

For their part, the paratroopers carried a supplementary load.

"The men were well-supplied," General Maxwell said later while analyzing the reasons for their defeat. The plan's organizers, meeting the requirements of Colonel Hawkins, had ensured that there would be enough of every type of supply on the beachhead to cover the first three days prior to the start of the general landing.

Within six hours, at dawn of April 17, 1961, the paratroopers' battalion was dropped over points north of where the swamp ended, and the embankments that crossed it were cut off to prevent any troops from moving in. Immediately, they established contact with the troops that had landed by sea.

Four days earlier, on April 13, when the Brigade's men were on the boats and ready to leave, Colonel Jack Hawkins rushed to write a memorandum addressed to the CIA's Director for Plans, Richard Bissell, saying, "My observations the last few days have increased my confidence in the ability of this force to accomplish not only initial combat missions but also the ultimate objective of Castro's overthrow. [...]These officers are young, vigorous, intelligent and motivated with a fanatical urge to begin battle for which most of them have been preparing in the rugged conditions of training camps for almost a year. [...] The Brigade is well organized and is more heavily armed and better equipped in some respects than U.S. infantry units. The men have received intensive training in the use of their weapons, including more firing experience than U.S. troops would normally receive. [...] The Brigade now numbers 1,400; a truly formidable force. I have also carefully observed the Cuban Air Force. [...] Lt. Col. George Gaines (USAF)[2] informed me today that

---

[2] This name has not been declassified, but I infer that it is General George Gaines.

he considers the B-26 squadron equal to the best U.S. Air Force squadron. [...] This Cuban Air Force is motivated, strong, well trained, armed to the teeth, and ready." [3]

As he stood there on the Puerto Cabezas dock, raising his arm to wave good-bye to the men and wish them luck, Col. Hawkins may have had a vivid picture in his mind —like something out of a U.S. war film, where the Americans always emerge victorious— of the attack on Okinawa. Smiling with satisfaction, he imagined the moment when, on Cuban soil, he would pin on his general's star.

According to the operational plan, on D-2, two days before H-hour, three squadrons of B-26 light bombers would attack an equal number of Cuban airfields with the goal of destroying aircraft on the ground. In order to avoid any surprises, however, the escort ships *Blagar* and *Barbara J.* were heavily armed with .50-caliber machine guns, five .30-caliber machine guns and two 75-mm recoilless cannons. Each transport ship had been outfitted with .50-caliber machine guns in its prow, port and starboard.

Between 15:00 and 17:00 hours on the first day of the landing, two B-26 bombers would arrive at the occupied airport to provide air support. Because they would be operating from a beachhead, they would not need auxiliary tanks for additional fuel, and they would have tail gunners for combat against the enemy's interceptor fighters.

Beginning on D+1, they would carry out daily exploration flights along the route of Cienfuegos-Aguada de Pasajeros-Jagüey Grande (the towns closest to the landing area), with the goal of hounding and destroying military objectives.

With that same purpose, they also would fly along the following routes: Havana-Jagüey, Havana-Santa Clara-Cienfuegos, Cienfuegos-Manicaragua-Topes de Collantes, Havana-Pinar del Río and Holguín-Cienfuegos. These missions would have the objective of preventing military forces from moving to the landing zone.

To execute these missions, Brigade 2506's Tactical Air Force had sixteen B-26 bombers; not only were they adapted to the story that had been prepared beforehand (that it was a privately-financed effort

---

[3] Tomás Diez: La guerra encubierta. Document No. 18. Urgent cable sent by the project director to [name not declassified] from Puerto Cabezas on April 13, 1961, declassified by the U.S. government.

6

by exiles), but they were also used in Cuba. They had two-man crews, eliminating the tail gunner to create space for extra fuel and expand their radius of action. Their main base, Happy Valley, was located in Puerto Cabezas, Nicaragua, 580 miles or two hours and fifty minutes flying time from Girón.

They could remain over Cuban territory from an hour to an hour and a half. The air force also possessed 12 paramilitary transport planes, six C-46s and six C-54s, the military version of the Douglas DC-4. They did not have any identification — no serial numbers on their engines or manufacturer's markings, and were equipped with cutting-edge technology. These planes would be used to drop the paratroopers.

The air force had sixty-one Cuban-born pilots, along with navigators, radio operators and maintenance troops. A half dozen mechanics were on board in the landing crafts; they were to attend to the planes that would land in Playa Girón's airport.

Six advisors and two dozen other U.S. technicians had remained with the pilots throughout their months of training and others were rotated. The force's operations were under the command of U.S. Air Force Colonel Stanley W. Beerli.

A second attack against Cuban airfields scheduled for dawn on this day had been permanently called off the previous afternoon by President John F. Kennedy, with the decisive intervention of Secretary of State Dean Rusk.

Photos taken by U-2 spy planes showed that only nine Cuban planes had been destroyed or damaged during Saturday's attack (a T-33, two B-26's, a DC-3, an F-47, a C-47, an AT-6, a Catalina and a Beechcroft). The Revolutionary Air Force maintained a certain degree of operational ability.

Destroying the rest of the enemy's airplanes on the ground had been the objective of the planned second air attack, which did not happen.

In reality, an extremely difficult mission was presented. The operation's commanders knew that the first of the two attacks was the main one, and with Cuba's stepped-up protection of its airfields, there was no reason to believe that the Revolutionary Air Force could be destroyed in the second attack. At the most important airfield, San Antonio, two new batteries of anti-aircraft artillery and one of 37-mm cannons had been installed between Saturday the 15th and

Sunday the 16th. The planes were camouflaged and scattered apart; their pilots remained on maximum alert under their wings.

If the first attack had the benefit of the element of surprise and was not very effective, it would be overly presumptuous to assume that a second attack would be.

The U.S. Central Intelligence Agency's Directorate of Plans claimed that some 2,500 to 3,000 activists in Cuba were engaged in anti-government resistance. In order to train these individuals in the use of modern weapons and explosives, organize the reception of air-dropped war materiel, and advise them on the most important sabotage actions in support of the invasion, thirty-five of the CIA's best Cuban-born agents, trained in the jungles of Panama and Guatemala, had infiltrated the island between the latter half of February and April 1.

The organizations of the underground movement knew that the United States was preparing an invasion of Cuba, and that they had the means to support it. The bombings of the airports forty-eight hours earlier were, for them and the Revolution's leadership, an unmistakable signal of the invasion's imminence. A message was to be broadcast shortly afterward, via the transmitter located on Swan Island, as the signal for the long-planned internal uprising. The message would say:

Alert! Alert! Alert! Take a good look at the rainbow. The first will be out soon. Chico is at home. Visit him. The sky is blue. Place notice on the tree. The tree is green and brown. The letters arrived fine. The letters are white. The fish will not take long to rise. The fish is red.

Another was to be broadcast at 3:44 a.m. with an appeal to the Revolutionary Armed Forces.

Take strategic positions controlling the highways and railroad lines. Take prisoner or fire on those who refuse to obey orders... All planes should remain on the ground.

Ensure that no fidelista airplane takes off. Destroy their radios. Destroy their tails. Break their instruments. Puncture their fuel tanks.

It was the last effort to try to neutralize the FAR.

A force of 300 counterrevolutionaries was believed to remain in the Escambray Mountains, although their possibilities were limited given the recent offensive carried out by the government, actions from which these forces had not recovered. Other groups of

8

insurgents were active and awaiting the invasion in Oriente, Camagüey, Matanzas and Pinar del Río. According to reports, there were eighty men operating in the area around the town of Jagüey Grande, thirty kilometers from the landing area, and there were more in Cárdenas and Colón. In the coastal cities of Cienfuegos and Trinidad, friendly forces were expected to cooperate with the Brigade as soon as the opportunity presented itself. These forces were expected to destroy the main railroad bridges and highways in the areas around Havana, Matanzas, Jovellanos, Colón, Santa Clara and Cienfuegos to isolate the landing area.

With the goal of ensuring the population's collaboration and breaking them from revolutionary ideas, a psychological warfare campaign had been carried out via radio stations prepared specifically for that purpose. One of them had gone on the air eleven months earlier: Radio Swan (Radio Free Cuba), which came in clearly, powerfully, and with a triumphal tone. David Atlee Phillips, one of the CIA's best propaganda experts, was put in charge of the project. The station broadcast false information about legions of non-existent guerrilla troops and battles that never took place, urging people to carry out sabotage and spreading rumors of all kinds.

Despite these efforts to reduce popular support for the Revolution, the CIA's chiefs knew that Fidel Castro had broad support. On March 10, Sherman Kent, director of the CIA's Board of National Estimates, had sent a secret memorandum to CIA director Allen Dulles titled "Is Time on our Side in Cuba?" In it, he said that Castro seemed to be getting stronger every day, rather than weaker. And he repeated his warning about assuming there would be anti-government resistance in Cuba.

This was why Fidel Castro's assassination was the goal of one of the largest subversive actions to be carried out in Cuba. Beginning in March, several capsules of synthetic botulinum —an effective poison that could be used in any food and kill its victim twelve hours after being ingested— had been smuggled into Cuba via Mafia contacts. The conspirators were supposed to wait for the revolutionary leader to visit a restaurant in Havana that he frequented and feed him the poison. The capsules were in the hands of determined individuals, and the order to proceed had been given days earlier. They believed that if Fidel's death coincided with the landing, the possibilities of a response from the Armed Forces and the militia would be significantly less due to shock over the loss of the charismatic leader.

Once the beachhead was consolidated, the plan was to do a sweep of towns that had been taken over. For that purpose, sixty-two men were on the last ship in the convoy, the *Atlantic*, waiting for the right moment to land. These men had been carefully selected, above all for their reliability. They comprised Operation 40. Their mission: to arrest, interrogate and physically eliminate —at their discretion— the revolutionary government's top military and civilian leaders, and to occupy the archives of its intelligence agencies, public buildings, banks, and communications and industrial centers. They were also prepared to carry out missions in the enemy's rearguard. For that, they had been equipped with sophisticated weapons: M-3 submachine guns and pistols with silencers, white phosphorus charges with detonators, and miniature flamethrowers that fit comfortably in their hands and could throw a column of white phosphorus fifty feet, a top-secret weapon. The members of Operation 40 were supposed to place trustworthy civilian personnel in key posts in the cities to get them running. As soon as hostilities ceased, the members of this operation would become part of the civilian intelligence force to be created in Cuba.

According to the operation plan, on the night before the D-Day landing, a force of 168 men would land near Baracoa, on Cuba's eastern tip. The objective was to confuse the Cuban government, causing it to believe that this was the main site of the invasion, and forcing it to move considerable forces and resources to that region. Once ashore, this invading force would head for the U.S. naval base in Guantánamo.

In anticipation of the formation of a pro-U.S. provisional government according to plan, by D+5 day the State Department had obtained promises from at least six Latin American governments to immediately recognize the new government. The CRC's designation of a press representative several days earlier had been the final step taken to cover up U.S. participation in the invasion, even though it would not be the CRC's leaders —who were concentrated and isolated on the Opa Locka military base in Florida— who would keep the media informed of the course of the battle that was about to begin.

The CIA had hired Lem Jones Associates, a publicity agency in New York. By midnight of April 17, H-Hour, it was preparing to issue its first press release, to be published at dawn. It said:

CUBAN REVOLUTIONARY COUNCIL
Via: Lem Jones Associates, Inc.
280 Madison Avenue
New York, New York
FOR IMMEDIATE RELEASE
April 17, 1961

Bulletin No. 1

The following statement was issued this morning by Dr. Jose Miró Cardona, president of the Cuban Revolutionary Council:

Before dawn Cuban patriots in the cities and in the hills began the battle to liberate our homeland from the despotic rule of Fidel Castro and rid Cuba of international communism's cruel oppression.

In order to come to the aid of the provisional government once it had obtained U.S. recognition, a U.S. naval group would remain in the waters off the Cayman Islands, south of the landing zone. It consisted of the LPH-4 *Boxer* amphibious assault helicopter carrier, from which a battalion of the Marines' 2nd Infantry Division would be transported to the beachhead once the provisional government was recognized and aid approved; the CVS-0 *Essex* aircraft carrier, which held forty combat planes; the destroyers DD-507 *Conway* and DD-756 *Murray*, and the *USS Wailer* and *USS Cony*; the DD-701 *Eaton*, which had led the invasion flotilla from Puerto Cabezas to Bahía de Cochinos; and the *Shangri La* CVA aircraft carrier, with a seventy-plane capacity.

In the waters off Florida near Bimini Island, the command ship GCI *Northampton* was anchored with the command of the U.S. Second Fleet aboard. It had been the command post for the deployment of destroyers and submarines charged with protecting and escorting the invading fleet from Nicaragua to the landing zone.

Early on the morning of April 17, something unusual was taking place in a Pentagon building in Washington. Proof of that was the fact that almost all the lights were on. This was Quarters Eye, the headquarters for Operation Pluto. Its War Room was located on the first floor in a restricted area with its own teletype machine. Large, acetate-covered maps covered the walls. Almost all of them showed the island of Cuba, and more than a few showed a specific region: the Zapata Swamp. It was from that room that the fleet's movements were monitored and contact was maintained with the invading air force. At this time, the Air Operations Section was finalizing the details for dropping a battalion of paratroopers over the forward points of the beachhead.

For the duration of the battle, ongoing communication would be maintained with the War Room via Grayston Lynch, who would retransmit from the *Boxer* helicopter carrier.

On the second floor of Quarters Eye was the Propaganda Section, with the mission of creating messages for broadcasting on Radio Swan and press releases supposedly issued by the CRC. The CIA agent in charge of writing them, David A. Phillips, had drafts prepared for the most important moments: the start of the patriots' struggle; the conquest and consolidation of the beachhead; the uprising in the cities; the arrival of the CRC in Cuba and the course of battles; the constitution of the "provisional government"; the first countries to recognize the new government; recognition by the United States; approval of the aid requested by the provisional government and the dispatch of the first U.S. troops to the liberated zones.

The drafts were soon to end up in the wastebasket.

Those occupying command posts in Quarters Eye were: Richard Bissell, the CIA's Director for Plans and the brains behind the operation; Bissell's assistant, Tracy Barnes; General Charles P. Cabell, deputy director of the CIA; Howard Hunt and Frank Droller, in charge of the Cuban politicians and front operations; David A. Phillips, in charge of propaganda; Jack Esterline, director of the Cuba task force; and several dozen other officials from the CIA and the U.S. Army, Navy and Air Force. They were in constant contact with generals Shoup, Wheeler and Gray —the latter presiding over the Pentagon's supervising group— Admiral Arleigh Burke, Navy commander, and General Lyman Lemnitzer, Chairman of the Joint Chiefs of Staff.

Arthur Schlesinger, Jr., assistant to President Kennedy and the author of Pulitzer Prize-winning biographies on John and Robert Kennedy —and who showed little enthusiasm for the plan to invade Cuba— said days later, "Historically, we have played a dual role in Latin America. Sometimes we are the good neighbor, sometimes the bully of the Hemisphere. Therefore, Latin Americans have a love-hate relationship with the United States. They respond warmly to Dr. Jekyll. They detest and fear Mr. Hyde. It would be the same with us if we were Latin Americans. Dr. Jekyll promotes the long-term interests of the United States; Mr. Hyde leaves bitter, anti-Yankee sentiments wherever he goes. The Bay of Pigs was the work of Mr. Hyde."

In our opinion, Mr. Hyde has been far more present on our continent than Dr. Jekyll, and in Cuba's case, it has always been the former. This was true even before our independence wars, and very markedly since the end of the one led by José Martí, when, through Washington's opportunistic intervention, the desires of the Cuban people were frustrated with the imposition of the Platt Amendment. And throughout the 20th century, it has been Mr. Hyde who has been present in Cuba with repeated interventions —in the prow of a coal-fired ship, from an embassy or at a Quarters Eye command post.

Operation Pluto, the most powerful plan ever organized by the U.S. Central Intelligence Agency, in close collaboration with and the approval of the Joint Chiefs of Staff of the Armed Forces, was underway. An army of exiles with a navy and an air force had been recruited, trained and equipped; a political front had been organized; a theoretical justification for the annihilation of the Cuban Revolution had been found and set down in a "White Paper"; and above all, the hand of the United States in the affair had been hidden. Everything had been anticipated.

Thirteen months had passed since President Ike Eisenhower signed the memorandum ordering the organization of a military force of Cuban exiles. The battle was inevitable. It was completely consistent with U.S. policy in face of such a challenge.

Thirty-four kilometers west of Playa Girón, on the other disembarkation point, Playa Larga, agent William "Rip" Robertson —whom the Cubans nicknamed Crocodile because of his scaly skin— and a group of frogmen had just signaled the best courses for the ships to follow. He then placed a luminous yellow sign, where the invaders could read:

WELCOME LIBERATORS
COURTESY OF THE *BARBARA J.*

That euphemism was not unfounded. It was based on the successful preparation of the military operation, the enormous quantity of war materiel involved, and the limited objective of the mission. It is worth repeating. The only thing that Assault Brigade 2506 had to do was occupy a beachhead and hold it.

One no less important psychological factor boosted the morale of the combatants who found themselves at a culminating moment on that early morning; from their first days of training, they had repeated it over and over: "The Americans are with us, and the Americans can't lose!"

A tremendous year

Nineteen-sixty was a tremendous year in Cuba. In a demonstration of sovereignty and independence, and in response to the Soviet solidarity in the form of aid to reduce the impact of U.S. economic aggression against the island, the revolutionary government welcomed one of the USSR's highest-ranking leaders, Anastas Mikoyan. When he laid a wreath at the monument to José Martí in Havana's Central Park, a small group of overwrought Catholic students burst onto the scene, carrying their own wreath in a show of defiance. Revolutionaries attending the event did not stand by with arms crossed, and the situation turned into a public commotion. The placards carried by some two dozen Catholic students —most of them from private schools and universities— were an accurate reflection of the political struggle in those turbulent months: "Mikoyan, what about Hungary?" "Down with Russian imperialism!" "Cuban like the palm trees!" "Fidel, say the last word."

One month later, at 3:15 p.m. on Friday, May 4, a flash of light followed by a red mushroom cloud with multi-colored bands appeared in the sky over the docks on the west side of Havana Bay. A split second later, an explosion shook the capital. It was the French ship *La Coubre*, whose holds contained thousands of grenades and rounds of Belgian rifle ammunition purchased by Cuba.

Thirty minutes later, as hundreds of firefighters, soldiers, militia members and civilians came to the aid of the victims and tried to put out the fire, another, more powerful explosion blew the ship into the air. Its propellers landed on the sidewalk of the street running along the docks. The two explosions killed more than one hundred people and injured twice as many, permanently maiming many of them. The Cuban people had never suffered such a devastating act of terrorism. Its source continues to be a mystery, although all indications point northward. Three months earlier, in January, the CIA had created a task force with the goal of unleashing a war of subversion against the revolutionary government. And on that tremendous March 4, when *La Coubre* blew sky-high, Fidel Castro had not yet said the last word. But the time was drawing near.

After the overthrow of Fulgencio Batista's regime, the U.S. government stopped sending weapons and replacement parts for airplanes, naval units, tanks, and artillery. In fact, the blockade against the island began with military supplies. The revolutionary government began buying arms in other Western countries, and for good reason: "We were buying Western weapons, we didn't want to go to a socialist country, remembering that one much-used argument involved a ship with Czechoslovakian weapons headed for, or that arrived —I'm not sure if it arrived or not— in Guatemala under Arbenz."[1]

The United States learned of these efforts and immediately began trying to block them. Allen Dulles, CIA director, had his own reason for doing so, an ethically questionable one:

Cypher
Top Secret.
November 24, 1959.
From Washington to Foreign Office.

Following personal for the Secretary of State from the Ambassador:

I had to see Allen Dulles this morning on another matter and took the opportunity to discuss Cuba on a strictly personal basis. From his own point of view, he said that he greatly hoped that we would decide not to go ahead with the Hunter deal.[2] His main reason was that this might lead the Cubans to ask for Soviet or Soviet bloc

---

[1] Fidel Castro: Academic lecture "Girón 40 Years Later." Year 2001. Transcription by the Council of State.

[2] This refers to Cuba's attempt to buy combat aircraft in the United Kingdom.

arms. He had not cleared this with the State Department, but it was, of course, a fact that in the case of Guatemala, it was the shipment of Soviet arms that had brought the opposition elements together and created the occasion for what was done. The same might be true in the case of Cuba, and the presence, for instance, of MIGs would have a tremendous effect, not only in the United States but with other Latin American countries...[3]

England did not sell the Hunters to the Cuban revolutionary government. Belgium, after lengthy negotiations, agreed to deliver a batch of light weapons. These included FAL rifles, anti-tank and anti-personnel grenades and ammunition that Batista's government had purchased from a Belgian company in 1958, making a partial payment. Despite pressure from Washington, the Belgian businessmen were not willing to lose such a profitable deal. *La Coubre* was carrying the third shipment of these munitions to Cuba. The previous ones had been made without difficulty. Fielle, a Belgian company specializing in explosives, had dispatched the cargo to Brussels in rail cars under the watchful eyes of customs police, the gendarmerie, and a special government inspector, and, in the port of Antwerp, it was transferred to the ship. Just six hours before *La Coubre* set sail, an American photographer named Donald Lee Chapman boarded the ship. In the port of Havana, the morning shift of unloading took place without incident. In the afternoon, ten minutes after the second shift began working on deck near the entrance to hold no. 6, the explosion occurred. Interrogation of *La Coubre*'s crew members by Corvette Captain Rolando Díaz Aztaraín revealed that all loading for the previous shipments had been done from barges in Antwerp harbor, while this time the ordnance had been loaded directly from the docks. Three months after that tremendous March 4, Commander Raúl Castro, minister of the Revolutionary Armed Forces, traveled to Czechoslovakia and the USSR in search of weapons.

It would be an error to attribute Cuba's close relations with the Soviet Union to the United States, and even more simplistic to blame

---

[3] Declassified British government document, part of the dossier given to Cuba by the U.S. side for the academic conference "The Bay of Pigs, 40 Years After."

the United States for the proclamation of the socialist character of the Revolution. Che Guevara, with his customary frankness and incisiveness, explained the reasons for those decisions to French journalist Jean Daniel in July 1963, when the two met in Algiers during Commander Guevara's tour of Africa. Jean Daniel asked him:

Guevara, do you believe Cuba could have done anything other than proclaim, in April 1961, the solemn and complete adherence of this Caribbean republic to Marxism-Leninism?

Che responded: "If you are asking me that question because we are in Algeria, and because you want to know if a Revolution can be made by an underdeveloped nation, in spite of imperialism, without joining the camp of the communist nations, in this case, I would say: Perhaps; I don't know anything about that; it's possible. I doubt it a little bit, but I am not a judge.

"But if your intent is to create an idea about the Cuban experience, then I would answer categorically: No, no we could not do it any other way, and at a given moment, we did not want to do it any other way. Our commitment to the Eastern bloc is one half the product of pressure and the other half the result of a decision. In the situation in which we find ourselves, and which has allowed us to learn more than anybody else about imperialism, we have understood that for us, it was the only way to fight effectively."[4]

Thirteen days after the explosion, and one year before Fidel had said the last word, a definitive decision was made in the White House to overthrow the revolutionary government.

"On March 17 1960," U.S. President Dwight Eisenhower recounts in his memoirs, "I ordered the Central Intelligence Agency to begin to organize the training of Cuban exiles, mainly in Guatemala, against a possible future day when they might return to their homeland. One suggestion was that we begin to build up an anti-Castro force within Cuba itself. Some thought we should quarantine

---

[4] Ernesto Che Guevara: *Obras* (in progress). Editora Política, Havana, 2001, Volume VIII, p.402.

the island, arguing that if the Cuban economy declined sharply, Cubans themselves might overthrow Castro."[5]

The use of certain euphemisms in this excerpt does not hide its true essence from the reader. What is being talked about here is invasion (return to their homeland), internal subversion and destabilization (building up an anti-Castro force within Cuba), and a total naval and air blockade (quarantine the island).

And this language was being used in the White House just fifteen months after the triumph of the Cuban Revolution, long before the island's commitments to the Soviet Union and at a time when the laws being passed by Cuba's leaders had given a nationalist character to its political process, one of profound social justice, with broad, undeniable popular support.

During this short period of time Fidel Castro had nationalized the electric company, lowered electricity and telephone rates, and cut rents by fifty percent, measures that had great social impact. He created the National Institute of Savings and Housing, using it to undertake a vast program of housing construction throughout the country. He reduced the Presidential Palace budget from almost five million pesos a year to 1.2 million. He ensured the approval of funds by the Council of Ministers for the immediate construction of 5,000 classrooms, mostly in the countryside, and 200 schools. He ordered price cuts of twenty-five to thirty-five percent for general education textbooks, created the Ciudad Universitaria de Oriente educational complex, reduced prices of medicines by fifteen to twenty percent, and created the Department of Reforestation, with the goal of preserving, protecting and increasing the nation's forest resources.

Fidel Castro organized a project for rehabilitating minors and launched a campaign to wipe out vice. The U.S. mafia, which controlled casinos and other types of dirty business, was expelled from Cuba. "A moment of decency" was how Ernest Hemingway described the Revolution at that time. In a July 17 session, the revolutionary government approved funds needed for developing a child welfare program. Tens of thousands of neglected children —shoeshine boys,

---

[5] Dwight D. Eisenhower: *The White House Years*. Doubleday and Co., New. York, 1966, p. 401.

street vendors, and beggars— began leaving the streets and enrolling in school. Begging, prostitution, gambling, and drugs, all plagues on society, suddenly stopped spiraling upward that first year of the Revolution, and analysts believed they would be totally eradicated in a matter of time, and a very short one, to be sure.

Fidel Castro was chiefly responsible for instituting the Agrarian Reform Law, vindicating the long-frustrated desire for land. More than 100,000 land titles bearing his signature were distributed to peasants. Tenant farming, sharecropping, squatting, and other inhumane forms of exploiting the land disappeared. Due to a lack of resources for compensating landowners —including major American monopolies— bonds were issued to indemnify over time those adversely affected.

During his constant travels throughout the country, Fidel ordered the construction of roads and highways in isolated areas; oversaw initial steps toward establishing rural medical services; advocated national tourism; founded the National Printing Office, National Institute of Agrarian Reform, Cuban Institute of Cinematographic Arts and Industry and National Institute of the Tourism Industry, and banned monuments, portraits in public offices or plaques honoring prominent living Cubans.

Months before President Eisenhower issued his order, *Bohemia*, the largest-circulating magazine in Cuba, had conducted its own survey. The results left no doubt about the charismatic leader's popularity; they showed that 90.2 percent of the island's population supported the government's work.

However, the CIA did not begin taking action against Cuba on March 17. Eisenhower himself was explicit about that: "Within a matter of weeks after Castro entered Havana, we in the administration informally began to examine measures that might be effective in restraining Castro."[6]

On January 14, 1960, a meeting of the National Security Council reviewed the evolution of U.S.-Cuba relations since January 1959. Roy Rubottom, assistant secretary for inter-American affairs, summed it up as follows:

"...the period from January to March might be characterized as the honeymoon period of the Castro government. In April a

---

[6] Dwight D. Eisenhower: Ob. cit., p. 404.

downward trend in U.S.-Cuban relations had been evident... In June we had reached the decision that it was not possible to achieve our objectives with Castro in power and had agreed to undertake the program referred to by Mr. Merchant. In July and August we had been busy drawing up a program to replace Castro. However some U.S. companies reported to us during this time that they were making some progress in negotiations, a factor that caused us to slow the implementation of our program. The hope expressed by these companies did not materialize. October was a period of clarification...[7] On October 31, in agreement with CIA, the Department had recommended to the President approval of a program along the lines referred to by Mr. Merchant. The approved program authorized us to support elements in Cuba opposed to the Castro government while making Castro's downfall seem to be the result of his own mistakes." [8]

The real issue was that any change to the U.S. system of domination in Latin America was seen as part of communism's advance in the Western Hemisphere. That perception drew a veil over their eyes, preventing them from understanding and accepting the undeniable reality that the Revolution had the support of the immense majority of the population. And this was a decisive factor. The most powerful country in the world could not allow the slightest hint of sovereignty or self-determination in what it considered its backyard. The Cuban Revolution constituted a radical program of national sovereignty and —as if that weren't enough— provided an example of an alternative model of social justice and development for Latin American nations. Cuba was no longer just a place for good times: rumba, mulattas, prostitution, gambling, pornography, and drugs. And for after dinner: coffee and cigars. From now on, it would be the main dish. People who dreamed of social justice came to drink at the fountain of eternal

[7] Coincidentally, that same month in Cuba a counterrevolutionary conspiracy led by Commander Hubert Matos, military chief of Camagüey, was aborted. Matos had close ties with wealthy ranchers in the region opposed to the Revolution's radical course, particularly the agrarian reform.
[8] Piero Gleijeses: *Ships in the Night: The CIA, the White House and the Bay of Pigs*. Journal of Latin American Studies, Volume 17, Part I, Cambridge University Press, 1995, p. 3.

emancipation, and headed home full of dreams and plans for rebellion. The Revolution had become a sounding board. Previously, it was as if Latin America didn't exist for the rest of the world. Now, Fidel Castro became the forbidden fruit. Carthage had to be destroyed. The battle that had commenced with President Eisenhower's signature that tremendous year was an inevitable one.

Rubottom's summary didn't mention the economic measures the Eisenhower administration implemented against Cuba as soon as the Revolution triumphed. Beginning in mid-1959, the U.S. government began carrying out a veritable economic war clearly aimed at making Cuba's domestic situation intolerable: to not make "a balance of payments loan to Castro... prohibition against public and private loans, discriminatory trade treatment, discouragement of investment and impeding of financial transactions...."[9] Further considerations of this official, I.D. Mallory, in April 1960 are on page 885 of the same State Department document: "The only foreseeable means of alienating internal support is through disenchantment and disaffection based on economic dissatisfaction and hardship... Every possible means should be undertaken promptly to weaken the economic life of Cuba... A line of action that makes the greatest inroads in denying money and supplies to Cuba, to decrease monetary and real wages, to bring about hunger, desperation and the overthrow of the government." These measures included public steps such as reducing and eventually canceling the sugar quota, cutting off oil supplies, and canceling the 1902 and 1934 trade agreements. In addition, sugar mills were strafed, canefields were burned, and innumerable acts of sabotage and covert warfare were carried out against vital industries. These measures, approved along with the program of subversion that culminated in Girón, laid the bases for the economic warfare that would be waged against Cuba from then on.[10]

[9] July 1, 1959, memorandum from the director of the State Department's Office of Regional Economic Affairs. See *Foreign Relations of United States*. Vol. VI, pp. 545-551.

[10] Andrés Zaldívar Diéguez: *La implementación de la guerra económica de Estados Unidos contra Cuba*. Cuban State Security Center for Historic Studies. Havana, March 2001.

The March 17 memorandum from President Eisenhower featured a premise adopted by both his and Kennedy's administrations: the hand of the United States would remain hidden. "There will be no palefaces on the beach," said Richard Bissell, the brains of the operation. The image for the world would be one of an affair among Cubans, an effort by exiles, financed by Cubans and Americans who had been adversely affected by revolutionary,laws. The matter would remain absolutely secret. At some point, there might be speculation that the source of aggression was at the highest levels of the U.S. government, but it would be impossible to prove. It was a fashionable theory at the time: "plausible deniability."

Immediately, the CIA made it a top priority to comply with the presidential order. Richard Bissell, deputy director for plans —the agency's number-two man— personally oversaw its strategy for overthrowing the Cuban government. After the expected outcome, everyone would see him as the logical successor to Allen Dulles, CIA director at the time.

Richard Mervin Bissell, from a well-off New England family, was a shy man. He graduated from Yale University and then worked as a professor there in the 1930s. In World War II, he was appointed executive director of Maritime Supplies, which provided for American military forces and their allies around the world. In 1946, he began working as a professor of economics at the Massachusetts Institute of Technology.

At the start of the Cold War he was summoned to Washington, and in April 1948 began working on the Marshall Plan. In 1953, Allen Dulles, a personal friend of Bissell's who had been recently appointed CIA director, invited him to join the agency. Five years later, he appointed Bissell deputy director for plans. Bissell oversaw plans for the first spy satellite, dubbed Corona, and came to be considered a pioneer of aerial reconnaissance, which contributed significantly to improving technical intelligence during the Cold War. Ironically, his fame does not stem from any of his successes. His name will forever be associated with his biggest failure: the Bay of Pigs invasion.

Months after the disaster, a CIA summary attributed much of the responsibility for the defeat to Bissell, and on February 28, 1962, he was forced to resign. Two months later, on the first anniversary of the failed invasion, President Kennedy awarded him the National Security Medal.

The covert action program approved by Bissell was prepared under his supervision by the WH/4 Task Force (Branch No. 4 of the Western Hemisphere Division). This unit had been created two months earlier, on January 18, and placed under the command of Jack Esterline, a former CIA station chief in Caracas, Venezuela.

Esterline was directly responsible for developing the plan. He would be one of Bissell's three key subordinates in the Cuban project. The other would be Colonel Jack Hawkins, who took over military planning after it was decided months later to invade a point on the island with a conventional strike force. The third was Colonel Stanley Beerli, in charge of air operations. This preference for the military aspect was no coincidence; it was present in the operation from beginning to end. What would be most decisive in settling the Cuban question was not the political aspect, but military aggression. Cuban exile leaders, in the hands of Howard Hunt and Frank Bender, would be used to make noise.

Only one non-military plan was important to Bissell: a propaganda program for psychologically softening up the Cuban people.

The WH/4 quickly grew: "In April the Director of Central Intelligence told a meeting of WH/4 personnel that he would recall people from anywhere in the world if they were needed on the project. From January 1960, when it had 40 people, the branch expanded to 588 by April 1961, becoming one of the largest branches in Clandestine Services, larger than some divisions. Its Table of Organization did not include the large number or air operations personnel who worked on the project and who were administered by their own unit, the Development Projects Division (DPD), nor did include the many people engaged in support activities or in services of common concerns, who, though not assigned to the project, nevertheless devoted many hours to it."[11]

The plan approved by the president had four basic aspects:

a) The formation of a unified political anti-Castro force outside of Cuba that could be used to counter him and to hide the participation of the United States.

[11] Central Intelligence Agency: *Inspector General's Survey of the Cuban Operation, October 1961*. Peter Kornbluh (ed.): *Bay of Pigs Declassified. The Secret CIA Report on the Invasion of Cuba*. The New Press, New York, 1998, p. 27.

b) Undermining the foundations of popular support for Castro through a vast program of gray propaganda. Measures included setting up a shortwave radio station with programming directed at Cuba.

c) The formation of an underground resistance force within Cuba for the job of subversion and the promotion of insurgency in the country's mountains.

d) The creation of a paramilitary force outside of Cuba. The intent was to train it to infiltrate the island and to organize and train resistance forces after active centers of resistance had been consolidated in mountain regions, and after underground movements had been consolidated in the cities.

The essence of this plan was to combine psychological warfare and internal subversion, infiltrations and an abundant supply of weapons, explosives, and communications equipment. These actions were backed by a relentless economic and diplomatic pressure aimed at isolating Cuba and leading to an imposition of sanctions by the Organization of American States (OAS). Additionally, it was not excluded that the OAS might take action on the grounds of the Caracas Resolution or by other means.

"The President said that he knows of no better plan for dealing with this situation", read the notes from the March 17 meeting. "The great problem is leakage and breach of security. Everyone must be prepared to swear that he has not heard of it."[12]

The CIA went to work.

The command post for the plan was set up with the best resources available at the time in a Washington building known as Quarters Eye. The building's sophisticated features included an electronic map room and a communications room. The maps, on a scale of one to 50,000, were recent (1957) and based on high-altitude aerial photos taken by the U.S. Navy. These were continually updated with new shots taken by U-2 spy planes and reports by agents in Cuba. The map room was surrounded by glass walls for better

[12] Piero Gleijeses: Ob. cit., p. 4.

lighting. Red lights indicated insurgent areas in the mountains and large-scale actions of sabotage and terror in the cities. Each point of light signified a column of insurgents, a destroyed economic target, the infiltration of a team, the place from which an agent was broadcasting or the site for air drops of weapons and explosives.

In the communications room, numerous telephones and radio and teletype equipment for encrypted messages linked Quarters Eye with security houses assigned to the plan and training bases in Guatemala, Panama and Florida. In other offices, propaganda plans were drawn up for psychologically softening up the Cuban people through radio programs, the press, television, film, and literature. This was the source of pamphlets dropped over the island, and where flights were planned for air-dropping supplies for insurgent groups and fire-bombing sugar cane fields.

Based on recommendations by CIA Cuba experts and State Department officials, a group of men was chosen to form the unified political front outside of Cuba; they were supposed to represent the broadest political spectrum of the anti-Castro opposition. Those involved in making this selection included William D. Pawley, former ambassador to Brazil and a friend of dictator Fulgencio Batista; William Wieland, director of the State Department's Office of Caribbean and Mexican Affairs; Roy Rubottom, assistant secretary of state for inter-American affairs, and James Noel, CIA station chief in Havana.

Five well-known individuals were chosen.

Manuel Antonio de Varona Loredo, fifty-two, was a traditional politician who had held the posts of Senate president and prime minister in the administration of former president Carlos Prío Socarrás. Varona was one of the few political leaders who remained in Cuba under the Batista dictatorship, moving in circles of the friendly opposition. As the repression became worse, his presence in Cuba helped him rise in his party's ranks.

He opposed Fidel Castro's insurrectional line, saying the solution to the Cuban problem would be provided by the military with a traditional-style coup d'état. Everything he did was aimed at becoming president himself. Varona was a rightist with aristocratic ideas and behavior, something reflected in his personal life. He owned an insurance company with a subsidiary in Puerto Rico, and had procured an extremely advantageous marriage. In the 1950s, while holding high-ranking posts in the Prío government, Varona became linked with the U.S. mafia bosses who controlled Havana's casinos. These ties ensured the growth of his fortune and created a relationship of dependency that would come due after January 1, 1959. It would be Varona, contacted by the mafia, who would have several capsules of the deadly poison synthetic botulinum sent to Cuba from Miami, with the goal of assassinating Fidel Castro before the invaders landed.

After the revolutionary triumph, Varona remained in Cuba as part of the legal opposition. He opposed laws that were passed to benefit the people and set himself up as a defender of affected property owners. On June 12, 1959, he appeared on televison, lashing out at the Agrarian Reform Law and saying it conflicted with the still-valid 1940 Constitution. He also criticized the National Institute for Agrarian Reform (INRA), "for having more power than the president of the republic and being controlled by only two people..." One of those people was Fidel Castro. Varona went even further that night and said, "I think that after five months and days of being in power, the revolutionary government should set a date for the end of its mandate."[13]

His corrupt past —like that of most individuals operating in Cuban politics in pre-revolutionary Cuba— and his resistance to the Revolution discredited him completely in Cuba, but won him supporters in the U.S. State Department and CIA. With the help of CIA agents stationed as diplomats in Havana, he created the Movimiento Rescate (Rescue Movement), which used clandestine methods and had a small but loyal membership. That is when he began conspiring. Soon afterward, the Agency asked him to leave Cuba and go to the United States. Varona recalled, "An embassy official arranged to meet me and proposed that I leave the country to lead an anti-Castro movement..."[14]

[13] Antonio Núñez Jiménez: En marcha con Fidel. Editorial Letras Cubanas, Havana. 1982, p. 190.
[14] Testimony of Antonio de Varona in the documentary "Girón, ¿derrota o traición?" broadcast on a Florida television station.

Another individual, selected for the group for very different reasons, was Manuel Artime Buesa, a twenty-eight-year-old former Rebel Army officer with a solid religious background. Artime was the nephew of a poet who was very popular at the time, José Ángel Buesa. Perhaps Buesa's pretentious verses, written in an outdated modernist style —although with undeniable formal values— contributed to the somewhat sickly sweet oratorical abilities of the accidental political leader.

In 1957, Artime joined the Party of Radical Liberation, which had Christian-Democratic leanings. He had a degree in medicine and hopes of becoming a psychiatrist when he decided to join the Rebel Army, in December 1958. In January 1959, he was assigned to be chief of Zone O-22, in the Manzanillo area, working under then-minister of agriculture Commander Humberto Sorí Marín and his agriculture director, Rogelio González Corzo. While there, Artime promoted the work of the so-called *Comandos Rurales* (Rural Commandos), a sort of Peace Corps comprised of young people, mostly from the Catholic University Association of Havana. They lived in pairs in the homes of local peasants, helping them with farm work and implanting religious faith. On the Sierra ranch, an estate spanning 2,350 *caballerias* (more than 120 square miles), they tested a type of agrarian reform that avoided touching the interests of large landowners, especially Americans. They did not know that a group of Fidel Castro's close collaborators were secretly preparing a proposal for an agrarian reform law that would soon be presented to the Council of Ministers.

After the defeat of a conspiracy in Camagüey led by Commander Hubert Matos, a close associate of Artime's, the Rural Commandos were dissolved. In the following months, more than a few of their members joined CIA-sponsored counterrevolutionary organizations. Rogelio González Corzo became the CIA's top agent in Cuba.

With help from the U.S. embassy, Manuel Artime secretly left Cuba for the United States. Evidently, his work in Oriente province had not been unconnected with CIA efforts to interfere with the revolutionary government's work. Once in the United States, Artime organized the Movement of Revolutionary Recovery (MRR), announcing its platform in Costa Rica. In its early days, the movement was made up of former members of the July 26th Movement, Rebel Army, and National Revolutionary Police. These were men who had fought against the dictator Fulgencio Batista, but some of whom had political ambitions and felt excluded; others were opportunists who had joined the revolutionary tide when it was evident Fidel Castro's strategy would be victorious. More than a few wanted revolution, but not too much, and all of them, to one degree or another, were extremely dogmatic anti-communists.

Within a few months, the MRR, under the control of the Agency that had sponsored its creation, organized followers all over the country. It received abundant supplies of military equipment and became the most belligerent counterrevolutionary and terrorist organization in the country. As with other such groups, however, it never posed a serious threat to the Revolution.

In the latter half of 1959, the CIA began supplying the MRR by air and sea. This included hiding M-1 rifles, grenades, ammunition, and explosives in automobiles transported by a ferry that traveled between Cayo Hueso and Havana. Weapons were also sent from different coastal points and air-dropped over the farms of members and collaborators.

MRR members carried out acts of sabotage, cultivated and maintained different rebel groups in the mountains, smuggled a dozen of its men out of the country to CIA training camps in Guatemala and Panama, and repeatedly plotted to assassinate the Revolution's top leaders.

Their actions had the support of the reactionary, Spanish-born clergy whose schools many of them had attended as youngsters. The MRR used methods of underground struggle taken from the fight against the Batista dictatorship; their members were organized in small, compartmentalized cells in a pyramid structure. Their men made contact in public places and their liaisons used public transport to move around.

José Ignacio Rasco, a history professor who represented the Christian Democratic Movement (MDC), was another "acceptable" politician for the project. Rasco had been a leader of the Catholic Youth, and when the Revolution triumphed, he supported the revolutionary government for the first few weeks, just like almost all the traditional politicians. Rasco was no different from them, with the exception that his hostility toward the government of Fidel Castro had the special hallmark of pitting the Catholic Church against the Revolution. He promoted the activities of the country's Catholic organizations: the Catholic Student Youth (JCE), Catholic University Association (ACU), and Young Catholic Workers (JOC). He was one of the main organizers of a Catholic congress held in late 1959 featuring a program, presentations, and conclusions that were openly provocative. He was attributed with creating a slogan during that event, "¡Caridad!" (Charity!) in opposition to the popular cry of "¡Paredon!" (To the firing squad!) After the congress, carrying out one of its decisions, Rasco set up and led the Christian Democratic Movement. He focused on organizational work, especially among the exclusive private Catholic schools in the capital, with support from the Church hierarchy. In a propaganda stunt, Rasco was given asylum in April 1960, at a time when he was carrying out public political work and faced no persecution whatsoever. The CIA, which maintained contact with him through the U.S. Embassy, had asked him to leave the country and join the Democratic Revolutionary Front (FRD).

Evidently, the Cuba program specialists thought that if they could convince religious people that Fidel Castro was the Antichrist, the Revolution would lose its base of popular support. This would turn out to be another CIA blunder.

At the triumph of the Revolution, Cuba's clergy was made up mostly of openly reactionary Spaniards with Falangist political ideas. Universities, schools, and other religious educational institutions were concentrated in the capital's most exclusive neighborhoods. One was Santo Tomás de Villanueva Catholic University, run by Augustine priests from the United States. A clash with the Revolution was not long in coming. During the first two years, a series of sermons expounded on the theme "Rome or Moscow," which in effect boiled down to "Revolution or counterrevolution." These sermons were published by hostile newspapers, especially *El Diario de la Marina*, with commentaries by its editor, José Ignacio Rivero, in his column "Vulcan and Lightning Bolts."

This counterrevolutionary preaching found a hearing among a good number of students at these schools, almost all of them from wealthy families. One former student at Belén School—the same one Fidel Castro attended in his youth—recalled an activity attended by a prelate who was one of the most energetic and active antigovernment opponents, Bishop Eduardo Boza Masvidal: "Those summoned to attend that event included the Lestonac, El Verbo Encarnado, La Salle, Los Maristas, Nuestra Señora del Rosario, and Nuestra Señora de los Ángeles Catholic schools. I remember how the nuns who stood out the most were from Nuestra Señora de los Ángeles and Nuestra Señora del Rosario; they jumped up and down exclaiming 'Long live Boza! Down with Fidel!' Afterwards, the students began imitating them. When the bishop arrived, they greeted him with applause and shouts of 'Long live Boza!' 'Boza yes, communism no,' and 'Boza, yeah, give it good to the reds.' During his speech, the bishop said we should carry out Christ's revolution, which is the only true one, because it is a revolution of love, of equality for all men. I remember very well that he said the rich had abused the poor a lot, that communism had emerged because of their selfishness, and that we had to help the poor. Most of the students who were present, children of the rich, didn't like that last comment very much and applauded very little at the end."

Members of the clergy who appreciated the humane work of the Revolution created a patriotic religious organization called *Con la Cruz y con la Patria* (With Cross and Country). These rank-and-file priests and laypeople believed they could be Catholics and revolutionaries, and they tried to get the Church to end its alliances with the interests the Revolution was fighting against. This attitude resulted in their being repressed and punished by the Church hierarchy. The same thing happened with students in private Catholic schools who identified with the revolutionary process; they were expelled from their schools.

The government led by Fidel Castro did not allow itself to be provoked. It dealt with the religious issue wisely, showing strict respect for the work carried out by churches and their congregations, something in absolute harmony with Fidel's own political views. On more than one occasion, he referred to the principles shared by Christianity and the social justice process under way in the country.

Hundreds of thousands of believers remained loyal to the Revolution, and Pope John XXIII did not excommunicate Fidel Castro, unlike what Pius XII had done with Juan Domingo Perón.

Another of the counterrevolutionary leaders selected for the Front was Doctor Aureliano Sánchez Arango, a traditional politician and a leader of the Triple A Party. Sánchez Arango had been secretary of state in the Carlos Prío government. He was the last politician of those selected for the Front to leave Cuba, in mid-1960. At that time, the Triple A became an underground organization. It carried out terrorist actions, such as arson attacks on economic centers like clothing stores, sabotaging electricity towers, and scattering tacks during carnival time. They also sold bonds. In late 1960, several men from this organization began spying on the newly appointed Soviet ambassador, with the intention of assassinating him.

The Triple A was infiltrated by Cuban state security agents from the very start. Before the invasion, they had an agent in its national leadership, facilitating the arrest of its top leaders in several operations carried out from March 19 to March 29, 1961, just two weeks before D-Day.

Montecristi was the name of another of the organizations contacted by the CIA. Its leader was Justo Carrillo. It is believed to have had no more than 100 members, all of them from the middle class, including Carrillo's family. Publicly, Carrillo tried to portray himself as the leader of a large organization. Under the dictatorship, Montecristi channeled all of its energy into collecting money. When the Revolution triumphed, the group's top leader was appointed president of the National Bank of Agricultural and Industrial Promotion (BANFAIC). Once in that post, he made every effort to place his friends in government jobs and showed few scruples in managing the funds under his control. After a number of clashes with the revolutionary leadership, he left for the United States.

Other counterrevolutionary organizations later merged into the FRD. Three that later acquired a degree of notoriety were the November 30th Movement (M-30-11), the Student Revolutionary Directorate (DRE), and the People's Revolutionary Movement (MRP). The MRP eventually became one of the worst terrorist organizations operating underground in Cuba. It was created in mid-1960 by engineer Manuel Ray Rivero, who had been a national leader of the July 26th Movement's Civic Resistance Movement during the dictatorship. After the triumph of the Revolution, he was appointed minister of public works, and as such began conspiring against the revolutionary direction the process was taking. His background was very attractive to the CIA. He was not tied to the Batista regime and he had initially given support to the Revolution. His social-democratic political leanings inevitably led to a clash with the Revolution. Knowledgeable about the strict rules for conspiracy and operating underground, he was able to build a tightly knit organization. He also enjoyed prestige, because he held that the real "leaders" of the opposition to Fidel Castro should remain in Cuba and assume the risks involved in such a difficult struggle. In every respect, it seemed like the CIA had found a man capable of matching Fidel Castro's demonstrated qualities, although more than a few at the Agency didn't like him, seeing him as the representative of a dangerous political line: "*fidelismo* without Fidel." But Ray's closest collaborators noticed that he began acting strangely. He made every move with extreme caution, seeking a degree of security that seemed suspiciously ridiculous, if not a sign of cowardice.

"He was hard to locate, and for some in the organization it began to be evident that after getting things moving by using the prestige of his name, he had decided to keep himself safe. In November 1960, just five months after the MRP's creation, he left the country without notifying the movement's leadership and with the help of CIA agents in Havana. He left a message saying he was going to the United States to establish contacts, but none of us who worked for him believed him."[15] Nevertheless, he appointed himself MRP delegate to the FRD, and from the comforts of an exile that supplied him with a none-too-shabby monthly allowance, haggled repeatedly over the leadership of the Front.

Meanwhile in Cuba, the MRP stepped up its actions to the same extent that the CIA was able to supply it with weapons and explosives. Its men, advised by a CIA agent specially trained in terrorist actions, carried out the largest act of sabotage in the country leading up to the invasion: using two pouches of plastic explosives, they reduced Cuba's largest department store, El Encanto, to rubble. Other terrorist actions they carried out included sabotaging tobacco warehouses, the national paper factory, several port facilities, and two of the capital's "Ten Cents" variety stores. The MRP eventually had cells of conspirators in such diverse industries as telephone, electric power, insurance, medical, transport, liquor, banking, graphic arts, shoe, leather, restaurant, construction, and civil aviation.

[15] Statement by Reynold González, national coordinator of the MRP. Ministry of the Interior Archives.

Howard Hunt, according to his memoirs, was the CIA agent assigned to the "five leaders" who initially comprised the Frente Revolucionario Democrático (FRD—Democratic Revolutionary Front). It was easy for him to meet with them; what was exhausting was the way they haggled over funds they were supposed to get from the CIA. They asked for $435,000 for activities outside the country, $200,000 for stepping up operations in Cuba, and $105,000 for incidental expenses, salaries, and maintenance of the Front's offices. All of this added up to more than $745,000 per month.

It was finally made clear that funds allocated to the Front were supposed to be used to set up offices in major cities of the Western Hemisphere, including the United States. Covered separately by the CIA were the cost of anti-Castro propaganda, weapons, ships and communications equipment for infiltrations, and subsidies for recruiting personnel and other paramilitary operations.

On June 20, the FRD and its "five leaders" were presented to the media. During the ceremony, the CIA agents who organized them and who would be their handlers remained in their rooms.

Moments earlier, the agents had given their approval to the press release and political manifesto, which called for the overthrow of Fidel Castro.

The FRD manifesto justified the group's actions with a theory created by CIA specialists. From then on, the anti-Cuba project was based on a moral pretext: the revolution betrayed. One of the manifesto's paragraphs claimed, "Soviet-style betrayal by the regime of Comandante Fidel Castro of the noble and original intentions of the Cuban Revolution."

Another section said, "it is not possible to remain indifferent to the most coercive legal, physical, and psychological terror ever known in our history." The document goes on at length with statements that reveal petty anticommunist verbosity more than rational thought or political principle.

It concludes with a twelve-point political platform to be implemented after the overthrow of the revolutionary government. Some points stand out for their unequivocal demonstration of the true intentions of these "freedom fighters":

— Elimination of the Communist Party.
— Review of sentences handed down for offenses committed before January 1, in the ordinary court system. (In other words,

a review of sentences received by the dictatorship's war criminals and torturers.)

— Preservation of the agrarian reform, but as described in the 1940 Constitution, "without divestments or outrages."

The use of the word "divestment" clearly shows the contradiction with the initial formulation. How could an agrarian reform be carried out without divesting large landowners, chiefly Americans, of their land?

The idea was to keep the same formulation, because the agrarian reform implemented by the revolutionary government had become so deeply implanted among Cuba's farmers. And of course, the advent of an old-style government would guarantee the bourgeoisie recovery of the power it had begun to lose on January 1, 1959. One low-level member of the FRD, Max Azicri, drew closer to the Revolution after becoming disenchanted over the years with so much hypocrisy in the counterrevolution's rhetoric. He confessed to this author many years later that he was once in one of the Front's houses in Miami, when he walked into a room and found a galaxy of prominent individuals, circumspect and well-dressed, who looked at him somewhat hostilely. Max quickly left and shortly afterward inquired about the distinguished gentlemen. "They're dealing with the issue of the return of their nationalized land and property," he was told. Max didn't like it, but he wasn't surprised to see them there.

The Cuban bourgeois elite were arrogant and aristocratic, racist and spectacular. If the Americans had a Capitol building, then they would build one to scale. The sumptuous Blanquita Theater, a national cultural emblem, was not only as dazzling as the Metropolitan Opera House but had four more seats. Cuban millionaires would send for architects from France to build small-scale replicas of palaces. They imported Carrara marble, German stained-glass windows, carved pedestals from Austria, and Limoges porcelain. They collected English paintings from the Romantic period, furniture from Versailles, and Bordeaux wine. The organizers of New Year's parties in exclusive clubs were obliged to try to recreate Broadway for their members. Despite the stifling heat, furs were the best-selling items at winter fashion shows. Cuban millionaires vacationed in the United States, where they did their Christmas shopping. Their children went to American universities. For all these reasons, it was not difficult to imagine where they would turn to recover the economic and political power they were losing.

With the goal of putting an even greater distance between the U.S. government and the project for overthrowing the Cuban Revolution, it was decided to set up the FRD's offices in Mexico City.

Soon afterward, branches were opened in different Latin American countries. While they had a certain degree of independence in their actions, it was the CIA that paid for everything, that set the rules of the game.

"Through Tony I convened the FRD Mexico City delegation and introduced Sam to them as their guide, mentor, paymaster and contact with me, the representative of the Bender group. Having set up fronts for me before, Sam went to work immediately. The delegation opened a downtown office and began producing a weekly newspaper named *Mambí*."[16]

From then on, the FRD was used as a front for U.S. aggression, a specific requirement of President Eisenhower.

Nevertheless, they weren't able to fool the Mexican government. Despite the best efforts of CIA agents in that country to hide the real nature of their relationship with the FRD (Hunt, for example, used his old cover of writing detective novels), they quickly came under suspicion. The Mexicans began making things difficult for and putting pressure on the CIA agents in charge. On October 3 of that same year, 1960, with President Eisenhower's authorization, the FRD's executive board was obliged to leave Mexico City and return to Miami.

The Front's "leaders" traveled from one place to another promoting their anti-Castro crusade. Propaganda delegations were sent all over the world.

Some of these Cubans really believed that they were the architects of a program of struggle. That was the case with ex-colonel Martín Elena, the confidence man of Antonio de Varona, who presided

---

[16] Howard Hunt: *Give Us This Day*. Popular Library. 1973, p. 52.

over the FRD's phantasmagorical general staff in Miami. Elena decided to draw up a strategy for the invasion. He drafted more than one invasion plan that ended up in the wastebaskets of Quarters Eye. "I regarded the colonel as a figurehead who ought to be kept busy in Miami with military plans. Cuban plans, in any case, were not the ones that would be used on I-Day, but plans that were being developed by the CIA and the Pentagon through the Joint Chiefs of Staff. Cuban military planning, therefore, was a harmless exercise and might proved tangentially useful if they became known to Castro's agents and served as deception material-disinformation. To paraphrase a homily: this was too important to be left to Cuban generals."[17] Further on in the same book, Hunt notes Martín Elena's words: "I don't see how I can pretend to command when in reality I do not."

With respect to the FRD's actions and organizing skills, nobody could better describe them than Hunt himself. In his book, he says, "Rasco, Varona, and Carrillo were seldom available until after midday. Artime, who had been up half the night attending to his growing flock, would appear red-eyed and unshaven, and Roberto de Varona would usually open the meetings by reporting how many new recruits for the camps his brother had gained the previous day. This usually provoked an outcry from Carrillo (whose Montecristi movement seemed to be limited to blood relatives). Next, Rasco would inquire wearily about arms and boats for his adherents in Florida. Finally, Artime, the junior member, would launch into an impassioned statement of why it was necessary to defeat Castro, and how this could not be done unless petty jealousies were put aside."

But unifying these individuals was impossible. Several of them were traditional politicians, and others had just joined the fray, but all were power hungry and ambitious, and some had records of corruption and larceny that were well known to Cubans.

They were convinced that their return to Cuban political life, to the old republic, would be on a U.S. warship or military plane. None of them was willing to cede the presidency. "While the project moved forward, acquiring boats, planes and bases, training men, negotiating with foreign governments, seeking policy clarification,

[17] Howard Hunt: Ob. cit., pp. 61-62.

training an FRD security service, publishing magazines and newspapers, putting out radio broadcasts, and attempting to move arms, men and propaganda into Cuba by sea or air, the FRD, in whose name most of this activity was being carried on, was making little progress toward unity."[18]

The CIA allowed the Cubans to make quite a bit of noise, but not as much as they wanted. After repeating over and over to themselves in exile that the anti-Castro issue was a strictly Cuban matter, they believed it. Then the CIA stopped them dead in their tracks.

In the camps, they went further: "Is it true or not that Capt. Oscar Alfonso Carol, first Cuban chief of the Trax base in Guatemala,[19] was removed from participation for demanding that the Cuban leaders should have a say on how operations were carried out and on the future of the struggle in our country? The answer is yes. I know it. I was there."[20]

Others met worse fates for expressing disagreement. At machine-gun point, they were disarmed and held in cells in the Guatemalan jungle. Years later, a journalist asked Tony Varona about relations with the Americans. The answer was, "They are not friends or enemies; they are Americans."[21]

However, while keeping these "political leaders" busy playing at war with Fidel Castro, the Quarters Eye men weren't wasting time. Military experts at the Pentagon and CIA were preparing and executing military plans. In fact, the CIA had begun planning its war of subversion without waiting for the formation of the Front. Beginning May 19, in complete secrecy, a group of exiles selected by the same counterrevolutionary organizations began rigorous training for insurgent and clandestine warfare on a semi-desert island near Fort Meyers, Florida: Useppa.

[18] Central Intelligence Agency: Inspector General's Survey of the Cuban Operation, October 1961, op. cit., p.33.
[19] Referring to the hierarchy among the Cubans. The Trax base was under the command of U.S. military officials.
[20] José Pérez San Román. *Respuesta*. Librería Cervantes, Miami, Florida, 1979, p. 23.
[21] Documentary: *Girón, ¿derrota o traición?*

Infiltration teams

The first recruitment sessions were held in Miami from April to May of 1960, and for them, the CIA used leaders of the organizations that later would be part of the Democratic Revolutionary Front.

"In early May of 1960, Manuel Artime came to see me—or better said, it was through one of the San Román [brothers], whose name is José, who later commanded the force that attacked Playa Girón—and he invited me to a meeting of former officers of the former Army... That meeting was led by Manuel Artime. He told us he was in contact with the United States government, and that he had called us together with the goal of organizing a force to fight the Cuban government."[1]

Other future recruits were sent from Cuba by counterrevolutionary organizations operating on the island. Manuel H. Reyes Garcia was one of them.

"In 1960, I began working actively in the MRR, serving as liaison between the coordinator in Oriente, Rogelio Gonzalez Corzo ("Francisco"), and an individual named [...]," he stated some time later to the [Cuban] Department of State Security. "[I found out] through Rogelio Gonzalez in March 1960 that I had to go to the United States as part of a group, to receive military training... I left for the United States in April 1960, and once I got there, I headed for the Centro Hispano, following Francisco's instructions, to make contact with a nun... They came to see me, along with a guy named Quintero,

[1] Statements by Miguel Angel Orozco Crespo, member of the infiltration teams. MININT archives.

and we went to a house... There was also a bed for Artime... On about May 20, the first group of ten left for training, and two days later, another group of ten was taken to the island of Useppa." Manuel H. Reyes was a radio operator for one of the infiltrated teams the day before the Bay of Pigs invasion.

On May 19, the first agent-recruits left for Useppa Island. At the house, they were picked up by a CIA officer who identified himself as Carl; the Cubans were instructed not to talk to him. During the days of training on the island, some of them learned that Carl had participated in training the mercenary forces of Carlos Castillo Armas in Guatemala.

After a five-hour trip by highway, the group arrived at a small dock where they boarded a ferry that took them to Useppa.

The island, located near Fort Myers, Florida, looked like a recreation area; it had a jetty, tennis court, and several cabins, along with other facilities. The new recruits had their fingerprints and photographs taken, and underwent different tests measuring their abilities and intelligence. More groups arrived, until the recruits reached a total of sixty-one, half of whom had been soldiers in the former Cuban Army. Some agents say their total was sixty-six.

Useppa was actually the first stage in the process of selecting and training the members of the future paramilitary groups. It operated as a center for physical and mental review; it was where they received their first telegraph and guerrilla warfare classes. All of them had to take polygraph, or lie detector, tests. They were repeatedly asked if they sympathized with communist ideas, had read Marxist literature, or had engaged in homosexual activities.

A few weeks later, the group was divided in two. The ones with the best abilities —some claim— or who didn't come from the Army —according to the testimony of others— numbering approximately thirty, remained on the island for a radio operator's course, while the other twenty-nine, all ex-soldiers, left in the second week of June.

In an unmarked Douglas C-54 plane, they flew for seven hours to a jungle area where they received an eight-week course in guerrilla warfare. They were moved in complete secrecy, and were not told where they were, but after constantly hearing the horns of ships passing through a canal, they realized they were in Panama.

American officers trained them in infantry weapons handling and shooting. They also received classes in explosives, especially for sabotage and demolition; guerrilla tactics; intelligence; counterintelligence; psychological warfare; evasion and escape; interrogation; clandestinity, and reception of air and sea drops.

They learned the technique of secret writing, including the most advanced method of the time, using special carbon paper with invisible writing.

Those who remained on Useppa became the radio operators of the teams. They received classes six hours daily and learned Morse Code, electrical theory, and other subjects related to telegraphy. On July 5, they left the island and, just like the former soldiers, flew for almost eight hours until they reached a landing field in the middle of the jungle. But they were not in Panama. The most curious were able to identify the country by the license plates of military trucks waiting for them on the tarmac. They were in Guatemala.

They were taken to the Helvetia estate in Retalhuleu, where the Trax base had been set up. Previously, they had been instructed to use false names to identify themselves among the almost 160 recruits already there. Immediately, the radio operation courses continued. On August 21, the twenty-nine trained in guerrilla warfare in Panama arrived. From then on, these men would take charge of training the entire troop, including new recruits who continued to arrive from Miami, under the supervision of their U.S. instructors. They were called "cadres."

In Miami, the recruitment centers seemed very active.

"Finally I was picked up —one of three or four people— and we were driven by car to the Homestead area, south of Miami, where we were taken to an empty house out in the middle of the woods. First we were assigned registration numbers. Mine was 2718... We were strip-searched by Cuban[-American] officers to make sure we weren't carrying any forbidden articles, like compasses or weapons... Later the same day our watches were taken away and we were put in an enclosed truck and driven for hours. Later we discovered that the truck had driven in circles... Soon after, we heard an aircraft taxiing up to the hangar... And off we went, directly into the airplane."[2]

[2] Felix Rodríguez Mendigutia: *Shadow Warrior: The CIA Hero of a Hundred Unknown Battles*. Pocket Books, Simon and Schuster, 1989, p.52.

Officially, the training for carrying out guerilla warfare and subversion in the cities began at the Trax base on September 19, and by the end of November, the recruits were ready to go into action. But for them to do so, it was essential to have created insurgency-controlled zones in Cuba's mountains, as well as a strong underground movement in the cities; this had not been possible.

The few groups that were operating in the Escambray were under continual harassment, and the CIA's air drops were repeatedly falling into the hands of the militias and the Rebel Army. In the cities, counterrevolutionary activities were limited by a combination of the work of State Security and the general population's response to the actions and provocations carried out by these groups. As a result the CIA chiefs had to change their concept of how to confront the Revolution.

On October 31, 1960, a cable dispatched from CIA headquarters in Washington to the agent in charge of the plan in Guatemala ordered a cutback in guerrilla training and the introduction of conventional training for an amphibious and airborne assault force. That was how Operation Trinidad was born. It consisted of a sea and air landing of a brigade, backed by its own air force, to occupy a beachhead in the Trinidad area, take over the airport there, and transfer a provisional government from Miami and install it there, where this government would ask for international recognition. Subsequent military support would be provided until Fidel Castro's government was overthrown.

A new stage began on the Trax base. The gray and black teams disappeared, and the agents, who were now recruits, were organized into companies and battalions. A thorough selection was made to form a limited number of teams —six in the end— with highly trained agents whose chief mission from then on would be to infiltrate into Cuba, make contact with the underground movement, train that movement's members, organize the reception of weapons and explosives, and participate in operations to sabotage vital objectives in support of the invasion.

Evidently, they were no longer supposed to organize guerrilla war or urban subversion; from then on, they would support it actively. They would be more than just reinforcement for subversive organizations operating on the island—organizations whose main leaders, in repeated, secret trips to the United States, were being training as rigorously as the agents in Useppa, Panama or Trax.

In fact, the paramilitary forces had been divided. Most of them were part of the Assault Brigade, and the rest made up the teams of special agents.

Eighty-three recruits were selected for the latter. They included some who had passed through Useppa Island and Panama, along with others who had stood out during their training at Trax base.

On December 5, they were transferred to the San Jose de Buenavista farm in the department of Escuintla, Guatemala. The place was known as Garrapatenango due to its abundance of *garrapatas* (ticks). There, the recruits underwent rigorous special training, consisting of survival exercises. For weeks they had to remain in constant movement without being noticed by the local population; they had to move weapons, equipment and messages, and organize the reception of air drops, which, moreover was the only way they were supplied. When the air operation failed, they were left without food, and had to survive on whatever they could find in their surroundings.

At the end of the course (two weeks), and once again using methods of compartmentalization —closed canvas-roofed trucks with darkened windows— they flew to Panama. Again, it was not difficult for them to identify the country where they had been taken after seeing a large ship in the distance moving slowly through a canal lock. They immediately ruled out the Suez Canal, due to an absence of sand and the presence of tropical vegetation. On the labels of discarded containers, they read: Fort Clayton-Canal Zone.

This time, training consisted of mastering the advanced weapons of the socialist countries and classes in clandestine operations, including how to track suspects in enemy territory. There were more classes on intelligence and propaganda, and they practiced shooting and receiving sea and air drops. They had six instructors, two Americans and four Europeans.

"We were at this camp for New Year's. The American instructors gave us beer and wine. I received a letter from my wife saying she had given birth to a girl. I was happy." [3]

For more than a few of them, this would be their last celebration. Most of them would serve prison sentences before celebrating another New Year's holiday.

[3] Testimony of Benigno Pérez Vivanco, member of the infiltration teams, 1994. Author's archives.

Before leaving Guatemala, they had been organized into six teams of 15 each, and the plan was to cut their forces by 50 percent.

In mid-January, the training was considered to be over, and 47 men were finally selected. The radio operators/telegraphists assigned to the teams were transferred to Louisiana, where they received classes in theory for a week to complete their training, at the Centenary College of Louisiana. On January 29, they flew to New Orleans and from there to Miami. Together with the telegraph operators, the remaining team members left Panama by airplane for an unknown destination.

"They told us we were going to Cuba, and placed the six members of my team, which was called Inca, on an airplane. The instructor Carl went with us. For weapons, we were each carrying a .45 caliber pistol, a .38 snubnose revolver, and an M-2; we had one set of civilian clothing and another of Rebel Army clothing with different ranks, along with the camouflage outfit we were wearing. After four and a half hours of flight, the bottom hatch opened, and we were ordered to jump out, first dropping the package with our belongings, then Carl and then us. On the ground, we picked everything up and entered a nearby hillock. We removed our camouflage clothing, put our civilian outfits on, and buried everything together with the parachutes and weapons, except for the .38 revolvers. It was then, half a kilometer away from where we had landed, that men dressed as militia members appeared, which at first really scared us, but afterward, when they approached us, they congratulated us, because we had completed the operation in less than an hour. We were then taken by truck to Retalhuleu Airport. They had dropped us over Guatemala."[4]

The next day, the teams were transferred to Miami and placed in a CIA security house in the Homestead area, where they were supposed to wait until they were to be infiltrated into Cuba. The house was comfortable enough to make their stay a pleasant one. It had a swimming pool, and the land around it was planted with tomatoes. They were given money and permission to visit families and wives. Around February 8, the commando units headed by Benigno Pérez, Manuel Blanco Navarro and Oscar Alfonso Carol —the latter two were former officers under the Batista dictatorship— were led to a wharf in Key West, and they headed for Cuba.

[4] Ibid.

The first attempt was on the north coast of Las Villas. There the group led by Benigno was to land with the idea of joining insurgent groups operating in the Escambray Mountains—groups who at the time faced a major revolutionary offensive known as *La Limpia del Escambray* ("the clean-up of the Escambray"). The choice of Benigno for this mission was no coincidence. He had battled the dictatorship's forces in those mountains.

The Inca teams had the urgent mission of organizing the reception of air-dropped weapons and explosives and providing training. They also carried a supply of weapons. The attempt to land failed and they had to return to Miami. The same fate was met by the teams of Blanco Navarro, in Pinar del Rio, and Oscar Alfonso Carol, also in Las Villas. The infiltration operation began under signs of uncertainty. But there were still several weeks to go before the invasion.

The infiltration of agents was done by sea and air, including by legal routes.

On February 13, 1961, agent Manuel Reyes García descended the passenger stairs of a commercial airliner that covered the Miami-Havana route. He was carrying false identity documents. Immediately, he established contact with the leaders of the internal counterrevolution and began his work.

The next day, Valentine's Day, a team made up of Félix Rodríguez Mendigutía, Segundo Borges, José González Castro, Javier Souto (radio operator), and Edgar Sopo infiltrated the country in the Arcos de Canasí area, bordering the provinces of La Habana and Matanzas. They unloaded two tons of communications equipment, weapons, and explosives.

They were met on the coast by a group of counterrevolutionaries who immediately set about moving and burying the supplies. A few days later, the supplies would fall into the hands of State Security, because one of the supposed collaborators worked for the G-2.

The commando unit was divided into two: Segundo Borges, Javier Souto, and José González headed for Las Villas, and Edgar Sopo and their chief, Félix Rodríguez, headed for Havana, where, on the following day, they met with Rogelio González Corzo, one of the main leaders of the underground movement.

Gustavo Enrique Casuso Pérez was sent as a radio operator for an insurgent uprising in the Sierra Maestra. He infiltrated north of Havana with the main organizer of that operation, Alberto Muller.

The uprising was supposed to happen in the days leading up to the Bay of Pigs invasion. Their main mission was to coordinate, via radio, air drops of weapons and ammunition for this unit, which was organized by the Student Revolutionary Directorate (DRE). The mission failed because the Brigade 2506 tactical air force squadrons were busy that first week of April transferring their base in Guatemala to the Happy Valley base in Nicaragua. There were no air drops because they were immediately arrested.

Oliverio Tomeu, the chief of the other team, was able to make it to Camagüey, along with his team.

At the end of February, Manuel Blanco Navarro made another attempt to land in Pinar del Río province. His boat received signals from another boat, as according to plan, but as the other vessel drew near, he saw its hull was an olive-green color, confused it with the Cuban Revolutionary Navy, and retreated.

Benigno Pérez and his group failed once again, and received orders over their yacht's radio to return to Key West. They were later taken to New Orleans, where each was given $200, and after a week's rest, they set out —according to his testimony— to visit every bar in the city.

Oscar Alfonso Carol was able to infiltrate in early March. At the same time, Juan Manuel Guillot Castellanos, who had been working for the CIA and conspiring in Cuba since late 1959 and had left for the United States February 13, secretly returned, along with three others who had been instructed to follow his orders.

In the first week of March, the CIA commando members and radio operators Adolfo Mendoza (Raúl) and Jorge García Rubio (Tony) were dropped by parachute over a farm in Santa Cruz del Sur, Camagüey. Dropped along with them was CIA agent Emilio Rivero Caro, who was leading a counterrevolutionary organization in Pinar del Rio, where he went after the infiltration. The three agents were carrying a supply of weapons.

Jorge García Rubio was supposed to be the radio operator for a major underground organization operating in the capital, led by Alfredo Izaguirre de la Riva and José Pujals Mederos, both recruited by the U.S. ambassador in 1959. They hid their assigned radio operator in Izaguirre's apartment in the Focsa Building, and hid the radio equipment on a farm in Santiago de Las Vegas, a town outside the capital. Soon after that, the group led by this agent prepared

—according to CIA instructions— to blow up the Tallapiedra electric power plant.

Jorge Rojas Castellanos was able to infiltrate, leading his group, which included Jorge ("The Sheriff") Gutiérrez Izaguirre, as radio operator, Abel Pérez Martín, Jorge Recarey, and José Regalado. About 200 meters from the coast, their rubber raft flipped over and they had to swim the rest of the way. They were soon picked up on the Via Blanca Highway by cars that had been waiting for them. Their missions included locating points for air drops of weapons and explosives for insurgent groups operating in the Jagüey Grande area, south of Matanzas. Rojas Castellanos did not know he was operating in the zone where the invasion would take place—in fact, at that point in March, the CIA had not yet chosen the invasion site. With the help of the group of a self-appointed colonel, Juan José "Pichi" Catalá Coste, he toured his assigned region for about 20 days. Like all of the CIA team members, before he left the United States he was given a .45 pistol, camouflage face paint, two additional magazines for cartridges, two boxes of .45 bullets, an M-3 light machine gun appropriate for urban battle, an ammunition belt with three clips, two MK2 hand grenades, a small knapsack, and materials for secret writing. Other team members were also able to infiltrate in late February and early March of 1960. These included Manuel Blanco Navarro, who had tried to do so before, Miguel Pentón, Jorge Cawy Comellas, and Antonio Díaz Pou, the latter in Oriente.

Miguel Ángel Orozco Crespo and his group approached the coast in an unmarked boat with the motors turned off, but they were not able to land because the contact failed to show up. Hours later, they returned to Key West. At the time of the invasion, Orozco was in a safe house in Homestead.

Shipments of weapons and explosives for the internal fifth column were made during February and March, now with the support of the infiltration teams. A good number of them entered the country through a coastal zone called Palmarejo —which appeared in CIA documents under the code name of Fundora— located between Santa Cruz del Norte and Arcos de Canasí on the northern coastline, about 80 km east of the capital. The area had dense vegetation, numerous caves and low hills and was sparsely populated. They were received there by an infiltration commando and one of the most active chiefs of the underground movement, Marcial Arufe.

Finally, on March 13, two of the top leaders of the underground movement infiltrated Fundora. Assigned by the CIA to unleash the largest operation in the country to back the invasion, they were former commander Humberto Sorí Marín, appointed as military coordinator of the FUR (United Revolutionary Front), and Rafael Díaz Hanscom, national coordinator. They were accompanied by commando member Manuel Lorenzo Puir Miyar. They brought 14 tons of weapons and explosives, which were hidden by Marcial Arufe.

Ten days later, on March 22, Benigno Pérez Vivanco, who had failed twice previously, was able to infiltrate.

"On March 22, we approached the coast at Palmarejo. We called it Punto Fundora. We were in a wooden boat, proceeding very cautiously, because we were afraid they might be waiting for us. We stayed out about five miles off the coast waiting for the receiving commando to signal us. When we finally saw two green lights and a red one, they ordered us to get quickly into a fiberglass raft. Behind us, another boat followed carrying 16 tons of weapons. Marcial Arufe was on the coast with a truck, onto which they loaded part of the weapons and the explosives. They took me and my radio operator, Rafael García Rubio, to Havana by car. They hid us in a safe house and we spent our time training different underground groups." [5]

The infiltrated agents tried to carry out the missions for which they had been trained for almost eight months: making contact with counterrevolutionary organizations in Cuba; establishing and ensuring communication with the General Staff; locating appropriate zones for weapons and explosives drops; organizing uprisings in mountain regions, mostly in the Sierra de los Órganos in Pinar del Río, the Escambray in Las Villas, and the Sierra Maestra in Oriente; training various underground groups in weapons handling and the use of explosives, and participating in major actions.

Up until the day of the landing, those who had not been detected maintained contact with the CIA using their radio equipment, via which they received instructions, warnings about security measures, and evaluations. José Pujals Mederos, who had a radio operator

[5] Ibid.

working under him, declared to Cuban State Security while in custody, "The CIA was very happy with the way the infiltration teams worked in Santa Clara…. Before Girón, around April 1, we received a warning to be careful about a false invasion south of Camagüey… Two days before the airports were bombed, a message was received, alerting us that G-2 had intensified its surveillance in railroad stations, airports and communications centers, and to avoid being in those places in order not to be detected."

The team agents organized air drops of weapons and explosives; trained dozens of underground activists in handling these deadly devices; and radioed messages with information on the military, economic, and political situation, and, above all, the morale and mood of the population. They also participated in dozens of sabotage actions, like one that reduced the country's largest department store to ashes, and instigated uprisings in the Escambray and Sierra Maestra mountains. There were some, however, who sought asylum in embassies as soon as they set foot on Cuban soil.

The final outcome of the teams may be seen in the strategic defeat suffered by the U.S. government and its intelligence services, and it is an eloquent example of the effectiveness of the incipient organs of Cuba's State Security.

Manuel H. Reyes García, the first agent who infiltrated —by entering the country legally— remained in hiding during the days of Girón, "inactive," as he put it. He later sent all types of messages until he was arrested. The commando unit that was supposed to go to Santa Clara under the command of Félix Rodríguez Mendigutía never achieved any of its objectives. The bombing of Cuban airports, which Fidel Castro interpreted as the prelude to the invasion, was not enough to mobilize the commando unit. Its chief, Félix Rodríguez, stayed hiding in the house of a conspirator, moving later to the residence of a Spanish diplomat, and from there, secretly, to the Venezuelan embassy. On September 13, he left the country. Edgar Sopo met the same fate, while Javier Souto managed to escape minutes before being arrested in Santa Clara. He later flew to Havana and was given asylum in the Ecuadorian embassy. Segundo Borges and José González Castro remained hidden in Santa Clara, together with Miguel Pentón, another member of the groups who joined them. The three were arrested on April 21 and taken to the offices of the G-2 in the city.

Segundo Borges made his first statements to then-lieutenant Aníbal Velaz, provincial Security chief. The minutes read, "That he was arrested on July 21, 1961; that he left Cuba in early August of 1959, returning in October of the same year for four to five days, and then going back to the USA; that in August 1960 he joined the movement of young Cubans against the Revolutionary Government; that they were taken to Guantánamo, where they received military training, then to another place unknown to him and from there to Key West and directly to Cuba; that he infiltrated with a certain Rogelio and others named Félix, Javier Souto, and Miguel Ángel González to open a front of insurgents on the northern coast; that the thing failed. He brought weapons in by beach and relied on instructions by radio."[6]

The subsequent history of these three agents was like something out of a movie. They were held in Santa Clara for twenty-five days until orders were received to take them to Havana. At Cuban State Security offices, an unusual event occurred, a reflection of the tension and organizational inexperience of the time. The three agents were not viewed with the importance they merited, and they were not interrogated again. On September 10, they were transferred to a place that was practically unguarded while their cases were considered.

Their cell was located next to a small garage full of auto parts. For six days, using an iron bar they removed from one of the beds, they bored a hole through the wall, and at 4 a.m. on October 11, they managed to escape. Entering the garage, they found just one guard, and he was asleep. Within a few days, they were given asylum.

Gustavo Enrique Casuso Pérez, the radio operator who infiltrated together with Alberto Muller, the leader of the counterrevolutionary Student Revolutionary Directorate (DRE), helped carry out several acts of sabotage in the capital in the month of March, especially targeting electrical cables. He then participated in an uprising in the Sierra Maestra on April 4, along with forty-five other men. His mission was to ensure communication and organize air drops of military supplies, but it was not possible to make the drops. In order to remain undetected, the unit did not enter combat. On April 21, a Rebel Army patrol encountered the insurgents and they suffered their first casualties. Days later, the rest were captured.

[6] Statements by Segundo Borges. MININT Archives.

The team commanded by Oliverio Tomeu did not carry out its orders to cut off the road to Camagüey; due to the arrests of other counterrevolutionaries, Tomeu fled to Havana and was given asylum in the Argentine Embassy.

Manuel Blanco Navarro, a former Army officer under Batista, was able to infiltrate after two unsuccessful attempts, but he was captured shortly afterward. Adolfo Mendoza, one of the radio operators dropped over southern Camagüey, was given asylum three days after setting foot on Cuban soil. He was replaced by Jorge "Tony" García Rubio, who also infiltrated by air. On April 15, the day the airports were bombed, he received a message saying he should turn his radio on every four hours. Arrests that were being carried out by State Security with the support of the Committees for the Defense of the Revolution forced him to move and hide the radio. Three months later he was given asylum in the Colombian Embassy.

On March 18, just five days after having infiltrated, two top leaders of the Unidad Revolucionaria group assigned by the CIA to unleash a vast program of sabotage and terrorism in support of the invasion —Humberto Sorí Marín and Rafael Díaz Hanscom— were detained in a State Security operation. In that same operation, the radio operator and group member Manuel Lorenzo Puig Miyar was arrested. So too was Rogelio González Corzo, the head of the underground movement and a CIA liaison, who had been working for the Americans for two years under the pseudonym of Francisco.

On March 19, Jorge Rojas Castellanos was surrounded in the area of Calimete and his commando unit was split up. One member was captured, and Jorge Rojas was arrested weeks later in Havana.

Benigno Pérez Vivanco, head of the Inca team, and his second-in-command, Rafael Ernesto Garcia Rubio, returned to a motel where they had spent the night with two women. It was six a.m. on April 21, and they headed for the house where they had been hiding since their infiltration on March 22. Since then, they had trained several groups in weapons and explosives handling and had broadcast information to the CIA center in Miami. The home where they were hiding was considered to be one of the most secure.

They entered the apartment and immediately a group of uniformed men knocked on the door. Marcial Arufe fired at the State Security agents and wounded three of them, but was hit by bullets from the others, killing him. Benigno and Rafael were arrested, and sixteen tons of weapons and explosives were seized.

Miguel Ángel Orozco Crespo, one of the most seasoned students in the CIA training camps, eventually became head of the CIA's anti-Cuba Special Missions Groups. On November 5, 1962, in the final days of the October Missile Crisis, he was arrested after landing in Pinar del Rio with the mission of sabotaging the elevated conveyer belt used to transport minerals from the Matahambre Mines.

Twenty of the thirty-five agents from the teams that infiltrated in the days leading up to the Bay of Pigs were captured by Cuban State Security. If we consider that three additional agents managed to escape after being arrested, the conclusion is obvious: two-thirds of the agents trained with such painstaking zeal by excellent instructors, equipped with cutting-edge communications equipment and supported by the CIA's top agents in the country, were discovered and captured by the youngest State Security agency in the world within eighteen months of the first infiltration.

The psychological environment

I intended to organize exile groups of women, workers, professionals, and students to act as propaganda fronts. I would support a number of exile publications. Radio broadcasts and, eventually, leaflet drops would be the vital operations. I would need my own airplane for the leaflet drops just before and on the day of the invasion, and a large medium-wave radio station...

I told Bissell that ... I would need a powerful transmitter, perhaps fifty kilowatts, to broadcast on medium-wave. Cuban listeners, unlike Guatemalans, were not accustomed to short-wave. Further, we would be competing with Fidel Castro...

'Do the necessary,' Bissell said.... 'How long will it take to create the proper psychological climate?'

DAVID A. PHILLIPS, *The Night Watch*

This conversation took place April 17, 1960, in the office of CIA Director of Plans Richard Bissell, who headed the operation to overthrow the Cuban Revolution. Philips's response was: "In Guatemala, it only took six weeks, but in Cuba, it would take about six months." Actually, it took Phillips a whole year to psychologically soften up the Cuban people; the invasion took place April 17, 1961, exactly one year after the meeting. Sixty-six hours after the landing, however, the Brigade was defeated by battalions of working-class militia members, pilots, and soldiers who remained loyal to Fidel Castro. Meanwhile, enormous support in the cities protected the rearguard. David A. Phillips went home and vomited in his bathroom. He was overwhelmed, bewildered, full of rage. He had never been defeated before.

What had gone wrong with Radio Free Cuba and the whole barrage of propaganda used to confuse or win over the undecided, neutralize the firmest, and encourage the disaffected? He found no answers.

For a year, he had worked with a team of propaganda experts, eighteen hours a day, often sleeping on a military cot in Quarters Eye. All resources he requested had been granted; millions of dollars had been provided to pay hundreds of journalists, writers, technicians, radio announcers, and editors. Yet nothing that had been expected happened.

For Richard Bissell, creating a radio station with broadcasts aimed at the Cuban people was the most important mission of the anti-Cuba operation. That's why he placed the project in the hands of one of the CIA's top propaganda experts, David A. Philips, a journalist and actor who had organized radio broadcasts hostile to Guatemala's Jacobo Arbenz in 1954. He knew life in Cuba well. He had been posted in Havana during the final years of the Fulgencio Batista dictatorship, and, following the triumph of the Revolution, had participated in several anti-government conspiracies, including one to assassinate Fidel Castro.

After the initial meeting with Bissell, Phillips devoted himself full-time to the task. The first thing he did was select the place from which to broadcast to Cuba: Swan Island, a small island in the Gulf of Honduras, located ninety-seven miles north of Punta Patuca in Honduras and south of Cuba's western tip. The island belonged to the United States, a claim disputed by the Honduran government,

A group of experts carried out a study and designed an antenna system. Technical help was provided by the U.S. Army, Navy, and Air Force. Phillips's team wanted a fifty-kilowatt transmitter equipped with antennas that would broadcast to all of Cuba, sufficiently powerful to ensure reception even if there were interference.

Once work had begun and the radio equipment was on its way from Europe, Phillips went to Boston to give the new enterprise a legal front. There he contacted an old CIA collaborator, the former president of the United Fruit Company, Thomas Dudley Cabot, who had also been director of the State Department's Office of International Security Affairs in 1951. After they reached an agreement, a shipping company called Gibraltar Steamship Corporation, located at 437 Fifth Avenue in New York, announced it had leased land on Swan Island to operate a radio station.

Phillips evidently overlooked one detail that attracted the attention of journalists: the shipping company claiming to be the owner of the radio station had not owned a single ship for ten years. Its "business manager" said the radio station would broadcast music, programs, and news.

"It is a strictly commercial enterprise," he told the reporters who pressed him. "We are looking to acquire sponsors. We don't have them yet, but we're in negotiations."

Sure enough, when the radio station went on the air, it broadcast ads for Coca-Cola, Colgate, the Pan-American Agency, Good Year Tires, and others. Coincidentally, these companies were among those adversely affected by the Cuban revolutionary government's laws.

While legal cover was being created for the planned radio station, CIA agents in Miami were recruiting several dozen Cuban exiles to be technicians, journalists, and announcers. The idea was to use voices that were known in Cuba, which, it was thought, would assure an initial audience. Those hired included journalists Sergio Carbó, Humberto Medrano, Ulises Carbó (who later went to Cuba as part of the invasion), Francisco Gutiérrez, and José Ignacio Rivero; announcers Arturo Artalejo and Alberto Gandero, whose voices had been heard on the island for years; Enrique Huerta, Ángel del Cerro, and Luis Conte Agüero, the latter a journalist who had managed to gain an audience in Cuba during the struggle against the dictatorship. And a woman, Pepita Riera, who was to be used to make rousing speeches to the people as a whole.

Phillips saw the possibility of using Riera to recreate the legend of Iva Toguri, a woman born in the United States to Japanese parents in 1916. During World War II, U.S. officials placed her family in an internment camp, along with thousands of other Japanese and Japanese-Americans who lived in the United States, for the sole reason that the two countries were at war. Iva herself was not interned because she was visiting Tokyo when the war broke out. Her mastery of English opened the doors of the Japanese Special Services to her, and she began to work for a radio network targeting U.S. forces stationed in the Pacific. They called her Tokyo Rose, and her harangues were so fierce and impassioned that once Japan had been occupied, her captors treated her as a criminal.

Repeating the Tokyo Rose experience was the idea behind the radio war waged against Cuba. The result, however, was a caricature of "Havana Rose," incapable of moving even her enthusiastic sponsors.

On the night of May 17, 1960, just a month after the meeting between Philips and Bissell, Radio Cuba Libre (Radio Swan) was heard in Cuba for the first time, at 1160 on the AM band. It came in loud and clear. Voices familiar to Cuban listeners could be heard on a wide range of news programs, commentaries, editorials and reports, carefully prepared to promote distrust of the Revolution. They were blatant lies, difficult to prove or disprove, with predictions of bloodbaths. The station had a markedly triumphalist tone.

The goal was clear: to psychologically soften up the Cuban people. The initial project continued to grow, and as the invasion plan progressed, the station also became a way of maintaining connection with insurgent groups operating in Cuba's mountains, with the internal counterrevolutionary movement in the cities and with clandestine agents for the CIA who were being recruited in abundance.

Phillips's network eventually controlled not just Radio Swan, but also WRUL, WGBS of Miami, WKWF of Key West, WWL of New Orleans, and WMIE. The latter still exists as a counterrevolutionary radio station in Florida, under the name of WQBA "La Cubanísima" ("the most Cuban of all").

These stations used a more moderate tone than Radio Swan and were not seen as being against Fidel Castro. Their aim was to influence Cubans of all types and convince them to support the invasion. Anti-Castro propaganda operations were stepped up all over Latin America, but the main strategic job remained in the hands of Radio Swan. For an entire year, it broadcast with the objective Bissell had assigned it: to create chaos in the minds of ordinary Cubans. Some news items it reported are eloquent examples of this goal. They were monitored by Cuban counterintelligence from June 1960 to April 1961:

Napoleon: I've sent, by the channel you know, a report on the communists, their informants and their locations in the region where you operate.

Teodomico: Remember that the ones who are coming are Cubans and not Americans. When they land, join them, because they are coming under the protection of heavy artillery fire.

Fidel Castro is going to create a church where priests and nuns will be nothing but government employees.

Cuban mothers! Listen to this! The next law passed by the government will be to take away your children ages five to eighteen.

On Kilometer Seven of the Rancho Boyeros highway, a militia member was found dead. And on 90th Street and 43rd Avenue, right in the middle of Marianao, three militia members were found strangled.

Militia member! Be careful when you go out! Do so as in Russia, in groups of three. If you don't want to die, come over to the ranks of the real revolution.

People can't visit their relatives in prison anymore, because they're being taken to Russia.

Che is traveling to Russia to save his skin, and to not be in Cuba on the day of battle, which is now approaching.

They are asking for a million coat-hangers. The people should not believe it is because they need them. They will be used to make barbed-wire fences to protect the rulers.

The United States has forbidden any shipments of goods to Cuba.

Fidel is looking for a way to destroy the Church, but this cannot happen: Cubans! Go to church and follow the instructions of the clergy.

A group of students in Camagüey was detained for burning buses.

Priest arrested in Pinar del Río for distributing food to the poor in that province.

In Cuba, even the peace of the grave is gone. During the most recent mobilization of militia members, they turned Colón Cemetery into a campground. They are preparing their meals over tombstones, they've installed beds in the mausoleum and it can be seen that certain areas are decorated with clothes hanging on clotheslines. There are as-yet unconfirmed rumors that some graves have been desecrated by the vandals.

Simultaneously with this last news item, one of the reactionary newspapers that was still circulating in Cuba published cartoons depicting militia members in the cemetery robbing jewels from graves. More than a few of these reports were so crude —such as this one— that someone had only to visit the cemetery to prove how false they were.

Newspapers and magazines in Cuba, like most of the media, had remained in the hands of their owners after the triumph of the Revolution. The only ones nationalized were those owned by dictator Fulgencio Batista, *Circuito Nacional Cubano*, and others whose owners were notorious figures of the dictatorship: radio stations Cadena Oriental de Radio, Unión Radio, and Reloj de Cuba, and newspapers *Ataja, Alerta, Mañana,* and *Tiempo en Cuba.*

The remaining major dailies and the magazine *Bohemia*, which were part of the Cuban Press Association, television channels, and the national radio networks CMQ and Radio Progreso all defended the prevailing economic system in the country —the cause of the country's worst social ills— and they submissively accepted political dependence on the United Sates. The boldest critics considered such dependence an inevitable evil.

Shortly after the triumph of the Revolution, the U.S. press began a ferocious campaign to slander the Cuban government. The Time-Life consortium, the magazines *U.S. News & World Report* and *Visión*, and *The Miami Herald* newspaper stood out in this effort. What eventually became an entire operation to psychologically soften up the Cuban population and create public opinion in the United States and Latin America had its start in those first months. The Miami-based newspaper *El Diario de Las Américas* published a UPI report in May 1959 reporting an early-dawn assault by police forces on a convent. The news was refuted by the bishop of Camagüey, but his denial was not published in the United States.

In the United States, the press sharply attacked the process under way in Cuba with the evident desire of discrediting it. The *World Telegram* described Fidel as a "liar," while another newspaper compared him to Hitler and Mussolini.

In Cuba, the reactionary media emulated their counterparts in the United States. The newspapers *Diario de la Marina* and *Avance* served as mouthpieces of the counterrevolutionary campaign. Under these circumstances, the Provincial Journalists Association decided on December 26, 1959 to issue notes from newspaper workers to clear up false or slanderous information about the revolutionary government that was being published. That was how "La Coletilla" ("The Tagline") was born, an original creation of the Revolution. The owners reacted by trying to shut down the newspapers. The response was an overwhelming one: the workers took them over.

Between January 18 and July 18 1960, all Cuban newspapers, magazines, radio stations, and TV channels that had joined in the anti-Cuba campaigns were nationalized. David Atlee Phillips encountered something that made his work on the island extraordinarily difficult: his media allies had been liquidated. The desired psychological environment would have to be created from the outside. In reality, however, this did not mean completely abandoning propaganda against the revolutionary government on its own home ground.

Cuba did not have sufficient or adequate radar equipment, and Phillips took advantage of that to create a program for air-dropping pamphlets. He had several small planes and the use of the Florida Keys. Hundreds of thousands of pamphlets began to be dropped over Cuban territory, urging people to carry out sabotage, set fire to sugarcane fields, attack militia members and leaders and spread lies. The operation was backed by Radio Swan, which was the main weapon in this psychological war. Without a doubt, it was able to create confusion among part of the population. That became evident during one of those campaigns.

Phillips was a true expert in the art of subverting the human mind. One of the radio campaigns that perhaps did affect part of the population —a minority to be sure, and for different reasons — was the one on parental custody. Because of its importance and connotations, it is necessary to examine it further here.

Planning for Operation "Peter Pan" began in Washington in mid-1960. It was named after the story of the boy who took the three Darling family children to Never-Never Land. This version of the story had at its core a sad irony: for many of the children who were taken from Cuba, the United States would be the land from which they would "never-never" return home. The operation was part of the arsenal of weapons used in the effort to psychologically soften up the Cuban people. The Quarters Eye Propaganda Department used the operation as part of a campaign to make ordinary Cubans believe that under a communist government children would become the property of the state, the same as was occurring with land, industry, businesses, and housing. For this reason, parents would lose custody of their children.

The CIA experts knew that if they were able to create doubt in at least part of the population, the issue would explode. It could, they felt, lead to an exodus of thousands of children, splitting up families, and weakening support for the government. Obviously, it would be an effective method of destabilization.

The first stage of the operation was to report alarming news over the radio that would be circulated by word of mouth. The Radio Swan 8 p.m. news show referred to the issue for the first time in October 1960.

Cuban mother, don't let your child be taken away! The revolutionary government will take him away when he turns five years old and will return him to you at the age of eighteen. When this occurs, they will be monstrous materialists.

Several days later, they made it a longer news item, adding a key word: law. What was heard was the following:

Attention, Cubans! Remember how on this same liberation program in the past, we told you about many of laws that were later put into effect by the government. That was the case with the Urban Reform.
Now we are announcing the next law. They will take away your own children from the ages of five to eighteen, and when they give them back to you, they will have been turned into fierce materialists. That is how Fidel Castro will become the supreme mother of Cuba! Do not let your child be taken away!
Attention Cubans! Go to church and follow the instructions of the clergy.

Over the following months, the radio station would broadcast the false news about parental custody over and over. By December, the experts believed that the issue had taken shape on the island and decided to go on to the next stage, which was to divide Cuban families and get some of them to confront the government. With an apparently legal cover and using the services of the Catholic Church, the exodus of children began. Operation Peter Pan functioned under a religious front, as supposed humanitarian aid from the Catholic Service Bureau in Florida. Its leading figure, the one who would "show his face," was Monsignor Bryan O. Walsh.

"I went in through one of the side doors of the State Department," he recalled years later. "It was very mysterious; it seemed like I was working for the FBI or something. In a three-hour conversation, they said that we could work on a project for getting kids out, that they could grant visa waivers[1] that would give us authority to issue those documents."

High-ranking officials from the State Department and Attorney General's Office participated in those first meetings, along with the CIA official in charge of the operation, who identified himself as Harold Bishop. His real name was David Atlee Phillips, and he could not be absent from the meeting: he was the one who created Radio Swan and Peter Pan. Years later, he would become a celebrity, after an investigator from the U.S. House Special Committee on Assassinations cited him as possibly being the CIA official who met with Lee Harvey Oswald in a building in Dallas two months before the assassination of President John F. Kennedy. That was how Phillips was included on the long list of U.S. Secret Service agents who were linked, one way or another, with the assassination of President Kennedy.

When the meetings with the State Department were over, Monsignor Walsh had the first 500 visas on his desk. The CIA had been clear: authorization would be given only to children and teenagers who were five to eighteen years old.

Coincidentally, those were the same ages mentioned by Radio Swan. Parents would not be included. They would remain in Cuba to swell the ranks of the opposition to Fidel Castro. At least they would have a moral pretext.

---

[1] Visa waivers. Certain people were authorized to issue them, in the name of the State Department, without going through the regular paperwork of U.S. immigration authorities.

Walsh contacted other bishops in Florida to find a steady, loyal collaborator in Havana to whom he could secretly send the visas. A month later, Ramón Grau Alsina,[2] who headed Catholic Welfare, the main Catholic church office in Cuba, agreed to take part in the project of advocating an exodus of children from Cuba. Mongo Grau had been conspiring against the Cuban Revolution since immediately after its triumph, and he was a member of one of the subversive organizations closely linked to the CIA via the Democratic Revolutionary Front (FRD).

Customs and immigration officials at the José Martí International Airport were surprised, on December 26, 1960, to see a dozen children traveling unaccompanied to the United States. But their documents were in order and their parents were there. That is why their passports were stamped.

The first delivery to Never-Never Land was under way. From then on, the CIA had the complicity of religious authorities in Cuba. "The priest from Santa María del Rosario traveled the entire island, but he never went to my house; he would send a female intermediary once a week who would sit in the little green living room of my house. I would give her the packet of visas, and she would give me the new list of names."[3]

A considerable quantity of visas was taken to Cuba by James Baker, an American who was headmaster of the Ruston Academy until it was nationalized. He eventually functioned as a sort of secretary for the operation.

By early 1961, the first 500 children had left. Monsignor Walsh, following the instructions of the CIA agent in charge, asked immigration officials for another 500. The official who received the request asked, "What are you people trying to do, take away all of Cuba's children?"

Some of the people who were conspiring against the government used the operation as a way of getting their children away from the dangerous environment in which they saw themselves obliged to live; other families, fearful of a possible invasion of the island —something talked about on a daily basis— opted to remove their children from that possible situation, and still others, out of ignorance,

[2] Nephew of former president Ramón Grau San Martín.
[3] Statements by Ramón Grau Alsina. MININT Archives.

really believed that the government would take away their children. More than a few of the farmers who joined insurgent groups in the mountains in late 1960 were motivated by the parental-custody campaign.

One of the people most involved in the operation was Leopoldina Grau Alsina, Mongo Grau's sister. Many years later, after she was released from prison, she was interviewed by journalist Luis Báez. The excerpt below reveals the true essence of the dirty operation.

Journalist: You were one of the main people responsible for the parental custody campaign against the Revolution.
L. Grau: That's true. We spread the rumor that the communist government had absolute power over the children, and that parents would lose their rights, that they would send their children to Russia. A fake revolutionary government law on that was even invented and printed.
Journalist: Did you really believe that?
L. Grau: Not really.
Journalist: So, why did you do it?
L. Grau: It was a way of destabilizing the government. For people to start losing faith in the Revolution.
Journalist: That's a pretty cynical attitude.
L. Grau: Maybe so, but we were at war with the government. And in war, everything goes.

Finally, D-Day came, and with it, the definitive test for measuring the effectiveness of the CIA's propaganda campaign. In the early morning of April 17, as the invaders were reaching the coasts of the Bay of Pigs, David A. Phillips ordered his agents on Swan Island to broadcast the message instructing the internal counterrevolutionary movement to advocate a popular uprising. It said:

Alert! Alert! Take a good look at the rainbow. The first will be out soon. Chico is at home. Visit him... The fish will not take long to rise. The fish is red.

Early on the morning of the landing, the radio station announced the "victorious advance of the invaders, the takeover of cities and the flight of the Revolution's top leaders."

The invading forces have occupied the city of Pinar del Río, capital of the province of the same name. The invasion of the provinces of Matanzas and Santiago is progressing well. (UPI).

An invasion force has arrived on Cuba's main highway, which runs from east to west, in an advance from the province of Matanzas, to cut the island in two. (UPI)

The Isle of Pines was taken over by the rebels and 10,000 political prisoners were freed, joining in the uprising. (UPI)

One thousand soldiers of former president Carlos Prío Socarrás landed in the province of Oriente. (AP)

Luis Conte Agüero is landing with his commandos in the Port of Bayamo and marching to the Escambray to unite the victorious invading troops. (Radio Swan).

In Happy Valley, Nicaragua, the operations base for Brigade 2506 air force, there were 11 million brochures ready to be dropped over Cuban territory. Their content openly incited the population to rebellion.

Shortly afterward, they would be fuel for the fire. "Immediately before D-Day, Radio Swan and other outlets were broadcasting 18 hours a day on medium-wave and 16 hours on short-wave. Immediately after D-Day, these totals were increased to 55 hours and 26 hours, respectively. Fourteen frequencies were used. By the time of the invasion a total of 12,000,000 pounds of leaflets had been dropped on Cuba."[4]

How did the Cuban people react after having been subjected to veritable psychological warfare for a year? Had they been softened up? The answer is well known, but to give an example of what was happening all over the country, we will briefly describe what happened in a small town, the closest to the landing zone: Jagüey Grande.

At about 1 a.m., a militia member who was on guard duty at the police station received a telephone call informing him that a landing was taking place and that he should report it to the battalion stationed

---

[4] Central Intelligence Agency: *Inspector General's Survey of the Cuban Operation, October 1961*, op. cit., p. 38.

at a nearby sugar mill. He immediately sent the message, and the battalion chief, without waiting for orders, immediately headed for the beach with his forces. Meanwhile, the news ran like wildfire through the town. A considerable number of its men belonged to another battalion and were enjoying a brief leave. The word was passed from house to house and they began moving any way they could to their headquarters and weapons.

Throughout the early morning, voices could be heard: "Get up, the invasion is here!" "The Americans are attacking!" "The Americans are in the swamp!"

The people gathered at militia headquarters, the city hall, and Rebel Army barracks to get weapons and instructions. The Federation of Cuban Women mobilized its members to go to the Red Cross. Ordinary citizens offered to protect the town's vital points, electric power stations, radio relay stations, water tanks, and fuel tanks.

At the Rebel Army barracks, boxes of rifles were opened and distributed to a group of citizens who said they knew how to use them. Totally spontaneously, thirty-two of them were chosen to leave shortly afterward in two trucks for the landing site.

By 10 a.m., the Committees for the Defense of the Revolution had arrested the town's most notorious counterrevolutionaries, and they were taken in a truck to the city of Matanzas. People in the streets cheered the militia members as they passed by on the way to the battlefront, with cries of "Be careful of the airplanes!" "Give it to 'em good!" and "Homeland or death!"

Dozens of men and women became medics and stretcher-bearers. They painted white crosses on vehicles that they had taken or borrowed from the counterrevolutionaries and went out to look for the wounded. The elderly took care of the funeral services and dug graves. At one point, more than 60 bodies —both of revolutionaries and of the enemy— arrived at the same time. They all received Christian burials.

Not one single resident of Jagüey Grande —not a soldier, or a militia member, or anyone on the battlefront— went over to the side of Brigade 2506.

That was the case all over Cuba.

Imitating Fidel

The heavily loaded plane received orders to take off. From the control tower, the agent in charge of the operation wished pilot Eduardo Ferrer luck. He would fly for four hours, from the Rethaluleu air base in the Guatemalan jungle to central Cuba, piloting a plane without any identifying marks on its fuselage and with the radio turned off.

Eduardo Ferrer had been a pilot with the Cuban commercial airline Aerovías Q, but had moved to the United States shortly after the victory of the Revolution. Now a CIA pilot, he was about to fly over Cuban airspace and run the risk of being fired on from the ground. His mission was to drop a load of weapons and explosives over an encampment of insurgent forces.

At close to midnight, he neared the Cuban coastline. He turned off his cabin lights and pushed forward on the controls. The four-engine plane began to descend. As he entered the Guamuhaya mountain range, he made several turns to avoid the peaks. Emerging from a cloud bank, he could see lights in the shape of a cross, shining like stars, that marked the landing area. The altimeter showed 400 feet. It was the right altitude. He pressed the green-light button and rang the bell. The PDOs (parachute dispatch officers) hooked the static lines and made their drops. A few seconds later, half a dozen parachutes ballooned in the darkness of the night. Ferrer turned the plane sharply and headed south over the Atlantic Ocean.

After gaining altitude, he turned on his lights, switched on the automatic pilot, sipped some coffee and lit a cigarette. He was satisfied. The mission had been a success, although he knew that real credit was due to those who had organized the rearguard.

Ferrer was right. The operation had been carefully worked out, step by step. What he and his superiors at Quarters Eye didn't know, however, was that Cuban State Security had taken part in its preparation.

The story of the air drop had begun a month earlier, when Benigno Balsa, an activist with the underground Movimiento de Recuperación Revolucionaria, Movement of Revolutionary Recovery, (MRR), had been summoned to a meeting with the group's coordinator. As he arrived at the majestic mansion on Avenue 17 and H Street in Vedado, Benigno thought about how this man would have many reasons for wanting to fight Castro.

Lino Bernabé, the house's owner and a national coordinator of the MRR, took him to the library and went straight to the point.

"The American Embassy" —as the anti-Castro agents somewhat euphemistically referred to the CIA station housed in that country's diplomatic offices— "asked me to find us a farm in the Escambray mountains to drop a shipment of weapons for the people under Commander Joaquín Benvibre. For now, the only thing the Americans need is a map with the name of the farm and neighboring farms. Evidently, they have the whole region mapped."

The next day, Benigno Balsa and a trusted acquaintance drove to the old colonial city of Trinidad in the foothills of the Escambray. At that time, it was the headquarters of the rearguard of the insurgent forces, which had been operating in the mountains for three months.

The city was euphoric with revolutionary ferment; placards with revolutionary emblems were hanging everywhere, and the footsteps of militia members could be heard echoing through its cobblestone streets. But the atmosphere was charged. In hushed conversations and street-corner murmurings, like a premonition of the storm that was coming, people were saying, "There are rebels in the Escambray!"

After visiting several houses, Balsa found the local head of the MRR and passed on the CIA's request. The man said he needed two days to make contact with the insurgents' chief and select a farm. Balsa agreed. Without a cover story to justify his presence in the city for two days, Balsa would definitely come under the suspicion of the people's guards in the Committees for Defense of the

Revolution, an organization recently created on every block of every city in the country. So he decided to continue on to the city of Cienfuegos, 100 kilometers to the west, where he had relatives and old friends. He also used the opportunity to make contact with other cells of the organization that were supplying the anti-Castro rebels of the Escambray with men and arms.

Forty-eight hours later he was on his way back to Trinidad, and, a few hours after arriving there, he began the trip back to the capital. Hidden in the engine of his car, a small, cylindrical talcum-powder container held the map requested by the Air Operations Section at Quarters Eye.

Days afterward, his superior, Air Force Colonel Stanley W. Beerli, located the name of the farm on the military map hanging from a wall in his office: El Lumbre.

Two weeks went by and Benigno was summoned again by the coordinator, Lino Bernabé.

"Go back to Trinidad. The drop will be within the next three days," Bernabé told Benigno before he could even sit down. The coordinator was visibly excited. "Tell them that they should dig four holes in the drop zone and light fires inside each of them, so that they can only be seen from the air. The distance between each hole should be 100 meters, in the shape of a cross. At 12 midnight, a group of men lined up over the imaginary cross will turn on flashlights behind their backs. The parachutes will be dropped over them."

Benigno left for Trinidad, and on the night of the action, he stayed hiding in one of the organization's safe houses, waiting to hear how it turned out. He couldn't sleep. The air-drop was the most important action he had participated in. It was considered decisive to maintaining the regional operations of the MRR column, and the MRR was the strongest of the organizations fighting the revolutionary government. That was why he was startled when, very early, someone knocked loudly on the door.

"We were getting ready to open the boxes when the first shot rang out," said the new arrival, somewhat calmer. "Then there were bursts of gunfire. They surprised us. They were milita members who were operating in the area, and apparently they heard the plane and saw the parachutes. Most of Benvibre's men who were part of the operation were taken prisoner, but he wasn't there. It was a miracle I was able to escape. And the worst thing is, we lost the boxes." Benigno scowled. The story was convincing.

"You escaped alone?" he asked skeptically.

"No," the other replied without understanding everything behind the question. "There were four others who came down with me."

Benigno began the journey back to Havana.

Before going to his appointment with Lino Bernabé, he met with a high-ranking State Security official in a safe house. Benigno was an undercover agent operating inside the MRR. He was head of supplies for the organization's forces in the Escambray.

This was an actual incident; it occurred in September 1960.

Three months earlier, the organizations that made up the Democratic Revolutionary Front (FRD) had promised the CIA they would start an insurgent movement in the Cuban mountains, particularly the Escambray.

Bisell believed it was possible to create such a movement, based on a campaign of guerrilla warfare as strong as the one Fidel Castro had led just two years earlier.

"If Castro defeated Batista with his guerrilla forces, why can't we bring him down with his own methods," he said in his Quarters Eye office. The reasoning may have seemed simplistic, but Bisell knew what he was doing. His guerrilla force would not have to get their weapons by capturing them from the enemy the way Fidel had to, or to save their pennies. His guerrilla fighters would be supplied by air, with hundreds of tons of weapons and explosives, and plenty of money and food. The anti-Castro movement would have leadership training camps and well-qualified instructors. To carry this out, the gray teams were trained on the Trax Base in Guatemala.

"If Castro was able to win with so little, why shouldn't he [Bisell], with so much? All he would have to do is imitate him."

The FRD members, following CIA instructions, set out to train their followers on the island to organize uprisings. Antonio Varona, the FRD's coordinator and top leader of Rescate, designated his brother-in-law José Ramón "Mongo" Ruisánchez, a lubricants salesman who was still in Cuba, to lead the subversive operation. Ruisánchez used the pseudonym of Augusto, and, with Varona's approval, was promoted to the rank of commander. He led operations from his luxury home, located in an exclusive part of Havana known as Country Club.

The attempt to imitate Fidel Castro had started off badly. The Cuban leader had marched at the front of his men, assuming the greatest danger.

The CIA station in Havana gave Ruisánchez a radio to communicate with the insurgent forces that were being established in the mountains.

On August 12, 1960, Osvaldo Ramirez, a former lieutenant the Rebel Army, joined the counterrevolutionary forces. He had fought against Batista with the Revolutionary Student Directorate. A few weeks after the victory, he had problems with the revolutionary authorities. He had forcibly evicted a group of farmers, burning their *bohíos* (thatched-roof houses), after they had occupied the property of a rich landowner in the Caracusey area, where Ramirez was head of the military post.

The same day that Ramirez joined the counterrevolution, a former commander, Sinesio Walsh, headed for the mountains along with a group of friends and relatives. On August 15, Evelio Duque Millar, who had close ties with the clergy, joined the antigovernment forces. Very soon afterwards, Commander Augusto appointed him military chief of the Liberation Army, keeping the post of civilian chief for himself. A month earlier, in July, two more former officers—Porfirio Remberto Ramírez, leading twenty-seven men, and Joaquín Benvibre, had taken up arms against the revolutionary government in a remote wooded area called Guanayara, the same place where they had made camp during the anti-Batista struggle.

Another central figure was Plinio Prieto, also a commander and a friend of former president Carlos Prío. Prieto traveled secretly to Miami stowing away on the merchant ship *Rio Escondido*. He met with CIA officials in the United States and was trained in the use of communications equipment. On his return to the island, he brought radio equipment that he set up in the Escambray and used to establish the coordinates for guiding the pilots who made weapons drops over the camps he commanded.

William Alexander Morgan Ruderth, a former paratrooper, adventurer, and braggart, had arrived in Cuba in 1958. He said he was there to "avenge the death of a friend at the hands of Batista's soldiers." He made contact with Eloy Gutiérrez Menoyo and soon afterward joined the rebel forces in the Escambray. Quickly, he was promoted to commander of the Second Front. After the victory of the Revolution, he joined an antigovernment conspiracy that could be traced back to the capital of the Dominican Republic and had the discreet and wary support of the CIA. Along with Menoyo, Morgan emerged as a hero for revealing the conspiracy and saving Fidel Castro. Others believed that when he sensed the plot could not be kept secret due to the number of people involved, he decided to go over to the other side and wait for further opportunities.

Apparently, these arrived in 1960. One night in September, Commander Morgan held a meeting at his Havana home with all of his personal escorts. He told them categorically that he had decided to rise up in arms against the government, and that he was absolutely sure that all of them would follow him, making it clear that those who didn't *se ñamaban* ("were no longer"). That phrase, spoken in his hurriedly-learned Spanish, was something he had picked up in the Escambray, where he would use it when sentencing to death those he believed to be spies or communists. Morgan, who enjoyed a certain amount of popular sympathy because of his boisterous personality, his corpulent body and childish round face, and his public admiration for Fidel Castro, ended the meeting by asserting the American Embassy would provide him with anything he wanted. It was not an exaggerated claim.

Days later, using his position as head of the River Repopulation Department under the National Institute of Agrarian Reform (INRA) —charged with tasks such as increasing the bullfrog population and the planting of gardenias in Guanayara Lagoon in the Escambray— he began transferring military equipment to the mountains. In the house of an old acquaintance and collaborator, Clotilde Pérez, he set up a center for recruiting and training the expected new recruits. Once the zone was consolidated, these recruits were to be trained by the black teams who at that time were completing their own training in the jungles of Guatemala. Morgan did not take up arms against the Revolution. He decided to take advantage of his INRA position and play both sides while continuing to move weapons and explosives into the Escambray.

Commander Evelio Duque found it strange, but not upsetting when José Ramón Ruisánchez ordered not to attack and to remain hidden. The order came from Quarters Eye, and the goal was to increase the insurgents' number without exposing them, to supply them with weapons, and to train them. If the government were alerted, it would be impossible to turn the situation around. But that had not been the course carried out by Fidel Castro, who, having barely regrouped the few forces remaining after the defeat of Alegría de Pío, went on to attack an enemy garrison, and was victorious.

The presence of the armed counterrevolutionary forces in the Escambray was not a secret for long. Military leaders in Las Villas province received information from farmers alerting them to the movement of people and weapons and even target practice. Immediately, patrols were dispatched.

"First we went to the home of Plinio Prieto's in-laws, but he had already left. So we went on to Clotilde Pérez' house. We got there and surrounded it; we captured two insurgents who were hiding there. The rest had left. We seized a shortwave radio, knapsacks, officers' stripes, and blankets. No weapons. We arrested 'La Gallega' Clotilde and took her with us. Afterward, we went out almost every day, but we didn't run into the insurgents. Then we got confidential information on where Plinio was with his troops. When we were getting ready to go out, an order came from Fidel to suspend operations."[1]

By September 1960, an insurgent force apparently had been consolidated in the Escambray Mountains. For the time being, they would try to avoid any encounters with the few patrols that went out after them. Their real combat mission was supposed to begin after the CIA teams arrived. But the tranquility in those places of lush beauty would not last for long. The storm that would hit the insurgents began on a farm in foothills known throughout the world for its celebrated tobacco crops. It was Hoyo de Manicaragua.

On September 8, the first serious force trained by the Revolution to combat insurgent groups finished its training and prepared to go

[1] Testimony of Rebel Army Lieutenant Rebelde Víctor Cortés, 1987. Author's archives.

into action. The news of the armed groups in the mountains had not gone unnoticed by Fidel Castro. In July 1960, after receiving the initial news and anticipating the danger, he issued instructions to organize rural militias in that mountain region. Close to 800 farmers were gathered on a farm called La Campana. There they received classes in infantry, assembling and disassembling weapons, tactics, and shooting. They were organized into twenty-five squads, each led by a Rebel Army officer who had distinguished himself in the guerrilla struggle.

"We were in the area of Guayabal de Yateras, Yateritas, close to Guantánamo, when Commander Filiberto Olivera received an order from Fidel to gather twenty-five of the Rebel Army's fittest officers; they brought us to La Campana."[2]

Most of these officers were from the countryside.

On September 5, as their training was coming to an end, Fidel Castro paid a surprise visit to their camp. Standing on a small hill, he talked to them about the political situation in the Escambray, the plans of the U.S. government and the quality of the weapons they were carrying, and he emphasized what their conduct should be with farmers' families and in combat. Elio Jorge was one of the farmers of the Escambray who appeared at La Campana in June 1960. He arrived alone, having come a long way. He had been plowing when a friend came up and told him "confidentially" to be very careful because there were insurgents in the area, and that they had their eye on him because they knew he was a revolutionary who supported the Agrarian Reform. He left his plow, untied his oxen and headed for his *bohío*.

"'I'm going to La Campana,' I told my wife, and I left. In La Campana I saw Fidel for the first time. He got up on a little hill and talked to us. He told us what we should do when we ran into the insurgents. Then he ordered a box of rifles to be opened and fired a Czech rifle. Then, he fired a mounted machine gun, standing up. He told us we had to respect the farmers, that we couldn't take anything without asking and that if they gave us food, to pay them in cash. That we had to respect the prisoners. I liked that."[3]

[2] Testimony of Rebel Army Lieutenant Addis Torres, 1987. Author's archives.
[3] Testimony of farmer Elio Jorge, 1981. Author's archives.

Fidel talked for about thirty minutes. Next to him, another farmer, Boliche Broche, held a canteen in his hands, which he would pass to him now and then.

After leaving La Campana, Fidel headed for the city of Cienfuegos, southwest of the Escambray, and in a fifth-floor room of the Hotel Jagua, he called an impromptu meeting of military leaders who would participate in the operation. With a map spread out over the bed, he explained the strategy to be followed. Fidel had decided to divide the battalion into squads and have them enter the mountainous region via different access routes. After combing the area, the squads would converge in Topes de Collantes, an elevated plain located south of the mountains, where a modern sanitorium had been built for tuberculosis patients.

While still in Cienfuegos, Fidel was informed of the presence of a group of insurgents in the region. Immediately, he organized a patrol and prepared to go out after them.

"Where are you going?" Commander Manuel Fajardo, recently appointed chief of operations, asked Fidel, as guide Juan Milián recalled.

"What do you mean where am I going? I'm the one in charge here."

The categorical answer permitted no more liberties. Fidel led the operation on the ground, and soon afterward a number of insurgents were captured.

On September 8, 800 farmers wearing uniforms of green shirts and blue pants left La Campana. Elio Jorge remembered how his squad traveled by train to the point from which they would climb Topes. Beginning at the very railroad line where they were dropped off, they began combing their assigned territory.

The idea of operating with farmers from the area was based on the revolutionary leadership's strategy of countering the counterrevolutionary forces with the local population, making it easier to penetrate the intricate world of family relations and traditions that tended to surround the struggle in these mountains.

The initiative was not a new one. It had been used for the first time on August 21, 1959, in Pinar del Rio. Fidel Castro was touring the

Great Cavern of Santo Tomás, and during a rest, farmer Leandro Malagón told him about the abuses being committed by Corporal Lara and his men, all of them fugitives of revolutionary justice.

Lara had been a soldier under the dictatorship and after the victory of the Revolution he was sentenced to death for the murder of twenty civilians. Before the sentence was carried out, he managed to escape and hide in the Sierra de los Órganos mountains. The search for him had been unsuccessful.

After listening to the farmer, Fidel told him to choose twelve men. The group received a little training and was given arms.

"'Negro, there's an order from Fidel to put together twelve farmers from the area to do a job. I came to get you,' farmer Leandro Rodríguez Malagón told me... Then we found out that the mission was to capture some counterrevolutionaries, who had risen up in arms under the command of the bandit Lara... After twenty-six days of training in the Managua military camp, we got a visit from Fidel, who confirmd we were ready and told Leandro, 'Malagón, you have three months to capture the counterrevolutionary band, and if you're victorious, there will be rural militias in Cuba.'"[4]

Weeks later, Lara was captured. The militias had been born in Cuba.

The Escambray was no exception. The presence of farmers who knew the terrain ensured the pursuit would be successful.

"In our camp in El Aguacate, I had stretched out in my hammock to take a nap and wake up at midnight. I knew that the insurgents moved at night. The barking of a dog in the distance woke me up. The barks marked where people were moving. After a silence, I heard more barking. Now they're close to so-and-so's farm, I told myself, and I woke up the unit. We advanced, following the line of the barking. Two hours later, the dogs had stopped barking. 'They've camped out on so-and-so's farm!' I told my troop, and we headed for it. We found the path made by the passing of the enemy troops. If you see the grass flattened, that's where they've just passed. I decided to wait for dawn before starting battle. With the first rays of light, I had the squads spread out and advance very cautiously.

[4] Testimony published in the *Granma* April 17, 1987, p. 4.

As we got near the insurgents' camp, I saw people rocking themselves in their hammocks. Then I remembered what Fidel had said: 'Throw yourselves down on the ground and open fire. Don't stop firing, and organize the battle.' That's what I did. One of the first to be wounded was the second-in-command of the insurgent column, which was demoralizing for them. From behind the bushes, their chief yelled at me, 'You filthy communists, look what you've done!' I knew Edel Montiel quite well, and I answered, 'Come out into the open, and let's have a showdown between you and me.' Montiel respected me from earlier times, and didn't accept the challenge."[5]

The effect of Elio Jorge's words was not long in coming. The insurgents were dispersed and several were captured. Edel Montiel was able to escape, and in December he left the Escambray to go to the United States.

After the capture of Sinesio Walsh, as he was being transferred to La Campana, the driver of the jeep tuned in Radio Swan, and, to the prisoner's surprise, he heard it being broadcast on the news that he was continuing to inflict defeat on the pro-Castro militias.

In the first ten days of October 1960, the former commander Plinio Prieto was captured and soon after, John Maples Spiritus, an American CIA agent who was carrying out secret missions linked to the activities of Commander William Morgan. Statements by Prieto and Spiritus led to the arrests of Morgan and Jesús Carreras, another commander of the Second Front involved in counterrevolutionary actions.

On September 30, a new air operation became a tragicomedy. The parachutes fell into a recently created cooperative. Immediately, the farmers picked up the boxes and took them to the administration office. Soon after that, Commander Manuel Fajardo, head of operations in the Escambray, appeared. He proceeded to open them and made an initial count. "One bazooka, two 60-mm. mortars, two light machine guns with bipods, two Browning automatic rifles, nineteen Thompson machine guns, six Garand rifles, eight Springfields, two .45 pistols, 108 hand grenades, 16 boxes of TNT, and plenty of ammunition."[6]

---

[5] Testimony of Elio Jorge. Author's archives.
[6] Archives of the Ministry of the Interior, Collection of the Office on Bandits

Enough to arm a group of forty-five men. Plus, there were seven sacks of black beans, three of rice, and one of salt. The commander took the weapons with him and distributed the food among the farmers of the area.

The reports that Commander Augusto, Mongo Ruisánchez, began receiving could not have been more discouraging. The silence around the presence of the insurgents in the Escambray had been broken. Forces made up of rural militias under the command of experienced Rebel Army guerrilla fighters had entered almost every access route to the Escambray and had combed every inch of the area. A number of clashes had taken place, almost 200 men had been captured, and their weapons, radio equipment, and encampments had been seized. And although several insurgent chiefs remained, including Osvaldo Ramírez and Evelio Duque, who had managed to evade the offensive, it was evident that under such conditions, the arrival of the teams from Guatemala could not be expected.

Ruisánchez rushed to communicate the bad news to the American Embassy, and from there, messages were radioed to Quarters Eye. The CIA had not been able to consolidate territory for the insurgency in the mountains of Cuba.

The first large-scale operation against the insurgent groups was coming to an end. In late October, 177 insurgents and their collaborators, including the commanders Plinio Prieto and Sinesio Walsh, stood trial in the Leoncio Vidal Garrison in the city of Santa Clara. Charges were being brought against William Morgan.

On October 31, a coded message was sent from Quarters Eye to the chief of the Trax Base, Colonel Frank J. Egan. It instructed him to begin conventional warfare training. The men were to be organized into an assault brigade.

The CIA and its director of plans, Richard Bissell, had abandoned their strategy of destroying the Cuban Revolution through guertilla warfare. This would not be completely discarded; it would be used from then on as a way of supporting the new plan. The invasion had been born.

It was clearly impossible to imitate Fidel Castro.

Trax Base

Irán found it strange that the house looked so empty; he looked at his watch and realized he was late. He hurried his step, opened the wrought-iron gate, crossed the garden, took the six steps in two bounds, and rang the doorbell. It was the house where he had signed up ten days earlier. After the medical exam, they told him to wait for a telegram. And now he was here again, telegram in hand, ready to go off into the unknown, but the mansion was empty. Suddenly an idea occurred to him.... He ran to a nearby telephone booth and dialed the number of the person who had recruited him. After a pause, a voice on the other end of the line gave him a different address and assured him that if he hurried he could make it.

"Make it where?" he asked naively.

"That's a military secret," the voice responded, hanging up. Irán looked at his watch. Coconut Grove was far, but he could get there by cab in twenty minutes.

"In different businesses and industries, management is implementing a policy, signaling to their Cuban exile employees that when they leave for Cuba —clearly, of course, as part of the invasion army, which was registered in the offices of the Front, located on 12th Street between 9th and 10th Avenues N.W. in the same city— that once they had signed up, they would be given more details outside the country, and that no further information would be provided in the United States. After about a week, more or less, he was called again to the same office. He arrived about 7 p.m., but he didn't find anyone, because they'd already left. They gave him a telephone number to call the place where they'd gone. When he called, they gave him an address, telling him that if he hurried, he could make it."[1]

Colonel Martín Elena, head of the FRD general staff, opened the door.

"You're late," he said reproachingly, making a gesture of disapproval. Irán had nothing to say. He had never been a soldier before, and it seemed ridiculous to find himself there, signed up for a war where he had simply arrived late. For a few seconds, the other man's disapproving look crushed him. He was about to turn around and leave when the colonel broke the silence.

"Come in," he said.

The large, white, two-story wooden house was a beehive of activity. More than 50 men were preparing to leave. After surrendering his passport, Irán received a sack. Inside, he found a khaki uniform, three dark green uniforms, two caps of the same color, two pairs of boots, a jacket, six pairs of socks, four changes of underwear, two blue caps, and two belts. A Cuban man then helped him fill out a form with the necessary information to receive a salary. It would be $175 a month, because he didn't have any children. If he had, they would have paid him another $75 for the first child and $25 more for each additional one. When they asked him where they should send the money, he said his parents. He thought, that way, at least the folks would be able to get through their difficult economic situation. Irán was not concerned about where the money was coming from. Some people had told him it was contributed by Americans whose property had been confiscated by the Revolution. Others said the U.S. government had to be behind the whole thing.

Finally, they gave him a dogtag, which he hung around his neck. Printed on it was the number that would identify him from then on.

Irán Gómez Rodríguez had left Cuba on June 24, 1959, six months after Fidel Castro triumphed, after realizing he had nothing to do there. Under the government of Fulgencio Batista, he had been a fifth-class administrator in the Ministry of the Treasury, directly under the orders of the minister. He had run for city council in the 1954 elections, and had been defeated.

---

[1] Statements of Irán Gómez Rodríguez, invader, 1961, Archives of the Ministry of the Interior.

After January 1, he was viewed as a Batista supporter and had to endure the condemnation of his neighbors. More unfortunately, his father, a former major in the police, was under investigation. So he went to Miami, where some 10,000 Cubans who had left the island over the previous six months were beginning to take over Eighth Street, in what would become the center of Little Havana. Irán began working at Delta Airlines for a weekly salary of $70, enough to live decently but not enough to satisfy the personal ambitions of a man who had tasted power and was thirty-one years old. So he didn't think twice after they talked to him about the recruitment offices on 17th and Biscayne Boulevard, 27 Flagler, and 3593 12th Street, among many others. He was in the United States, and it seemed like it might be the beginning of his return to Cuba.

At the recruiting office, they gave him a medical exam and then, in a laboratory, they took blood samples and examined his lungs. He waited for ten days before they finally told him, in a phone call, to come to the 12th Street office again. He was surprised that they had asked him to come at 6 p.m., and that they told him to bring a toothbrush and a razor.

Irán looked at the number on the dogtag again, and when he thought about death, he shuddered. A short while later, he was being subjected to a detailed body search, for which he had to undress, so that they could be sure that he was not carrying any forbidden items, such as a compass or weapon. He placed his watch in an envelope with his personal documents. It was time to leave. That was when he saw the first American, right when it was time to leave the house. The mission assigned to the Cubans ended there, with the noise of the recruiting centers. From then on, the more important part would begin, and that was a matter for the Americans.

The man, through an interpreter, specified how many men went into each truck. Irán and fifteen of his comrades settled into one with a Hertz logo. The American closed the door and locked it. Irán breathed a sigh of relief. In the last few days, as he had been waiting for the telegram, he had been on the verge of believing the Front's propaganda that the force to free the homeland was exclusively composed of Cuban exiles. It made him sleepless. He could not imagine disembarking in Cuba from a recreational yacht, armed with a shotgun. This wasn't Moncada or the *Granma*. That had nothing to do with him. That's why, even though the American seemed skeptical and had locked him into the truck without telling him where he was going, or even saying good-bye or good luck, Irán felt relieved.

"It looks like the Americans are in on this," he commented to the young man sitting next to him, Alberto Julio Bolet Suárez, who agreed with a smile. He, too, felt relieved. At the age of twenty-one he had no desire to lose his life in an enterprise of dubious prospects. He had agreed to the risks, because danger was assumed, but "if the Americans were in the mix, then getting Fidel Castro out of power would be a walk in the park." Then he would get back what was his.

"He and his family went to live in the city of Miami on July 22, 1959, for reasons that were economic more than anything else, given that when his father's chicken farm —which sat on three-fourths of a caballería [about 25 acres]— was nationalized, he was left without work... He signed up at the Front's office, because he felt the Revolution had hurt him, and he believed there was a communist dictatorship in Cuba run by the Russians, Chinese, and Czechs. This was the product of the extensive propaganda carried out in Cuban and American newspapers, on the radio and on TV newscasts, and also, of the fact that several of his friends had signed up and were being held prisoner.[2]

Unlike many of the others who were there, Albertico had not had to travel to the United States. When the Revolution triumphed, he was studying civil engineering at the University of Miami.

"And do you think that the Americans are going to land with us?" another passenger in the truck asked shyly. He was Manuel Menéndez Pou, 21, who had decided to return to Cuba to get something back.

"He claims he left the country because his father was laid off from Aspuru & Co. S.A., which he was president of, having been left out after the company was nationalized... That he subsequently received an offer from Miami to be an export representative for different companies in South America, and that was why he went

[2] Statements of Alberto Julio Bolet Suárez, invader, 1961. Archives of the Ministry of the Interior.

to that country with his family. Later, on October 24, 1960, the subject under interrogation left for the same place to both seek work and find out why he hadn't been accepted as a recruit to the Front...

[...] This occurred in the context of a wave of systematicand false propaganda that the militias in Cuba were discontented...and that the island was full of Czechs, Chinese, and Russians."[3]

"I think we'll be the first to land. They'll be behind us," was the comment of Néstor Pino, another passenger. After graduating from high school in 1957, he enrolled in the National Army's School of Cadets; he had decided to follow in the footsteps of his father, a retired lieutenant colonel. But Néstor Pino was not able to see his military dreams come true. On January 21, 1959, a bearded officer gave him his discharge order. After the Rebel Army took over the School of Cadets, Néstor did not hide his disdain for these slovenly guerrillas, who did not stand rigidly at attention before their superiors and who were so popular with the girls. Soon afterward, Néstor was arrested and held at the La Cabaña Fortress, accused of being involved in a conspiracy against Fidel Castro organized by Dominican dictator Rafael Leónidas Trujillo. Four months later, he was released and his case dismissed for lack of evidence.

In August 1960, after several months of conspiring, he learned that exiles were being recruited to organize an army against Fidel Castro and he went to Miami to join it. Later that month, Néstor was dressed once again in a military uniform, only this time as a recruit of the future expeditionaries.

"The Americans are invading Cuba because they're not going to let their property be taken away," José Ramón Pérez Peña chimed in from the other bench as he lit a cigarette, disobeying the American's order to not smoke in the truck. "And we're going to give them the means to do it." José Ramón was twenty-five years old, and a native of Sagua la Grande. He had been an employee at a Ten Cents store, part of the Woolworth chain, in the city of Camagüey. When the revolutionary government nationalized the Ten Cents stores, he left for New York along with twenty other employees.

---

[3] Statements of Manuel Menéndez Pou, invader, 1961. Archives of the Ministry of the Interior.

The company had offered work to anyone who wanted to go to the United States. He began working for a weekly salary of $90, but quit after two friends invited him to go sign up at the Front's office.

Arturo Menéndez Rodil did not seem to be paying attention to the conversation in the truck. His thoughts were on the café on Eighth Street where his girlfriend worked. Arturito was hopelessly in love with her. That is why he followed her to the United States. He was not interested in politics. He had signed up because she had left him. Arturito felt disappointed and depressed. That was the only way to explain the step he had taken. He believed that when she found out about his decision to join the crazy military adventure, she would come looking for him and everything would work out. But there he was in the truck, with that sack on his lap, on his way to the unknown.

The trip lasted two hours until the van stopped at one of the hangars on an airbase that none of them were familiar with. They thought they must be far from Miami, but the Opa-Locka base was actually only thirty minutes from downtown. What had just happened was part of the plan to misinform the recruits, in case Castro's spies had infiltrated the group. The truck's driver, a CIA agent from the paramilitary group operating in Miami under the command of Colonel Rodrick, had orders to keep driving in circles outside the city before going to the airport.

For that same reason, the first order that the American gave when the truck's door was opened inside the hangar was for the recruits to place all of their personal objects in an envelope, including their watches. That way they couldn't time the flight that would take them to the training base. Without the slightest embarrassment and in a professional tone, the officer in charge ordered them to undress. Shortly afterward, four Americans thoroughly searched their bodies, clothing, and bags. From then on, it would be impossible for any Castro spy to transmit information about the operation under way. He could only do so by managing to get out of the camps —something that was almost impossible— or wait until they landed on the island. And by then it would be very late.

An hour after opening the back gate of the truck, splitting the word "Hertz" in two, another American closed it again. The recruits sat inside in silence. They were feeling uncomfortable after the strip search. After all, none of them had reason to be working for Fidel Castro. After a brief trip, the truck made a turn, stopped, and slowly backed up until it came to a halt. The back gate was opened again. "Out, out, move it, do not look to your left or right!" another American standing by the truck yelled in Spanish. The recruits began moving from the truck to an airplane. They could not see anything on either side of them because curtains had been hung. Inside, the plane's captain showed them where to sit. The man didn't look American or Cuban. Later on in the camp, they guessed he was a European, maybe a White Russian or from Poland. They were right. The pilots hired to fly the recruits from Miami to the training base were Cold War veterans from Europe.

Thirty minutes later the four-engine military Douglas C-54 rolled over the tarmac until it lifted off; in its belly it carried some fifty new recruits. None of them could see the view; the windows had been sealed. But Arturo Menéndez Rodil was not aware of that. Lovesick, he settled in without caring about who was sitting next to him. He was preoccupied, thinking about his girlfriend. But he started when he felt the plane touching down. They had only been flying for forty minutes. "They've dumped us in Cuba!" he exclaimed. The faces of those who could hear him tightened. It wasn't possible. Except for the former soldiers, none of them even knew how to shoot.

When the plane was opened, the recruits were surprised to see the same face that had shut them in. "Move it, move it!" the American yelled again, and the recruits returned to the truck. They were taken to a hangar where about 100 cots had been readied. "Because of a problem with the plane, the flight is suspended until tomorrow night," one of the Americans told them. "Until then, nobody leaves here. Tomorrow you'll have a tasty breakfast, lunch, and dinner. Rest and don't think too much. Good night."

The hangar doors were closed and locked.

The next night, the recruits departed again, this time with better luck. After a flight of almost seven hours, the C-54 touched down on a landing strip in the middle of a jungle. When the cabin door was opened and the sunlight poured in, the men who were closest shut their eyes. For the previous seven hours, they had been sitting in near darkness, lit only by a few weak bulbs.

At 7 a.m., José Ramón Pérez Peña stretched and breathed in the fragrance of the wet jungle, and then saw several airplanes lined up on the landing field.

"What are they?" he asked Néstor Pino, who was next to him.

"They're B-26 light bombers."

"And why aren't they marked?"

The question from Manuel Menéndez went unanswered. An American dressed in green coveralls took the group to breakfast. Bacon and eggs, ham sandwiches with cheese and pickles, juice and coffee. A paradise of a breakfast in the middle of the jungle. The men quickly devoured it, even Arturito, who set his heartbreak aside for later.

Before getting into trucks, the more curious of the recruits observed that their license plates were Guatemalan. Some of them wondered what all the mystery was about, while others guessed it was more disinformation.

In the vehicles, it took about an hour and thirty minutes to climb up to Trax Base from the Rayo Base, located in Retalhuleu, crossing through a town of the same name with some 4,000 inhabitants. The Cubans were struck by the poverty of the townspeople. The children ran alongside the trucks, barefoot and half-naked, asking for cigarettes.

The recruits were given a strange order before the trucks entered the town: to remove their hats. "Why?" someone asked. Nobody ever knew for sure what the answer was. Apparently it was one of the many crazy and ineffective measures used to try to trick those Guatemalan Indians, whose lives of dire poverty made them closer to Fidel Castro than to Quarters Eye.

Once on the base, the recruits were lined up and their Cuban superior, José Pérez San Román, addressed them.

"Recruits, from this moment on, you are part of a regular army whose objective is to invade Cuba to overthrow the communist dictatorship and get rid of Fidel Castro once and for all. Our mission is exclusively military. We are not interested in any political ideas that you may have. We are anticommunists and friends of the United States, and that's good enough. Meanwhile, it is possible that we may have to fight in other places to defend our great friends, the Americans. In a few hours, you will be assigned to your respective units. Let me remind you that any type of political or ideological indoctrination is strictly forbidden on this base. And for those of you who may doubt our possibilities of victory for one instant, I am just going to tell you one thing, which I want you to remember well: the Americans are with us, and the Americans can't lose."

Trax Base, named as such because its purpose was training, was located on a farm called Helvetia. Its owner was Alberto Alejos, the brother of Guatemala's ambassador in Washington. It had three levels, taking advantage of the way the land had been terraced. The target practice field and marching ground were on the first level. The barracks, dining hall, kitchen, infirmary, and other offices were on the second. The third and highest level held the dormitories and offices of the CIA agents, who had their own dining hall and even a small projection room.

By August 1, 1960, the first forty recruits had arrived at Helvetia. They were temporarily housed in Alejos's country home. They would leave early in the morning to head off to the mountains and return at dinner time. On August 15, the first barrack, Section K, was ready, and the group that was still on the farm was transferred to Trax. These first Trax trainees, who had passed courses in Useppa, Florida, and Fort Gulick, Panama, were assigned to be instructors for the other recruits that began to arrive.

During those days of August 1960, Dulles and Bissell briefed President Eisenhower on their initial strategy for overthrowing Fidel Castro's government. The document they drafted to inform the president outlined the operation as follows:

"The initial phase of paramilitary operations envisages the development, support and guidance of dissident groups in three areas of Cuba: Pinar del Río, Escambray and Sierra Maestra. These groups will be organized from concerted guerrilla action against the regime. The second phase will be initiated by a combine sea-air assault by FRD forces on the Isle of Pines coordinated with general guerrilla activity on the main island of Cuba. This will establish a close-in staging base for future operations. The last phase will be air assault on the Havana area with the guerrilla forces in Cuba moving on the ground from these areas into the Havana area also."[4] This plan was

[4] Central Intelligence Agency: *Inspector General's Survey of the Cuban Operation, October 1961*, op. cit., p. 30.

quickly discarded, particularly the idea of occupying the Isle of Pines. The revolutionary leadership, anticipating the threat, had sent considerable forces and arms to defend that piece of territory. The plan for an air raid on the capital was never mentioned again; it was simply a ludicrous idea. For several months afterward, the CIA's strategy continued to be based on creating a powerful insurgent movement in Cuba's mountains.

By early October, almost 500 men were on the base training for guerrilla warfare. Reveille was sounded at 5:45 a.m., with the first light of day. Fifteen minutes later they had breakfast and training began. Physical exercise included daily marches of twelve kilometers at an altitude of 7,500 feet. They were trained in assembling and disassembling weapons and in target practice and they were given classes in theory by U.S. Army Colonel Valeriano Vallejo, a Filipino who had distinguished himself in the guerrilla war fought in his country's jungles against the Japanese occupiers. Vallejo taught them about intelligence, air drops, camouflage, propaganda, and recruitment, among other topics.

The Americans commanded the entire facility. They planned the courses, controlled the weapons, and controlled communications with Quarters Eye, where the real decisions were made. The base commander was U.S. Colonel Frank J. Egan; the commanding officer of the Cuban instructors, Oscar Carol, a former lieutenant in the Cuban regular army; the aide-de-camp, José Abréu; the head of military intelligence, Manuel Blanco Navarro; the head of supplies, Ramón Ferrer Mena; and chief of operations, José Pérez San Román. The military records of these cadres reflected the importance that the CIA chiefs had placed on the military aspect. They set aside other considerations, such as possible opposition among the recruits to these former military officers, some of whom had been part of the Fulgencio Batista regime. However, the CIA had made an effort to recruit former officers who had clean records and had mostly been trained in American schools.

On Trax Base, the future guerrilla fighters were organized into infiltration teams. By mid-August, the first pilot recruits arrived. They remained on the farm until the air base was finished.

On August 19 training officially began. They organized the men into twelve teams, with each team divided into two. They were called the gray teams and the black teams. The first were made up of eight to ten men and the second of twenty to twenty-five. The grays were composed of an intelligence officer, a psychological warfare officer, an armaments officer, a demolition officer, a radio operator, and a commanding officer. The intelligence officer's mission was to obtain as much information as possible on the military bases, armaments, military capacity, as well as on the individuals who wanted to join the counterrevolutionary forces and training they had received. The psychological warfare officer would be in charge of propaganda aimed at destabilizing the civilian population, the Rebel Army, and the militias. The armaments officer would teach civilian personnel how to use weapons and the explosives officer would oversee preparations for sabotage actions and train any Cubans who joined. Finally, the radio operator would maintain communication with the rearguard base, sending all information obtained and receiving instructions.

Once the gray teams reported the establishment of minimal conditions of security and support, the black teams would infiltrate. Their mission was to train those who joined the fight against the revolutionary government, expanding the guerrilla warfare until the government had been overthrown. The gray teams would infiltrate first, paving the way for the black teams.

After being captured, Eulogio Lavandeiro Torrijos recounted the plan of action for the guerrilla war that the teams were supposed to carry out.

"They planned to land in three different places in Oriente: the Sierra Maestra, Sierra Cristal and Guantánamo… In Camagüey, they planned to land near the Sierra de Cubitas…and in Las Villas, they would land near the Escambray, and then, the Cienaga de Zapata (Zapata Swamp). In Matanzas, they planned for one gray team to land and then a black team. In Havana, two teams would land, which were to operate in the city. In Pinar del Rio, one would land by Sierra de los Órganos, and finally, the Isle of Pines would be infiltrated with the mission of freeing prisoners from the National Penitentiary…" Lavandero was on the latter team.

Each team was identified with the initials of a word corresponding to the international phonetics code: A—Alpha; B—Bravo, C—Charlie;

D—Delta; E—Eco; F—Foxtrot; G—Golf; H—Hotel; I—Indio; J—Juliet; K—Kilo; L—Lima.

They underwent physical training and marched through the jungle at an altitude of 7,000 feet. The third week of October, they practiced firing various weapons, including pistols, submachine guns, M-1 Garand rifles, .30-caliber machine guns, mortars, and 57-mm. recoilless cannons. They received training in explosives, communications, basic survival skills, and parachuting. Special attention was given to guerrilla warfare, with practical exercises; intelligence; a very brief class on propaganda, with emphasis on the most effective way to carry it out on different types of people; psychological warfare; clandestine demolition; maps and reception of air and sea drops.

The recruits listened attentively to the stories of Chino Vallejo and other instructors, including Lithuanians, Ukrainians, and other Europeans, and, of course, the Americans.

The teams' missions would be determined by the type of area in Cuba they were to operate. There were also some general principles. These included uniting dispersed groups and training them in such guerrilla tactics as ambushes, interrogations, attacks, reconnaissance, use of weapons and explosives, clandestine operations, and communications. The main mission for those operating in the city was to contact the different underground groups and train them.

For parachute training, they were transferred in groups to the San José de Buenavista farm. They made the three jumps required to pass the course in an area over the La Suiza farm, located on the Halcón base.

The main base, Trax, was guarded by Guatemalan soldiers. "Every day, they picked up eight Guatemalan soldiers and dropped them off in different places to guard the roads that connected Trax with Suiza Base and Aurora Base."[5]

Despite the vigilance, on Saturdays and Sundays the recruits would escape from the camp by bribing or tricking the Guatemalan

---

[5] Statements of Carlos Hernández Vega, invader, 1961, Archives of the Ministry of the Interior.

guards. They would head for the town of Mazaltenango, where they sold pistols to buy drinks and be with women. On one occasion, the chief of the rural police in that town reprimanded a group of Cubans for carrying guns and creating a scandal. The recruits threatened him with their rifles and forced him to do pushups. These types of incidents endangered the secrecy of the operation. And since the operation was highly controversial, given its very nature and the course of action chosen for it, the sentries were ordered to shoot any man who tried to leave the camp. A small jail was built, surrounded by a fence, for locking up those who tried to escape. The most dangerous men were taken to Petén, a detention center in the middle of the jungle, where snakes abounded.

The recruits watched films, especially ones about war and the fight against communism. On Sundays, priests officiated mass at 7:10 a.m.

In the camps, bulletins and propaganda with heavily anti-Castro content were given out, and they listened to Radio Swan. They had been warned that their correspondence would be censored, and were strictly forbidden from giving out any information about where they were or what they were doing. Pablo Organvidez Parada, an FBI agent, had been assigned to monitor the Cuban recruits.

"Letters from their relatives were reviewed in Miami before being sent to the Retalhuleu air base. If they had any problems, they didn't leave Miami. The ones sent by recruits were delivered in Guatemala City to the U.S. military attaché, McQuady. Recruits that showed any evidence of having problems, McQuady would instruct FBI agents like me, and then we would infiltrate the unit where the men were that we had to watch."[6]

In early November 1960, the training ended. Twelve teams made up of almost 600 agents were ready to begin infiltrating into Cuba. Troop morale was good. Radio Swan made daily announcements of fresh outbreaks of insurgency, and trumpeted victories against the Fidel Castro regime, which apparently was crumbling.

On black team C-Charlie, Arturito Menéndez showed little interest in being infiltrated into Cuba. He had written many letters to his beloved, and was anxiously awaiting her answer.

[6] Statements of Pablo Organvidez Parada, FBI agent and invader, 1961, Archives of the Ministry of the Interior.

In early November, the alarm sounded on the base, and the recruits ran to line up in formation. They were told that the time had come; strangely, however it would not be for Cuba, but for the president of Guatemala, Miguel Idígoras Fuentes. A group of young officers had led an uprising of several army units in Puerto Barrios. One hundred men were selected to retake the military airport in that town, which had been occupied by the rebels. Another 100 remained at Trax Base, ready to leave if necessary. The decision to use the Cubans had been made in Washington.

The C-47 planes, carrying 100 men, took off.

"Roughly three months after I arrived, our unit saw combat for the first time. But not against Castro. We were called in to help put down a coup attempt in Puerto Barrios, close to the Honduran border, against Guatemalan president Miguel Ydigoras Fuentes... Two hundred of us were selected. We were issued weapons, then trucked to Retalhuleu air base where we were to board the planes that would take us to Puerto Barrios...

"At the air base, we waited for our orders... The plan was for about a hundred of us to fly to Puerto Barrios —three C-46s of us, roughly thirty-three to a plane— take over the airfield after it had been softened up by our own Free Cuba air force of B-26 light bombers....

Finally we arrived over Puerto Barrios, and the day's first screw-up occurred. The B-26s hadn't finished bombing and strafing the area, so we had to circle above the bay and wait for them to complete their mission.... My friend Nestor Pino was in the doorway, one hand tight on the rope, the other holding a Thompson submachine gun...

"The rear wheel came down and the pilot reversed the engines, the sound of the props roaring in our ears. Quickly the plane taxied down the runway.... Then, suddenly, a Guatemalan officer shouted above the noise: 'We're taking fire! They're shooting at us! The plane reached the end of the runway and spun around...

Later, when we returned to Retalhuleu, I was one of the people who checked the fuselage of the aircraft thoroughly—and we discovered not a single bullet hole. Even though we hadn't actually seen any fighting, we were assembled the following day and the Guatemalan minister of defense showed up and congratulated us for our help."[7]

[7] Félix Rodríguez Mendigutía: Ob. cit., pp.57-61.

The men remained in Retalhuleu for a week, ready to go anywhere to help the Guatemalan government, but it was not necessary. Idígoras sent messages of thanks to the Cubans on the base and promised he would visit soon. Years later, some investigators tried to create the myth that the help of the Cuban recruits, including bombings by the Brigade's air force, was decisive to crushing the rebellion.

When all signs seemed to indicate that the moment of departure was near, the recruits began noticing unusual movements on the base. All of them were surprised when Colonel Vallejo, the guerrilla warfare expert, was replaced by U.S. Marine Corps Colonel Jack Hawkins, who was introduced under the pseudonym of Frank, and who would soon distinguish himself by his severe sense of discipline and poorly disguised disdain for the Cubans. But Hawkins knew nothing about guerrillas. Evidently, a major shift in strategy had been decided on in the offices of Dulles and Bissell.

The CIA had decided to destroy the Cuban Revolution in a single, overwhelming blow: an air and sea landing, with the aim of establishing a beachhead.

On the base, the gray and black teams were dissolved and the men organized into squads, companies, and battalions. Néstor Pino, Alberto Bolet, and Manolito Menéndez Pou were incorporated into Battalion One, of paratroopers. Irán Gómez and José Peña were in Battalion Two, infantry, and Arturito Menéndez Rodil was assigned to the armored battalion. But Arturito had ruled out the idea of setting sail for Cuba. His fiancée had written him and begged him to come home. The only thing Arturito could think about was rejoining his girlfriend as he looked for a way to escape the camp.

On Trax Base, a new language was being spoken: tanks, airborne troops, engineering corps, and heavy weaponry.

The recruits did not understand the change, and even today, some of them believe that the guerrilla warfare tactic would have successfully overthrown Fidel Castro's government. It was because of the Radio Swan broadcasts. At that time, not a single insurgent group in any mountainous region of the country had been able to conquer even a small zone of operation for the infiltration teams to occupy. The drops had been catastrophes, and most of the weapons and explosives had fallen into the hands of the militias.

But soon, everyone on Trax Base was enthusiastic about the invasion idea. To take a beachhead and hold it for several days and then receive the support of U.S. troops would not be a difficult task. Some of them managed to get their hands on cameras. Snapshots of themselves on the conquered beaches would doubtless make great souvenirs. That was what Colonel Hawkins must have thought too, when he said that each battalion should have its own war correspondent with his own movie camera.

Using the insurgents who were operating in the Escambray Mountains was still on the CIA's agenda. The city chosen for the landing was south of those mountains. The insurgents would come down to support the invaders. That way, guerilla warfare was not ruled out.

The cage

On September 8, 1960, military operations to wipe out insurgent groups in the Escambray began on La Campana farm. Within weeks, on October 14, Fidel Castro, as prime minister, signed a resolution creating the Escambray Plan (Las Villas-29 Agricultural Development Area). The Plan was a state project to transform that backward mountain region. In the Escambray, there was no electricity. Tens of thousands lived in dirt-floor *bohíos* (huts) with plank walls and thatched roofs. Infant mortality rates were astronomically high. Gastroenteritis, diarrhea, malaria, tuberculosis, parasitism, and polio were endemic. There were no doctors or hospitals. Few could read, the area was culturally isolated, and it had virtually no means of communications.

In a little more than five years, despite the irregular struggle that was taking place there, results were achieved. Several dozen villages of comfortable, completely furnished houses were built, with electricity and sewage. Five school complexes and seventeen rural schools were built, along with five hospitals with modern equipment that provided free services. Six hundred kilometers of local roads were built. Public transportation was introduced, dozens of sports facilities were built, and several recreation centers were set up.

Six improvised movie theaters mounted on four-wheel-drive trucks equipped with generators began touring the villages and providing shows. It was the first time the immense majority of the Escambray's inhabitants had seen images on celluloid. A theater group was set up in the mountains; its plays were staged wherever there were settlements of human beings, no matter how remote. Electrification began in the Escambray, and in a little over twenty years, the statistics were completely different; more than 80 percent of the territory had electric power. The first television sets appeared, as did many more radios. More than 7,000 young literacy teachers from the cities fanned out throughout the Escambray in early 1961 in ten months they taught 28,000 of the region's habitants how to read and write. These social improvements steadily and irreversibly undercut the bases of support for the insurgency.

In late 1960, however, the Escambray Plan was just beginning. And the CIA and Pentagon strategists in Quarters Eye had selected a very old city, close to these mountains, as the point at which to invade Cuba. Trinidad was located to the south, on the coast, just fifteen kilometers from Topes de Collantes, the most active peak in the Escambray. Its nearness to the Port of Casilda a bit further south, its beautiful beaches, and the fact of having an airport were decisive to the CIA's choice.

The Guamuhaya mountain range played an important role in the new strategy. The idea was to create a group of anti-Castro forces who at the right moment would support the invasion by completing the siege and isolation of the city. Two insurgent chiefs, survivors of the military pursuit that had begun September 8 in La Campana, remained indisputable leaders of the counterrevolutionaries: Evelio Duque Miyar and Osvaldo Ramírez.

In November 1960, Quarters Eye told the CIA station in Havana to have José Ramón Ruisánchez quickly prepare the new uprisings and coordinate the supply of weapons and explosives by air and sea. In Miami, Howard Hunt pressed leaders of the Revolutionary Front to get their organizations in Cuba —which, by this time, had underground movements— to mobilize some of their members to go to the mountains.

In November and December, several hundred counterrevolutionaries were taken from the cities to the foothills of the Escambray, where groups of collaborators guided them through the region, which was a labyrinth. Others who joined were local residents, encouraged by relatives and friends already in the insurgent camps. On Swan Island, the radio station created by David Atlee Phillips stepped up its "psychological softening-up" work.

"They were going to take away our children and send them to Russia. They were going to get rid of money and give out vouchers. To go anywhere, you'd need permission from the government. They had given out land for us to work, but they would take it away again. That was what people were saying all over those hills. Radio Swan came in better than the radio stations from here."[1]

The CIA gave its approval when Ruisánchez appointed Evelio Duque as commander-in-chief of the Escambray Front. During the Batista dictatorship, Duque had not exactly stood out for his aggressiveness in combat. After the triumph of the Revolution, he had a brief career as a revolutionary. He did not support the Agrarian Reform, which took land from his family and friends.

In the skirmishes of September and October, he managed to avoid engaging in combat with the militias and kept himself safe. In this new stage, however, where confrontation was inevitable, it would not be easy for him to keep his position as leader.

Clashes with Osvaldo Ramírez, a hot-tempered man, were not long in coming. On December 10, the two were in a place known as Dos Arroyos.

"Evelio reminded Osvaldo that he was commander-in-chief, and Osvaldo replied, how could that be, if he had never fired a single shot. 'I've got documents here that say so,' Evelio retorted. The argument heated up and Osvaldo took out his pistol. Then we intervened and calmed them down. Osvaldo wanted to shoot him. When we were leaving, Evelio told Osvaldo that he was the one who was recognized out there, and Osvaldo told Evelio that if he came into his territory, he'd smoke him."[2]

Commander Augusto (José Ramón Ruisánchez) knew about the disagreements between Evelio and Osvaldo Ramírez —who at the time was the commander of the strongest insurgent column— and he had reported it to the agents in the U.S. Embassy. Things began to look bad. Their plans required united forces capable of coordinating actions that would be carried out prior to and on D-Day.

During these December days, the CIA learned that one of the underground organizations operating in Havana had recruited a

---

[1] Testimony of José Reboso Febles, insurgent, 1987. Author's archives.
[2] Testimony of Demetrio Clavelo Solís, insurgent, 1987. Author's archives.

Rebel Army commander. In Quarters Eye that was welcome news, because the man fit perfectly with their plans for the Escambray. He had fought there as part of the forces of the Revolutionary Student Directorate, was outstanding in combat, and had won the sympathy of local farmers; moreover, he was from a nearby town, where many people looked up to him. And there was something more: this commander had fought in World War II on a U.S. Navy destroyer. Plus, the CIA chief for Central America and the Caribbean had met with him in the Cuban capital and the report he delivered after returning to Langley was extremely optimistic.

Bissell and his team made a decision: they would get the commander to join the Escambray insurgency, and if everything turned out well, they would appoint him commander of the Front. By then —year's end— Evelio Duque had decided to leave the mountains and Osvaldo was not opposed to the new appointment. He knew Commander Tony Santiago from the war in those mountains and got along with him.

Santiago joined the insurgency on January 27 with almost 200 men. He had just returned from a brief visit to the United States, where he had finalized details on how the Escambray forces would support the invasion.

December 1960 was a crucial month for the CIA's plans in the Escambray. If the insurgent group could build a structure and consolidate its positions, the invasion could be carried out in the first weeks of the New Year. The takeover of Trinidad would be a given. The insurgent forces would come down from the mountains and attack in three directions: to the north, to surround the city and support its occupation by the invading forces; to the east, where other groups would cut off the Sancti Spíritus-Trinidad highway; and to the west, where a third force would block the arrival of reinforcements from the city of Cienfuegos. As part of the operation, they would blow up the bridges over the Agabama and Manatí rivers as well as the San Juan.

The arrival of substantial numbers of Rebel Army troops would take time, because they had to be sent from the city of Santa Clara in the center of the province. Small groups might come from the cities of Sancti Spíritus and Cienfuegos, located to the west and east, respectively. But they would be stopped by the Escambray insurgents, in coordination with the paratroop battalion that would be dropped over the advance positions.

A brief year's end report written by an anonymous Cuban Security agent describes the prevailing tension and the real reason why more than a few counterrevolutionaries headed for the mountains.

CONFIDENTIAL:
Matter: information from an infiltrated agent.
...That the units referred to had a paper addressed to Commander Evelio Duque and signed by Commander Augusto, unaware of the latter's identity... Many of this organization's elements will rise up in arms in the coming days to attack when the invasion arrives.

Waiting in the mountains, rifle in hand, for the Americans to come would be the guarantee of a secure job in the armed forces, the police or —why not— politics. In the new republic, everything would be like it was before.

General Douglas MacArthur, certainly one of the most outstanding military figures of World War II, once said: "The history of failure in war can almost be summed up in two words, too late. Too late in comprehending the deadly purpose of a potential enemy. Too late in realizing mortal danger. Too late in preparedness. Too late in uniting all possible forces for resistance."

In post-1959 Cuba, nothing was being done too late.

A number of factors clearly influenced the decision by the Revolution's leader to launch a powerful offensive in the Escambray. He was convinced the U.S. government was preparing an invasion of the island. Signs of this were the persistence of insurgent movements in the Escambray and reports of their growth. It was obvious that these weren't spontaneous or native-born movements; they were in one way or another part of a planned invasion. In addition, there was the recent death of the Rebel Army's chief of operations in the region, Commander Manuel Fajardo. He had been killed in a confused incident, but one that could be exploited by the counterrevolution to encourage further uprisings.

Angel Martínez, a combatant in the Spanish Civil War was attracted by the Cuban Revolution, had arrived in Cuba months earlier, and was working as adviser to the Rebel Army's central region commander. In a diary he kept at the time, he noted details of preparations for the projected operation.

"The plan was basically political and military," Martínez said in a 1977 interview. "In fact, there was a principle, an element that was weighty in the commander-in-chief's choices in selecting the militia units that were coming from Havana; it was the proletarian, working-class character of these Havana militias..."

On December 2, 1960, in the middle of the theater of operations, which he frequently visited, Fidel issued specific instructions:

- Press the struggle constantly; don't give the enemy time to recover.
- Don't move at night, only during the day, to avoid confusion.
- In case it is necessary to carry out nighttime deployments, do them along previously determined roads.
- Carry out another mobilization of farmers in the area that same month.
- Protect the population in the area. This measure will go hand in hand with the construction of villages on the recently created farms to gradually eliminate isolation. Always act on the basis of absolute agreement on the part of the farmers.
- Incorporate volunteer teachers to begin a vast educational and cultural effort.
- Concentrate the forces of the battalions in strategic locations.

The location of the insurgent camps had been determined in large part in September and October. This information was updated by farmers who lived in the mountains, statements from prisoners, and from documents that had been seized. To a lesser extent —due to their initial stage of organization and development— State Security agents who had infiltrated the counterrevolutionary forces also provided information. Two examples were Orlando Hernández Lema and Reineirio Perdomo, agents "Tito" and "Cabaiguán."

Orlando Hernández Lema had been a collaborator of the March 13 Revolutionary Directorate forces during the struggle against the dictatorship. After the triumph, he decided to remain where he was and work the land. The capital held no attraction for him. But peace did not last very long. The Escambray was on the CIA's agenda. In mid-1960, Víctor Manso, the grandson of a wealthy landowner from the area who resented the Revolution because the Agrarian Reform had taken part of his property, told Orlando that four captains were preparing an uprising. Orlando didn't think twice. He went down to Trinidad and took a bus to the capital. Without losing any time, he found the Directorate's leader, Commander Faure: Chomón, for whom he had served as an escort in the mountains, and told him about the conspiracy. A few hours later, he was having lunch in one of Havana's best restaurants, Maracas. His lunch partner was the head of the G-2, Commander Ramiro Valdés.

In early November, Orlando left his home and headed for Manacal de Piedras, another rugged area where Evelio Duque, commander-in-chief of the insurgent forces, had his camp. Orlando, known as "Tito," was perhaps the first State Security agent in the Escambray. Duque knew him from the revolutionary war. He knew that Orlando was a brave, honest, and modest man; he was not ambitious and he had a little education. This made Duque suspicious. There was something about Orlando that didn't sit right with their counterrevolutionary war. But he became even more suspicious after Orlando offered him a load of weapons.

"Don't worry about weapons; I've got plenty, and more will be coming soon."

Orlando remained in the camp, but they didn't give him any weapons. He became the collaborator of a Spanish priest, a fanatical supporter of Franco who held Mass for the insurgents. Orlando would read for him during the liturgy. He remembers today how each evening he would mentally go over the events of the day, lying in his hammock. He would go over every detail: the messengers who had come and gone, the weapons, the plans, the discussions on internal disagreements, references to the Americans, inconsequential conversations.

One day they took photos. One of the photos went to the American Embassy and from there to Quarters Eye. The agent in charge of propaganda, David A. Phillips, took it upon himself to circulate it throughout the world, with a caption saying that it was the general staff of the insurgent forces in the Escambray. Agent Tito could be seen clearly.

In late December, a few days before Christmas Eve, he and another agent left the camp to carry out a mission. A few hours later, they arrived at a farmer's *bohío*.

"The area is full of militia members," the man said without looking them in the face, realizing from the way they were dressed that the two must be insurgents. That was reaffirmed for him when they hastily left. Tito deliberately lagged behind, and after his companion was out of sight, turned around and went back to the house.

"Where are the militia members?" he asked the farmer, who stared at him without understanding. After a few seconds of silence, Tito added, "I want to turn myself in." The farmer lowered his head again; he lit a cigar stub and said resolutely, "There aren't any operations going on around here, the militias are far away. So turn yourself in to me—I'm the only militia member in this whole area." Two days later, Orlando was talking to the recently appointed head of State Security in the Escambray, Lieutenant Luis Felipe Denis. He was one of the many sources of information that was getting to Fidel Castro.

Reineirio Perdomo had no problem selecting a pseudonym for the job he was about to do as a secret agent. He took the name of the town where he was born: Cabaiguán.

"We don't use liaisons, so don't identify yourself to anybody; record everything you see and hear in your mind. If you need an important piece of documentation, hide it on your body. When you have enough data, leave the insurgency. To make sure they don't shoot at you, take off your shirt and turn yourself in with your hands up, completely unarmed."

"'And the Bible?' I asked him. 'If it doesn't fit in your pocket, leave it behind, but turn yourself in with your hands up and shirtless. And remember, you can't fight, even if they demand it.' Anyway, I couldn't fight because I'm cross-eyed and I have eyeglasses that are like bottle-bottoms. Those were my instructions from Aníbal Velaz."[3]

[3] Testimony of Reineirio Perdomo, former DSE agent, 1987. Author's archives.

On December 24, as the rum was flowing and pigs were being roasted in the backyards of Caracusey, a little town at the foot of the Escambray, Cabaiguán greeted the nephew of Julio Emilio Carretero, a former policeman under Batista who was now the righthand man of Commander Osvaldo Ramírez. Reineirio Perdomo turned down the glass of rum. He was a Pentecostal missionary, and it was against his religion.

As soon as it was dark, the two began the journey to San Ambrosio, a remote, rugged area where the insurgent column was camped.

They walked all night, stopping twice to rest in the homes of family members who collaborated with Osvaldo. At dawn, they arrived at the camp and, without stopping to rest, Perdomo was led to the chief of the column. Quickly, Cabaiguán realized that the man didn't like him. He admitted that his somewhat ungainly and fainthearted appearance betrayed him for what he was. Reineirio was not a man of action.

After confirming that he had been sent by trustworthy people, Osvaldo Ramírez prepared to assign him to a squad, but Reineirio quickly said, "I can't fight, commander; I'm a missionary, you know." Osvaldo looked him over and then put his hand on his shoulder. Then he looked at Carretero, who was standing next to him. "Give him a Winchester and put him on guard duty."

During his free time, Cabaiguán walked absent-mindedly around the camp with his Bible open, recording everything in his mind.

By the first week of December the final details of Operation Jaula [Cage] were ready. The area that would initially be surrounded covered approximately 2,400 square kilometers, and this "caged-in" area was in turn divided into three smaller cages. The traps would be subdivided into areas or sectors, which would then be searched inch by inch. Access to water, access to sources of supply, and the roads would be closely monitored. Ambushes would be carried out, particularly at night, when the insurgents usually made their moves.

Militia battalions began arriving in mid-December. Further determinations on the ground led to an expansion of the original cordon. The Escambray was completely surrounded by a ring of militia members from the coastline in the south to the outskirts of the city of Fomento, forty kilometers to the north; and across eighty kilometers of uncultivated land from east to west. A decisive factor in the success of the operation would be the support provided by the part of the population that remained loyal to the Revolution despite the intense radio propaganda and the pressure from old friends, employers, relatives, and acquaintances —very strong ties in a dark and backward world.

With this in mind, extremely important instructions were issued on relations between the troops and the farmers. These were:

Offer protection to families and their goods; teach people how to read; explain the projects of the Revolution; teach first-aid; take part in agricultural tasks and teach hygiene. The way farmers were treated —even knowing they had relatives among the insurgents, or that they sympathized with them— was to be guided by strict norms of absolute respect. In the case of those who supported the Revolution, they were to be protected against any attempt to intimidate them. Militia squads were stationed in every *bohío*, and at night, ambushes were set up around them.

"Batista's soldiers never went into the mountains; the militia members did. During the government offensive, we would hide everywhere. I hid on a rocky cay far away from a friend's house, and every other day I would go to his house, through the back, for food. My job was to monitor the militia member and catch him off guard, and then I would signal my friend and he would bring me some food. We would sleep on the ground, covered with a piece of plastic; sometimes we would bathe once every two to three weeks. In the Escambray, there is food and fruit everywhere. There are a lot of trees that have fruit you can eat. Some are bad and others aren't. An insurgent has to eat everything. You couldn't go to people's houses, because there were militia members everywhere. One night, we went walking after midnight, and we were caught by surprise by militia members who were lying in ambush. We realized that by the gunfire. I was in between Gavilán and Berto; the militia fired a lot of shots. Berto fell in front of me, and Gavilán behind me. When you fall and don't say anything, it's because you're dead. You die the day you're supposed to die. We had some people who used to say to us that so-and-so was a snitch. But sometimes it was because our man owed him 2,000 or 3,000 pesos, and what he wanted was for us to kill him. And people were killed without looking into things too much."[4]

In Quarters Eye, the maps of the Escambray region began to fill up with colors indicating the presence of enemy forces, and some officials wondered what would happen on the day of the invasion if this unusual concentration of troops were still there, just a few kilometers from the city of Trinidad. Others wondered whether Fidel Castro had evidence of the CIA's goals. But this was totally impossible. Knowledge of the area chosen for the landing was limited to a select group of high-ranking officials. In the White House itself, only part of the administration's people knew about it. No, an infiltration was impossible. In reality, what was happening, and was beginning to worry the Agency's staff, was that the Cuban leader was showing signs of being a military strategist to be reckoned with.

Perhaps it was the danger hanging over the Escambray that made Bissell and Jack Esterline decide to rapidly execute an operation to drop a major arms shipment over the camp of Osvaldo Ramírez, recently appointed Commander of the Escambray Front. Ramírez had sent repeated messages asking for weapons to Commander Augusto, who, in turn, had passed the request on to the American Embassy.

Ramírez's camp was in the San Ambrosio area, an almost inaccessible region of thick vegetation and sharp peaks. After receiving the dispatch from Ruisánchez, he issued instructions to build an improvised landing strip in Paso Hondo. It was December 31, 1960. It had been a tremendous year for the Cuban Revolution, but not the decisive one. That one was about to begin.

As a group of insurgents cleared the ground for the landing strip, the news spread from mouth to mouth. There was a communist teacher in the area. It was a safe bet that the boy had no idea that Osvaldo Ramírez and his column of more than 300 men were nearby. Carretero, one of Ramírez's deputies, received the order to capture the teacher. It was no coincidence that he'd chosen Juan Emilio Carretero; the man had captured a lot of people. He had been a policeman under the Batista government. He was a professional. Despite

[4] Testimony of José Reboso Febles, insurgent. Author's archives.

Commander Augusto's instructions to the counterrevolutionary chiefs to not admit any Batista followers into their ranks, from the moment he joined the insurgency five months earlier, Osvaldo had brought along Carretero. Any order could be sent from the capital, including the stupidest.

That night, New Year's Eve, Carretero and three of his men —Macario Quintana, known as "Flatfoot"; "The Sailor"; and Tomás San Gil— burst in to the house of farmer Erineo Rodríguez [Heliodoro Rodríguez, whom everyone called Erineo], who had been housing the volunteer teacher. The teacher belonged to a Peace Corps or missionary-type youth group; after undergoing difficult tests to adapt themselves physically to harsh conditions, these young people would go out to the most remote° parts of the island with the mission of opening schools and teaching children and adults.

"Not only a communist, but black," Carretero snarled when he saw him. The teacher had jumped out of his hammock and was trying to pull his boots on.

"Let's go," Macario said dryly, giving the youth the first shove. The teacher fell to the floor.

"Where are you taking him?" the farmer asked timidly.

"You really are a stupid ass," Carretero snapped.

The wife's pleas and children's crying were to no avail. The teacher and farmer were quickly led to the camp. With the help of the other men, they improvised a cage for holding them. Osvaldo had decided to get rid of the problem the next day. They couldn't allow revolutionary teachers to flood the Escambray, much less allow farmers to house them.

He had decided to set a precedent for anyone who dared to defy his authority. But the problem couldn't be resolved the next morning. In the dawn of December 31, they had their first clash with the militia forces who were trying to rid San Ambrosio of insurgents.

Demetrio Clavelo Solís was a relative of Osvaldo Ramírez. He was working as a driver in the Sancti Spíritus area when he found out Osvaldo had joined the insurgency. He didn't give the matter much thought. One day, he went into a bar frequented by prostitutes with his friend Macario Quintana, nicknamed "Flatfoot" because of his big feet. Macario was an imposing mulatto who drank freely and had an extremely violent character. He was a typical thug. What Clavelo Solís—known as Valoy—didn't know was that his friend was carrying a .45-caliber pistol in his belt. They sat down at a table and two women immediately came around. After downing their first beers, the two men were in a good mood. Then Eddy Quiroga came in and walked up to the bar. Macario's face changed; he went pale. Without saying anything, he got up and approached the newcomer. Valoy had his back to them and didn't hear the argument, because the music from the phonograph was like a solid wall. But he heard the shot. He jumped up and turned around. Eddy was staggering toward the door. Then he heard a second shot. Eddy couldn't stand up. Gun in hand and beside himself, Macario pushed Valoy out of the bar. Once in the car, Valoy asked him what to do. "Step on it, to the Escambray!" Macario ordered, nervously fingering his gun. "We have to join the insurgency."

That was how Demetrio "Valoy" Clavelo Solís became an insurgent.

"Osvaldo was happy to see me. He made me his assistant. There were about 300 men in the camp, but not all of them were armed. The weapons came a few days later; Máximo Lorenzo brought them, and he'd brought them in a truck from Havana. Afterwards, more came in from Camagüey. The Americans had gotten them into the country over the coast, and the MRR people had gotten them to the Escambray. They also brought a generator unit for a radio, one of those crystal and pedal ones. They put that in a separate place, in a hut; we hung a sign that said, 'no entry.' Osvaldo organized the people into fourteen groups or bands, as you called them later. He placed them strategically, in the shape of a horseshoe, to defend the entire area. He had decided to defend the area, at least until the Americans made the weapons drop. I think it was December 31 when they informed us that the militia was coming, and that Fidel was in the lead, and people were even saying that Fidel wanted to meet with Osvaldo. Afterwards we found out that all of that was a lie. Actually, Fidel started bombarding us with mortar fire. The first shootout was on the night of the 31st, and soon after that, another band clashed with the militias in a different spot. Osvaldo realized that they wanted to surround us. I went to the rear, to organize the retreat. That's why I didn't see when they brought the teacher."[5]

---

[5] Testimony of Demetrio Clavelo Solís, insurgent. Author's archives.

The messages sent back and forth between Osvaldo and Ruisánchez are eloquent testimony to the drama that that was taking place in those mountains:

> "Important not to let the enemy see or enter combat with you. It might slow down Operation Silence."—Commander Augusto

> "Friends indicated Three Kings Day and three days more; that is, 7th, 8th and 9th." —Commander Augusto

> "Weapons drop will be done around 500 feet in 800-pound bales." —Commander Augusto

On January 3, the battles intensified. The situation got worse for the insurgents. For Osvaldo Ramírez, maintaining control of the area was a life-or-death question. If he left the area, he would lose the shipment of weapons and explosives, most of them destined to reinforce other columns so that they could await the invasion in a position to be able to give it support. He would only have to hold out for three more days. But the situation became desperate on January 5. The militia members and Rebel Army soldiers were preparing their final assault.

The topographical conditions that seemed exceptionally good for irregular warfare were not insurmountable for the revolutionary forces. On January 6, when the parachutes with weapons came raining down—a Three Kings Day gift from the CIA—it was the militias who received them. Messages exchanged the following day bear witness to how the drama unfolded.

> "Newspapers today have photos weapons captured dropped by plane Escambray. I suppose they're for 'Operation Silence.' If 'Operation Silence' fell into the enemy's hands, we're lost. I'm confused. Investigate and report." —Commander Augusto

> "Situation has changed. They are trying to surround us. All 'Operation Silence' packages fell enemy. Enemy preparing offensive with thousands militia members. Looks like everything will be lost, including life." —Commander Osvaldo Ramírez

Before the retreat, Osvaldo Ramírez ordered the teacher and the farmer to be put on trial. He was angry.

He needed to raise the troop's morale, and the teacher had provided him with an excellent opportunity. Before the trial, a messenger approached the cage and told the teacher that if he backed down from his communist ideas and condemned Fidel, his life would be spared.

At dawn on January 4, they placed the two men onto an improvised platform. Nearby, an insurgent took minutes on an old typewriter. The "court secretary" prepared to take statements from the detainees. There were about one hundred armed men there, tired from the battles of the day before.

The teacher spoke with his hands tied. He was nervous. There was no doubt. The young man, just eighteen years old, was scared. He said he was from the city of Matanzas, and that he had decided to leave school to take a course for volunteer teachers, because he thought teaching reading to children who had never had teachers was something just. The "prosecutor," waving a reading instruction booklet taken from Erineo's house, interrupted him, shouting, Didn't he know it was communist indoctrination?

The teacher, speaking a little louder so that he could be heard over the increasingly loud and abusive voices, answered that he had been teaching children their vowels, and spelling out words with them. Once again, the "prosecutor" silenced him, reading aloud a sentence from the booklet: "The Agrarian Reform Is On!" Once again, the shouting went up. The teacher looked around at the men who had surrounded him threateningly. "Are you a communist?" the "prosecutor" asked loudly, and the people calmed down. Suddenly, there was silence. The teacher lowered his head, and then looked over at the farmer. A rock hit his face, and he staggered for a moment, but didn't fall. Macario came up to him and gave him a blow to the ear. That time he did fall. Others got up and kicked him as they called him a communist, black, *Fidelista*. The trial was over.[6]

That night, as a thick silence presaged the final assault of the militias, the teacher was lying in the cage. He was breathing with difficulty, and a thin line of blood ran down his ear. His nose was

[6] Testimony of Reineirio Perdomo, former DSE agent, idem.

broken and his face was terribly swollen. They had broken several of his ribs, and he could no longer stand up. But the worst pain was in his testicles, squeezed over and over by Macario Quintana's powerful hands. The farmer, kneeling down next to him, wiped the boy's face with his dirty handkerchief. The guards had moved away a prudent distance, in order not to hear the teacher's moans. Once in a while, someone would approach the cage with curiosity, yell out an insult, and keep going. As morning dawned, one man silently approached, opened a Bible he was carrying and began to read. From a distance, one of the guards who was sitting under a tree shouted something at him.

"I'm going to perform his religious rites," the other answered, and the guard closed his eyes again. After making certain that he couldn't be heard, he put his face up against the wire netting that separated him from the prisoners.

"I'm not an insurgent," Reineirio Perdomo would later recall saying to them. He was actually agent "Cabaiguán," and a witness to the crime. "I can't do anything for you." The teacher opened his eyes, and for a few seconds —which felt like forever to Perdomo— he looked at him with a strange expression. Then he moaned again and closed his eyes. Cabaiguán saw a tear run down his cheek. The farmer asked for water, and Perdomo threw his canteen over the fence.

"Are you finished?" asked the guard, who had approached, and was standing next to the agent.

"At dawn, when the shooting began and it was clear that the militias were advancing, the order came to retreat," Reineirio recalled. "Then Carretero, Macario, "The Sailor" and Tomás San Gil pulled the teacher and the farmer from the cage, beat them and hit them with their rifle butts, once again showing the teacher no mercy. In fact, they bayoneted him, and cut off his genitals. I think that when they hung him, the teacher was dead. Then they strung up the farmer".[7]

A few hours later, the insurgent column left San Ambrosio.

A week later, agent Cabaiguán was able to leave the insurgents and turn himself in to a militia troop. After he insistently requested, he

[7] Ibid.

was taken to the head of State Security in Las Villas, in Topes de Collantes, the headquarters of the general staff of the Clean Up of the Escambray campaign. "Hey guy, you're still alive?" was the question from Captain Aníbal Velaz, the man who had trained him as an emergency agent.

He remained in Topes for three days, recounting everything that he had seen and heard to a clerk. He was still doing that when someone told him that Fidel had arrived. Shortly afterward, Aníbal was taken to the Commander in Chief.

"Tell me about the teacher's murder. I want you to write the names of the men who beat him, tortured him, and mistreated him, even the one who threw a rock at him."[8]

The murder of the young teacher moved public opinion and was a catalyst among the contending forces.

Fidel Castro was able to grasp —better than anyone else— the drop in morale that began to happen among a good number of the Cuban insurgents.

Early on in the conflict, several Rebel Army officers were meeting with Commander Fidel Castro. Raúl Menéndez Tomassevich, who was later a division general and is now deceased, was giving a report on the insurgency. He remembered that he used the terms "insurgents," "insurrectionists," and "guerrillas" interchangeably, but was not able to find an adequate, all-around word to describe them. Then Fidel interrupted him and said, "Don't call them guerillas anymore; we're the guerrillas. They're bandits."

On January 6, government forces took over the camp of Column 7, led by Osvaldo Ramírez, where there had been more than 300 men. Pursuit of the column began immediately. The enemy chief divided his troops into two groups. One under his command, with approximately 100 men, was caught a week later in a place known as Limones Cantero, and was decimated. The second group, with a similar number of men, began a slow nighttime march to the central region of the Escambray, where they began to split up after successive clashes with the militias. That was how the strongest column had been defeated. Others met the same fate. Columns 1 and 2 were

8 Ibid.

decimated, but their leaders, Evelio Duque, Edel Montiel, and Joaquín Benvibre, were able to get past the cordon and leave the country. Captains Zacarías García, Juan Cajiga, and Nando Lima, commanders of Columns 3 and 6, were taken prisoner in February. That same month, the commanders of Columns 5 and 8 were surrounded during skirmishes and captured. Captain Ismael Heredia, commander of Column 4, was killed in an ambush. In total, by the end of March, twenty-five counterrevolutionary groups had been defeated in one battle after another.

Despite the fact that the Escambray had been occupied by the revolutionary forces in January 1961, the CIA continued to carry out the air operations it had planned in order to reinforce its troops in the mountains. After detailed preparations, on January 6 they made an air drop of a sizeable load of weapons and explosives over the San Ambrosio area; its success was recorded in one of the last messages radioed to Osvaldo Ramírez. In early February, they made another drop over the Santa Lucía area, close to the city of Cabaiguán. A week later, on February 13, several parachutes fell over El Naranjo. Four days later, another considerable load was dropped over Sierrita, in the southwest region of the Escambray. On March 4, a drop was made over Charco Azul. They were all received on the ground by the militias.

According to CIA pilot Eduardo Ferrer in his book *Operation Puma,* from September 1960 to March 1961, 68 missions were carried out to drop weapons and explosives over Cuba's mountains, and 61 of them were resounding failures.

Even though he was well-protected in Havana, José Ramón Ruisánchez, Commander Augusto, sensed that the "clean-up" could hit close to home. Some of the leaders and liaisons who were now fleeing knew him, and if they were taken prisoner, they could inform on him. So he decided to leave secretly for the United States.

The Clean-Up of the Escambray campaign was too much for the insurgents who had been operating since the months of June and July, preparing to play an important role during the invasion of Trinidad. Enormous pressure had been put on them by the "cages," combined with relentless persecution, a well-conceived system of ambushes, strict monitoring of sources of water and food, constructive relationships with farmers who weren't committed to one side or the other, and the neutralization of those who supported the insurgents. The diary of one of their commanders is eloquent testimony to the brevity and intensity of that military operation:

"February 20. Matasiete deserted, and we had to leave the camp. Today Pedro and I went out to see if we could escape; there are militia members everywhere. We're surrounded and low on ammunition and have been without food for many days.... Only eight of us remain from what was a column of forty-some men, and they are discouraged... Today is March 1, and apparently nobody is coming to help us. The exiles are living too well to come and have a hard time here... Tonight, the two of us who are left are going to see if we can find a better area than this one. If it's all the same, we're either going to have to shoot ourselves or turn ourselves in."[9]

In late March, it became evident that the belligerence of the counterrevolutionary forces in the Escambray had diminished considerably, while information continued to be gathered about an imminent invasion. For that reason, in early April, the order was given for all troops participating in Operation Jaula to return to their home provinces.

Considerable forces had been allocated to defend Trinidad from late 1960 to early 1961. These forces remained in their combat posts until after the invasion was defeated. One of the arguments used to justify the invasion's defeat is that invading Trinidad would have been a better plan than the Bay of Pigs. There is nothing more untrue.

For the defense of the Trinidad/Cienfuegos region, six battalions had been allocated, and a defense system had been organized with a vast network of trenches set up in three stages near the coast, and protected by the foothills of the mountains. They had a communications network, three tank companies, mortars, antiaircraft machine guns, bazookas, and 57- and 85-mm. cannons. The Trinidad city airport was well-defended.

"The Brigade that landed at Girón had no possibility whatsoever of landing in Trinidad. They wouldn't even have made it to land. We were waiting for them, and anxious to shoot. Imagine the state people were in: several days before the invasion, we accidentally

---

[9] Campaign diary of Julián Oliva, insurgent. Museum of the Struggle Against the Bandits.

shot at a boat that was passing near the coast and we almost sunk it. If, after being defeated, they had gone to the Cienfuegos region in order to get to the Escambray, they would have seen the end there, too. We would have surrounded that whole region. Remember, we even closed the bay."[10]

The war in the Escambray lasted another four years. During its most difficult period, the conflict involved 100,000 troops and cost the country approximately one billion pesos. The last group of insurgents, made up of a dozen men hiding in a cave, was captured in early March 1965. Their leader, who was brought before Commander Lizardo Proenza, chief of operations, was wearing a wide-brimmed hat and a star, symbols of his military rank. Proenza, in a good-natured tone, stood at attention and asked him, "How are you, commander?"

The man answered, "The only commander here is Fidel."

[10] Testimony of Brigade General Valle Lazo. Author's archives.

The key to entering the CIA

On December 10, 1960, José Méndez, a member of the underground organization Rescate —led from outside of the country by Dr. Antonio de Varona— paid another visit to Commander Santiago in the latter's office where he was overseer of a prosperous trucking company that had just been nationalized. For several months, Méndez and other counterrevolutionary conspirators had maintained contact with Santiago, who they knew as an outstanding fighter in the Escambray during the guerilla war against dictator Fulgencio Batista. They also knew that in World War II he had enlisted in the U.S. Navy, distinguishing himself as an artillery officer on a destroyer in the dangerous waters of the Pacific.

Since their first meeting on October 13, a little earlier that tumultuous year, the conspirators had tested him in various ways, and nothing had changed in their lives. They felt safe. This time, therefore, José Méndez took the plunge. He told Santiago that his brother Juan had been appointed national coordinator of the Democratic Revolutionary Front (FRD), and that he was using the pseudonym Jorge Piloto. Perhaps to press him a bit, he added that Juan had returned recently from the United States, where he had met with high-ranking CIA officials.

The commander listened attentively and asked no questions. When Méndez was finished, Santiago used the atmosphere created to also dive in, in his own way. He talked about how he was upset with the revolutionary leadership for ignoring, marginalizing, and overlooking him, placing him in a job that was far below the level of what he had done before. He added, with an expression that could leave no doubt about his sentiments, that he had two choices: to leave the country or rise up in arms again.

José Méndez was impressed. The commander had succumbed. He was about to recruit a man who held the highest military rank in the Rebel Army, the kind of authority that could open any door in Cuba. And that was not something that happened every day. Méndez tried to hide his excitement and began flattering the commander. He asked him not to leave the country, and admitted that the Americans knew about him. Santiago interrupted him and said resentfully that the U.S. government had deprived him of citizenship because he had joined the Rebel Army. Méndez was solicitous. He assured him that he would resolve the matter, and that he would also ensure that Santiago's wife and two children obtained residency. Finally, he told him what the true objective of his visit was, and the reason behind so much amiability: the FRD wanted him to agree to be the commander of the Escambray Front, to give a significant boost to the guerrilla war in those mountains and to end all internal struggles once and for all.

The commander seemed enthusiastic about returning to the mountains. He was definitely a man of action. He inquired about the weapons situation, and Méndez told him it was precarious, but that one of his first actions would be to coordinate with the Embassy for air drops of weapons and explosives.

"This action will give you more authority, because it will make it clear to everybody in the Escambray that you have the support of the Americans."

For the next three days, Commander Santiago and his assistant, José Ramírez López, a man he trusted completely, worked on a plan for the uprising. It was to be submitted first to the FRD leadership on the island, and then, in all certainty, to the U.S. Embassy.

On December 13, the commander went to a house on Línea and Tenth streets in Vedado, very close by the main offices of Commander in Chief Fidel Castro, who occasionally stayed there overnight. Previously, following the instructions of José Méndez, he had picked up a woman who turned out to be an old friend now working actively against the Revolution. At that point, he had no doubt. Knowing his anti-communist inclinations, she had been the one who proposed him to the conspirators. Waiting for them at the house were José, his brother Juan, the national coordinator, and another individual, a member of the anti-Castro organization Revolutionary Recovery Movement (MRR). The woman was the first to speak. She explained to everyone there that Vladimir Rodríguez, whom they called the "Little Doctor," had been arrested. This was because a shootout had taken place on the corner of Línea and Paseo, and apparently the presence of Vladimir's car made him a suspect. Everyone there regretted it, but it was to be expected, given the aggressive and violent personality of the arrested conspirator, who had led an anti-government group somewhat independent of the FRD. The commander commented that Vladimir had proposed that he work with him, but he'd said no, and he'd predicted that sooner or later, Vladimir would be caught by State Security.

The matter was considered over, and the group was prepared to listen to the commander, who told them about his plan for the rebellion and the Escambray Front. Santiago pulled a sheaf of papers from his briefcase. He proposed forming an insurgent group with 200 men who were loyal to him, and he had a farm available for that purpose in the foothills of the Escambray. That is where they would gather. Once in the zone of operations, they would meet with commanders Osvaldo Ramírez and Evelio Duque and organize the general command. He would make a considerable number of his men available to those two commanders to be distributed among the different groups operating in the mountains. That would significantly reinforce those troops, aiding them with experience and combativeness.

He talked about his men, many of whom were working in the enterprise that he had been part of nationalizing, about their qualities. He went over details of the military actions he would undertake once the uprising took place. He outlined the methods to be used for maintaining contact with local groups of the FRD in cities near the Escambray; and for maintaining contact with the capital for basic supplies. And he outlined information and propaganda work with farmers from the area, many of whom he knew from the war against Batista. Antonio spoke for a while longer, and, when he was finished, those present were visibly satisfied. The MRR leader was the first to react. He placed the explosives factory that

117

his organization possessed at the disposition of the commander. Without hesitation, Santiago asked him for several cases of napalm for igniting gasoline, which he would test on some of the trucks belonging to the enterprise he directed. Shortly afterward, the meeting ended. In entering that house, Commander Antonio Santiago had reinitiated his conspiratorial activities, but this time against Fidel Castro's government. In leaving the house three hours later, he was one of the counterrevolution's top leaders.

That same afternoon, Juan Méndez went to the American Embassy to provide information on details of the meeting. At that time, the CIA chief for Central America and the Caribbean, Louis C. Herbert, was in town. In a secure room, he listened, via a recording monitor, to the fascinating story that Juan Méndez told the attending agent about the recruitment of a rebel commander, a hero of his country's army who was willing to fight Castro in Cuba's mountains. When the meeting was over, Herbert picked up Santiago's dossier again and reread some of the documents. He realized that he had something really substantial in his hands. This was no ordinary man, consumed by resentment over losing his property or by fanatical anti-communism. The commander was idealist, charismatic, and brave. Moreover, he was popular in the mountainous region of the Escambray, where the CIA had not been able to consolidate a powerful insurgent nucleus for providing support to the invasion when the time came. During those days of December 1960, the final preparations were being made for launching the invasion of the city of Trinidad, next to the Escambray region. Commander Antonio Santiago was the missing piece to the puzzle. His most dangerous defect, perhaps, was his temperament, given a certain tendency to explosions of anger and rage. But if he managed to keep it under control, this side of his personality could be used to benefit their plans. "Make contact with him," he told the agent on the case. "Gain his trust."

Events accelerated. Two days went by, and on December 15, as Havana was getting decked out to usher in Christmas, Juan Méndez called Santiago, and in a very brief conversation consisting of implications and allusions, said that he would visit him that night in the company of a very important person. It was Tony Sileo, who introduced himself as Marcos Behar from the U.S. Embassy. There were three things about him that the commander noticed: the pipe that he expertly lifted to his lips, the gold watch that shone on his wrist, and his elegant manner of dressing. He suspected —and with good reason— that Behar was an important CIA official at the Embassy.

The U.S. official proposed speaking on Santiago's front porch. It was an appropriate place, and Behar saw no danger of their conversation being recorded there. He had no doubts about the Cuban, for whom he felt a twinge of sympathy. These were simply the inviolable rules of the profession. He told Juan Méndez to stay in the house, and after a sip of his *España en llamas* cocktail, he settled into a rocking chair. Santiago lived near the airport, in the exclusive residential neighborhood of Fontanar on the city's outskirts, one of the last such areas built before January 1, 1959. It had become celebrated for a gigantic pine tree that was lit up with colored lights every December. But beyond that, darkness reigned in its broad avenues, and it was not possible to monitor the house without being discovered. That was why the official asked Santiago about the man who was sitting on the porch of the house across the street, openly watching them.

"That is José, my assistant," he answered. "If you look closely, you'll see he's got a Thompson machine gun. He will be protecting our meeting." Sileo/Behar tried to hide his surprise. Actually, it was an audacious thing to do, but he realized that he couldn't expect otherwise. The commander was a man of action, and that was precisely what was needed in Cuba.

Tony explained the insurgency plan again, and the American seemed satisfied. He made some observations which the Cuban gladly accepted. Suddenly changing the subject of conversation, the American asked him his opinion on the international situation, which meant, in a few words, in those turbulent years of the Cold War, finding out what side his interlocutor was on.

Santiago was convincing; he wasn't pretending. At least, that's how it seemed to the experienced CIA official.

His assistant José had darkened the porch of the house where he was sitting and was now gently rocking, caressing the cold metal of the machine gun resting on his lap. He had smoked his fifth cigar of what was sometimes —like this tense evening— more than a dozen daily.

Santiago and Sileo finalized the details on a major air drop of weapons and explosives. The commander offered to make available the farm he owned in the vicinity of the Escambray. The official told Santiago that during the same flight as the air drop four agents would be parachuted, and they would be responsible for training the forces that joined the insurgency. He spoke well of these men, saying they would be very useful and completely trustworthy. Sileo/Behar, no doubt, was alluding to members of the infiltration teams, who at that time were finishing their training in the jungles of Panama.

The meeting ended right at midnight. In an unusual gesture, Marcos Behar/Tony Sileo provided the commander with a set of Embassy telephone numbers.

"When the operator answers, ask for Marcos Behar's extension," he said, adding with a smile, "If I don't answer, you should say, 'Tony, it's Tony.' Actually, my name is not Behar; it's Antonio Sileo, Tony, like you."

That morning, the official reported the outcome of his meeting with the Cuban to the CIA official in charge of Central America and the Caribbean, Louis C. Herbert. Shortly afterward, the high-ranking official went to Washington. There, he met with Bissell. Forty-eight hours after that, a coded message was sent to Tony Sileo. It confirmed Commander Antonio Santiago as head of the Escambray Front, as well as the date for the uprising and the plan that would be carried out on D-Day, the date of which was still a mystery. And it included something unexpected, evidence of the importance the Cuban commander had acquired: he was to leave secretly for the United States to finalize details of his participation in the plan for supporting the projected and now almost imminent invasion.

Meanwhile in Cuba, Commander Santiago was still uninformed of the trip, and on the recommendation of his diligent assistant, he had sent his secretary to Miami to get personal documents certifying him as an American citizen. Along with his Social Security card, these included his driver's license, Navy records and decorations. Two years previously, he had had to leave them behind when he decided to return to Cuba to join the struggle in the mountains against the dictatorship.

On December 24, José Méndez called him very early in the morning and asked him to go that afternoon to the Sagrado Corazón Clinic, where his brother would be waiting for him. When he got to room No. 706, Commander Santiago found Juan lying down. He was genuinely sick; he was suffering from a kidney stone attack. The sick man told Santiago that being hospitalized was an ideal situation for dealing with confidential matters, and that Marcos Behar would soon be there. However, the afternoon went by, and the American didn't appear. Later, it was learned that he had discovered he was being followed, which he considered routine, because he had left from the embassy, but it was risky for the commander. So after circling around, he returned to the embassy.

Realizing that the American was not coming to the appointment, Méndez used the opportunity to lay out details of the actions that the underground movement would carry out on D-Day. For the commander, an old sailor, there was no doubt whatsoever. D-Day would be the day of the landing. He therefore prepared to hear about actions supporting the invasion.

1. Occupy civilian and military vital points. Each organization would occupy one part of the capital. For this purpose, it had been divided into eight areas.
2. The insurgency's command would be located in the basement of the Focsa, one of the two tallest buildings in the country.
3. Water and electricity supplies to the city would be cut off for 48 hours —along with other measures— with the goal of checking popular reaction in support of the revolutionary government.
4. Simultaneously, the guerrilla detachments operating in the Escambray, by then under the orders of Commander Santiago, would take over nearby towns, and then march to the provincial capital, Santa Clara, where they would receive support from the urban underground groups.
5. The same action plan designed for Havana would be carried out in the other provinces, with Las Villas being the most important for contingency plans.
6. Simultaneously, the La Cabaña Fortress and the San Julián and San Antonio de los Baños military airbases would be bombed. The destruction of La Cabaña was aimed at

preventing any response to the attack, given that it was located at the mouth of the capital and could bomb the insurgent groups. By bombing the military airports, they would destroy the Revolutionary Air Force, thus guaranteeing control of the air.

7. The bombings would indicate that the invading forces had left Guatemala and Florida, by air, to reinforce and consolidate the movement.[1]

The plan was not completely crazy, at least not from the perspective of CIA analysts in the United States, who believed these actions would generate an unstoppable movement of support for the invaders once these forces had landed. They unquestioningly believed that "due to the temperamental characteristics of Cubans, more given to indolence and apathy," a good part of those who supported the government would incline to the winning side once action had begun.

In order to impress the commander and show him that no detail had been left to chance, Méndez explained to him what would happen to the *Fidelistas* who were captured. After their interrogation in the same place they were captured, they would be sent to the command, together with the records of their initial statements. These would be taken down on paper of different colors. Those who arrived with records on red paper would be shot on the spot, without trial. Blue paper, in contrast, would mean they would be put on trial; and white, that the prisoners would be subject to investigation.

There was no question: the counterrevolutionary wave would reenact the tragic end of the Paris Commune; blood would run through the streets. As it was getting dark, Méndez told him that he had sent a letter to the Escambray to inform Evelio Duque and Osvaldo Ramírez of the order to unite as a single command under the orders of Santiago, once he had risen up in arms.

Perhaps in the whirlwind of events, Tony did not notice the importance the American plan placed on Las Villas province and particularly the Escambray. It was still early for such an assessment. What is certain is that during those final months of the year, the plan was for the invasion to take place on the coast near the city of

[1] FRD Plan. MININT archives.

Trinidad, near the Escambray. But that information was TOP SECRET, and knowledge of it was limited to a select group of high-ranking CIA and Pentagon officials at Quarters Eye. Now Bissell and his collaborators would decide on how much and what they would report to Santiago in the meeting that one of the men would hold with him, with the goal of finalizing the details of his participation in the siege of Trinidad on D-Day.

The FRD in Miami was informed of the acquisition of Commander Santiago for the ranks of the belligerent opposition. Antonio Varona, FRD coordinator and a top leader of Rescate, which was led in Cuba by Juan Méndez, was euphoric. He gave instructions for Santiago to prepare conditions—once the Escambray region was secured—for the landing of an airplane that would bring a provisional government from the United States.

He, Tony Varona, would lead it. When the matter was communicated to the commander, he was impressed. He no longer had any doubts; the main trump card for the CIA's plans was the Escambray. Santiago was close to hot, but not yet boiling.

Days later, confirmation was received about the trip to the United States. When notified that they were coming to pick him up, Santiago said he had boats and fishermen who were loyal to him.

In another meeting between the two, Marcos Behar/Tony Sileo proposed that Santiago get his wife and children out of the country to avoid any reprisals by the government if it was discovered that he was conspiring. Santiago thanked the American for his concern but turned him down. He had discussed the matter with his wife and she was unwilling. She would not leave him. Nevertheless, he had decided to send her to the house of some friends in Las Villas who would hide her and watch out for her and his two small children until everything was over.

Behar had more important news. The next day Tony was to meet with the head of the underground movement and the CIA's representative in Cuba, who he identified by the pseudonym of Francisco.

The wave of events was unstoppable, and Commander Santiago was overtaken by unusual tension. He had to continue overseeing the nationalized trucking company, give orders, monitor shipments, organize meetings, listen to workers' complaints, and inform the Ministry of Transport. Given his status as a Rebel Army commander, there were frequent activities he had to attend, along with maintaining relations with old comrades-in-arms who were loyal to the Revolution. There was no lack of reproach over a certain fight in a nightclub that undercut his prestige, or over certain friendships. Successfully dealing with these situations, and finding time to attend to his family and to sort out the threads of the conspiracy being hatched, without a single mistake, was not an easy task.

At a January 2 mass rally, Fidel Castro announced the government's decision to not allow more U.S. diplomats in Cuba than the number of Cubans who were accredited in Washington, of which there were eleven. This meant that in one fell swoop, some 300 officials from the U.S. Embassy would have to leave the island, including the staff of CIA and FBI agents and officials for whom almost all the other personnel worked.

The enormous rally had begun with a military parade that showed, for the first time, weaponry recently acquired from the Soviet Union and Czechoslovakia: bazooka companies, mortar batteries, four-barrel antiaircraft guns, antitank cannons, and heavy artillery. People in Cuba had never shown so much enthusiasm over weapons. The atmosphere reached a peak when the T-34 and Stalin tanks made their appearance. Then the Youth Army of Labor brigades, known as the "Cinco Picos" (Five Peaks), carrying bazookas; the volunteer teachers, armed with submachine guns; the women's militia battalions, known popularly as the "Lidia Doce" brigades; and dozens more militia battalions, made up of workers, students, and farmers. Suddenly, the crowds that were lined up along the entire parade route began singing a rhythmic, rumba-like tune, in a tone of determination and victory: "Rifle, shotgun, cannon; Cuba is respected; rifle, shotgun, cannon; Cuba is respected."

French philosopher Jean Paul Sartre, who was visiting Cuba during those months, later wrote, "If the United States didn't exist, perhaps the Cuban Revolution would invent it; it is what preserves their freshness and originality."

As this was happening, Commander Tony Santiago and Juan Méndez were waiting for the head of the underground movement in a house on 62nd Street between 11th and 13th. By 11 a.m., the man had not appeared, and Juan Méndez agreed to contact Francisco again, because he was the one who wanted to meet Tony.

At the same time, Santiago was rushing to leave for the United States. He was convinced his plans for an uprising and insurgency in the Escambray would be successful only if he could combine them with the Americans' plan. In short: to adapt them to the invasion plans, which would mean a certain level of knowledge about top-secret CIA and Pentagon plans. And that's why he was going.

Everything was prepared for January 5. They would leave from the Caibarién post and head for a point in American waters; presumably, the U.S. Coast Guard would intercept them.

As he was about leave for Caibarién, some 350 kilometers east of Havana, Juan Méndez told him that the meeting with the head of the underground movement would happen soon. Santiago seemed reluctant to postpone the trip, but he gave in to Méndez's insistence. Without a doubt, the meeting was very important. The delay, of just three days, would cost him his life.

On January 6, as a C-54 plane dropped several tons of weapons over the Escambray into the camp of Commander Osvaldo Ramírez —which was in the hands of the militias— Commander Santiago was meeting in Havana with the head of the underground movement in Cuba. This was Francisco, who was actually Rogelio González Corzo, and who acted suspicious of the commander. He only talked about plans that Tony knew about. Finally, he asked Tony for one of his company trucks, to transport 500 pounds of gelatin and sixty M-3 submachine guns. Tony agreed, but on one condition: his assistant would head up the operation. If this was a step to test his loyalty, he would guarantee its success.

On January 8, a militia company operating in the San Ambrosio area of the Escambray was taking a count of boxes of weapons and explosives that had been dropped by an unknown plane over the insurgent camp that had just been taken over after three intense battles At the same time Tony Santiago and his assistant José were leaving for Santa Clara, the first stop on their journey to the port of Caibarién. At that time, Cuba was on a war footing. All signs seemed to indicate that the invasion was imminent. Fidel Castro and his military chiefs believed that Dwight Eisenhower's Republican administration, which on January 20 would hand over power to Democrat John Kennedy, would use the transition to invade the island and eliminate the Cuba question before Eisenhower's mandate was over. World public opinion would have nobody to condemn, because the president-elect would not be responsible for his predecessor's last decision, and it would be the Republicans and not the young, inexperienced Kennedy who would put an end to the Fidel Castro regime. That was why the Revolutionary Armed Forces and national militias were on a war footing; hundreds of antiaircraft batteries were placed on the coasts, pointing at the sky alongside tanks ready for combat, as was the small air force. All main bridges had been dynamited.

Commander Santiago and his assistant, José, had to cross one of these bridges, the one stretching more than 300 meters over the Bacunayagua River. As they approached the bridge, the militia member on guard duty signaled the Chevrolet. Recently filled holes along the road indicated to the two passengers that it was impossible to cross there. José asked the commander to stay in the car while he talked to the patrol chief. He identified himself and explained that he urgently needed to get to Santa Clara; that it was a government matter. The young militia member slung his submachine gun over his shoulder and said reluctantly, indicating the narrow lane that remained from the original pavement, "Two wheels over the central divider and the other two over that strip. If you let one of your tires slip, you'll go flying through the air."

José went back to the car and asked Santiago to let him drive.

"It's no problem, it's easy," he said.

For several minutes, the car moved slowly as the militia members, who had taken their distance, looked on with astonishment. When it made it to the other side, José stuck out his lower lip and blew out heavily. His face was covered in sweat. Next to him, Commander Santiago was admiring the beautiful scenery.

When they arrived in Santa Clara, they registered at a second-rate hotel. It was where they were supposed to meet with the local head of Rescate, who was awaiting Tony's orders to join the armed insurgency. But the man didn't show up. They had lunch and continued traveling to Placetas, where the commander was very popular; it was where he had been born and grown up. When he came home from World War II, he could be seen in the park, surrounded by friends listening to his stories of that adventure, or playing basketball in the gym, where one night he invited a beautiful girl who was only fifteen to dance. Even though he was twenty-three at the time, he was impressed. Six months later, they got married.

After touring the town, greeting old friends, and making contact with conspirators, they held a meeting in a *bohío* on the city's outskirts with the coordinator for supplying the group operating in the mountains. He told them about the insurgency's operations, the deployment of forces, and relations between Osvaldo Ramírez and Evelio Duque, the main leaders. These two already knew Santiago had been appointed head of the Front, and had expressed their satisfaction at the decision.

In the meeting, the local chief promised to find a farm with all the required security for hiding the shipment Tony would bring from the United States. Together with the air drops, it would be a significant reinforcement.

That night, they arrived in Caibarién and headed for the port. Soon after that, Commander Santiago toured the forty-foot boat on which he would leave Cuba. It seemed appropriate. As he was leaving, he stopped and turned to look at its prow: *El Pensativo* —"The Thoughtful One," he read. He smiled and headed for the car. Certainly, the trip by sea would provide him with the only hours of rest he had had in the last four weeks. And as they crossed the "big hole," as Hemingway used to call the Straits of Florida, he would think about everything that had happened.

On his return to the capital, he brought along an insurgent who was wounded in one leg. The man was talkative, and throughout the three-hour trip, recounted for Commander Santiago details of the situation in the mountains. When they arrived, Tony asked his assistant José to get him into a Latin American embassy so that he could leave the country as a political exile.

The day of departure finally arrived. As planned, this time he made the trip to Caibarién with Juan Méndez, who, following embassy instructions, was also to go on the *El Pensativo*. At midnight on the dot, they arrived at the dock where the old fishing boat crew was waiting. Juan Méndez boarded first, as Commander Santiago walked along the dock. Twenty meters away, his assistant José was waiting, after having traveled to the city in a separate car. He was not leaving. Marcos Behar/Tony Sileo had been categorical; the U.S. Coast Guard would only take two people aboard.

They hugged in a tight embrace. As he was about to turn around to board the boat, Tony Santiago said in a low voice, to avoid being heard, "Tell Fidel I'll be back."

The supposed assistant, whose real name was José A. Veiga Peña, a Cuban State Security case agent, watched in the darkness of the night as his agent Oliverio, Commander Santiago's nom de guerre, jumped determinedly onto the *El Pensativo*.

Three months earlier, when Veiga, who used the pseudonym of Morán, had written the code name on the dossier for the G-2's top-secret files that would identify the case created to fight a group of conspirators with the underground organization Rescate, he had a hunch that Commander Santiago would go far. Morán had been a gambler years ago in the United States. That was why he wrote "Key Case" on the folder. Yes, Tony Santiago would be the key that would open the doors of Langley to Cuban State Security. And now, as he watched the boat head out into the waters of the Antilles Sea, northward bound, he had no doubt that the long-sought key was on its way.

He was far from suspecting that it would never open a door again.

In reality, Key Case rolled right along from the beginning. The commander's personality, a record tying him to one of the most extraordinary pages of U.S. history, and his status as a U.S. citizen, without any connections to communists, all gave great confidence and assurance to the men who were leading the anti-Cuba operation from Quarters Eye. Nobody there would suspect such a move by the inexperienced Cuban State Security forces, who actually made only one mistake, which turned out to be fatal.

Commander Santiago's departure was prepared by Cuban State Security. With the goal of ensuring the trip as much as possible, a crew was chosen that was made up of fishermen familiar with those waters who were revolutionaries. This was something that the fishermen of the port of Caibarién knew well, including some who had left the country and were navigating those waters in armed speedboats, hunting Cuban fishing boats.

Ten anguished days went by for Morán with no news of Commander Santiago or the *El Pensativo*. A deadly silence had begun to surround the affair when, on January 18, the administrator of the Caibarién fishing cooperative showed up in a State Security office and set a box on the guard officer's desk, the kind used by fishermen in that port for throwing small fish back into the sea.

It had been found near Cayo Coco, north of what was formerly Camagüey province. "There's one thing I'm sure of," the weather-beaten seaman said, looking at the piece of wood. "This belongs to *El Pensativo*."

Immediately, several boats were sent to inspect the maritime zone where the box had been found. Two fuel tank covers were found, along with a piece of railing, a piece of the sail, and the coal-hole. The carpenter who had built the *El Pensativo* recognized them.

What happened on the boat remained an absolute mystery for six months. Morán, saddened, and at the same time convinced that his agent had not betrayed him, closed the case. Osvaldo Ramírez was confirmed as head of the Escambray Front, but he could not do anything to support the operation to invade Trinidad. Moreover, he was preoccupied with staying hidden after the defeats suffered during Operation Jaula, the "clean-up of the Escambray." The invasion would target another area: Bahía de Cochinos, or the Bay of Pigs.

Everything seemed to be over when, on June 14, 1961, the crew of the *Petra María* fishing boat was kidnapped by the crew of an armed speedboat that had come from the cays near Florida. One of the kidnappers, whose henchmen called him "El Guajiro" —the peasant— told the fishermen he was from Caibarién, and boastfully admitted to sinking a boat from that port months ago, because it was "full of communists." It was the *El Pensativo*.

Destiny, so perverse, had dealt a bad hand to Commander Antonio Santiago. The key had sunk to the bottom of the ocean.

En route to the Southern Coast

It was 2:45 p.m. when the 2nd Battalion received the order to begin their march. In formation and at a walking pace, they began descending the small hill that separated them from the open area in front of the Brigade's headquarters. It was where they had staged a demonstration for Guatemalan President Idígoras Fuentes and where they had held their victory parade. José Ramón Pérez Peña turned and silently bid farewell to the barracks that had been his refuge since arriving at the camp eight months earlier in September 1960.

It was April 12, 1961, and Assault Brigade 2506 was preparing to leave for an unknown destination on the island of Cuba. In front of the building that housed the top officials, Colonel Jack Hawkins, the brigade's military leader, watched closely as the men approached their trucks. Even though he was the brigade's leader, Hawkins was not going to the beach himself. The man who would head the brigade on the beachhead was José Pérez San Román, who Hawkins had trained painstakingly. When the strategy for overthrowing Fidel Castro had changed in November, Hawkins had organized the troops into combat battalions, companies, platoons, and squads, and trained them for conventional battle.

The squads were made up of nine men each and two of them —the 5th and 6th— were armed with Browning automatic rifles. In combat, each squad was divided into two fire teams of four men each with the squad leader in the center. Each soldier carried 160 rounds of ammunition and a knife or bayonet. Each company's 4th Squad also carried two .30-caliber machine guns for defending the most dangerous areas, reinforced by heavy machine guns and recoilless guns. This structure would provide a barrage of fire much superior to that of the militia battalion squads.

The leader of José Ramón's squad was Edgar Buttari, the son of a former minister in the Carlos Prío government and a man of great wealth. Like the others, E Company was equipped with two bazookas, two .30-caliber machine guns, a 57-mm recoilless gun, an 81-mm mortar and a 60-mm mortar.

The 2nd Infantry Battalion, José Ramón's, was made up of five companies, for a total of 166 men.

The men began climbing into the trucks in order. The paratroopers, who were not in formation, said goodbye to old buddies. They would be the last to leave the camp. José Ramón shook hands with Julio Bolet, the student from the University of Miami; Manuel Menéndez Pou, whose father was president of the Aspuru Compañía S.A. (nationalized), and Irán, the former city council candidate.

The three were now part of the paratroopers' battalion. José Ramón asked about Néstor Pino, the former Cuban Army officer, and they told him Pino was now the company's second-in-command.

"Have you seen Arturito?" he asked. His friends repeated what he already knew. Arturo Menéndez Rodil had escaped a month earlier after receiving a letter from his girlfriend. He intended to cross the border into Mexico and go to Miami. He was declared a deserter and a week later was captured by Guatemalan authorities ten miles from the Mexican border. He was taken to Petén, a prison in the middle of the jungle from which it was very difficult to escape. After a month there, he was given a choice by an American officer: stay in prison until everything was over or return to the camp. He chose the second. He was put into the 5th Battalion, which had been put together recently out of newcomers hastily recruited in Miami. Two weeks later, he asked to be transferred to the armored battalion, complaining that the majority of the 5th Battalion's men had been soldiers and policemen during the Batista dictatorship. The recruits had dubbed it *Esbirrolandia*—"Thug-Land."

As José Ramón got into the truck, the ground shook slightly. It was a tremor from the Santiaguito Volcano. The soldiers began singing the national anthem. They were determined to free Cuba of Fidel Castro, but they also had another goal, one that depended on the overthrow of the Cuban leader. One hundred of the invaders owned vast expanses of property, holdings that had been expropriated, with the land distributed to those who worked it. Another sixty-seven owned tens of thousands of rental homes, which the Revolution had given over to the people who lived in them. Two hundred and fourteen were from wealthy families who used to control commerce, banking, and industry; 194 had been in the armed forces that had kept dictator Fulgencio Batista in power, and another 112 had been involved in businesses eradicated by the Revolution such as prostitution, gambling, and drugs.

In statements after their capture, the men spoke spontaneously and freely about what they had owned and many other things. Almost all of them admitted to having signed up for the invasion; they condemned the U.S. government and said they agreed with the compensation given to the revolutionary government for the resulting damages. Several brigade members were notorious criminals of the Batista dictatorship, such as Ramón Calviño Insua, a murderer and torturer who had raped women and castrated men; Emilio "El Muerto" (Death) Soler Puig, the murderer of labor leader Aracelio Iglesias; and Antonio Valentín Padrón Cárdenas, a murderer and torturer. These men are now considered martyrs of the Brigade.

"This past September was the twenty-third anniversary of the execution by firing squad of several brigade members who were taken prisoner... They are: Ramón Calviño, Jorge Kim, Rafael Emilio Soler Puig... May these brigade comrades be warmly remembered by those who continue to struggle for Cuba's freedom."[1]

The military caravan took the only useable road, which ran along steep and jagged cliffs, but the men didn't notice the danger. They had traveled it many times to climb hills and ford rivers during their long training marches. Soon after that, the sound could be heard of an improvised and unmistakable conga rhythm banged out on wooden boxes. They were definitely Cuban.

The paratroopers were the elite group. Their battalion was created in November 1960 when the men selected were transferred to Halcón Base, located on the La Suiza Farm about fifteen kilometers downhill from Trax Base. In December they were moved again, this

---

[1] *Girón* magazine, official organ of Brigade 2506, No. 1, Miami, Florida, October 1984, p. 11.

time to Garrapatenango Base, which was actually called San José de Buenavista, about forty kilometers from Trax, near the town of Quetzaltenago. That is where they practiced their jumps. These transfers were made because the main base, Trax, was in the mountains, making large-scale operations impossible. It had been chosen for training guerrilla fighters, not a conventional force.

The San José de Buenavista Base was not heavily guarded and the recruits' escapes to the town nearby began to alarm their American officers. That was why José San Román assembled the brigade and said the U.S. government would punish anyone caught off base. The punishments included halting financial aid to their families or deporting them.

In early February all the battalions were in Garrapatenango except for the tank battalions, which had gone to Fort Knox, Kentucky. A month later, in March 1961, training was over. The men were given two days' rest at Sipacate Beach on Guatemala's Pacific coast, where they were taken in open trucks in plain view. That was a month before April 13, when they said their final good-bye to Trax Base.

When they entered the town, children came to meet the trucks, stretching out their hands. Several brigade members threw cigarettes to them, including José Ramón. It was a common scene during the almost ten months since the first recruits had arrived. The brigade members were not shocked; they had seen this in Cuba, too. Most of them were ignorant of the deep-going changes that had been taking place in Cuban society. The only images they had of Cuba were from Radio Swan.

The trucks took almost three hours to arrive at the brigade's air base in Retalhuleu. Two armed Guatemalan soldiers halted the caravan. After identifying themselves, they drove into the military zone and stopped in front of a hangar. Battalion leader Hugo Sueiro and his second-in-command ordered the men out. After instructions were issued for their next move, the men spread out on the base. They found it strange not to see any combat aircraft; there were just a few C-47 transport planes. José Ramón commented that the fighter planes must have been transferred somewhere closer to Cuba. He was right.

Fifteen days earlier on April 1, the American commander of the Rayo air base, General Reid Doster, informed Manuel Villafaña that in the next twenty-four hours all pilots and planes would be transferred from the training base to the base from which they would fly to Cuba. The pilots realized they were being moved closer to the island. The next day, April 2, the B-26, C-46, and C-54 squadrons took off from the Rayo base and disappeared over the horizon. The pilots did not know their destination. Each squadron leader had received a sealed envelope containing maps and flight plans to get to the new air base and ordered to open them only after they were in the air. Several hours later, the planes began landing in Puerto Cabezas, Nicaragua. The pilots were informed that the base was called Happy Valley.

Back at Retalhuleu, the order was given to the battalion at 8:10 p.m. to return to the designated area. Shortly afterward, the men began boarding the three planes, one at a time. The planes were unmarked and paper was taped over their windows. Only the pilots knew where they were going. Once on board, the men began speculating. Some thought the invasion would be launched from the U.S. naval base at Guantánamo; one ventured that they would be divided up and land at different points. Little by little they became quiet and most of the men surrendered to sleep. Several hours later, the crew announced they would soon be landing.

It was 2 a.m. and it was cold at the Puerto Cabezas air base on Nicaragua's Atlantic Coast. It was from there that their ships would set sail for Cuba and their B-26 bombers would take off. For that reason, there was a lot of movement on the base; trucks were coming and going and Nicaraguan guards with floodlights watched over the landing strip and base entrances. A few minutes after getting out of their planes, the men were surprised by an order to get into trucks and soon they were driving through the town of Puerto Cabezas. The brigade members noticed that most of the houses were two stories high, made of wood and very small. Extreme poverty was evident. There was not a soul in the town's dirt streets. The townspeople had gone to bed early. The noise from the trucks was not letting them sleep, but they didn't dare go outside. The most curious peeked furtively through their windows. Somoza's soldiers had taken over the town.

Fifteen minutes later, the trucks began stopping in front of the town's train station. Inside and around the building, more Nicaraguan soldiers were standing guard with rifles. As he climbed into an old train car with the windows closed, José Ramón commented that anybody who was thinking about deserting at the last minute should forget about it. The word had spread. They were in Nicaragua, and its ruler was dictator Anastasio Somoza.

For José Ramón, Somoza was the same as Batista, but he knew that very few members of the brigade cared whether Somoza, Stroessner, or Trujillo was involved. The important thing was to overthrow Castro.

José Ramón and the rest of his company got as comfortable as they could in their assigned train car. They were warned not to smoke or turn on any lights. Slowly the train began to roll, stopping about thirty minutes later at a dock that jutted out like an arm into the sea. It was the port of Puerto Cabezas. The waters that bathed those shores were from the Caribbean Sea. Out beyond, in the mouth of the Gulf of Mexico, those same waters caressed the beaches of Cuba's southern coast.

The battalion walked down the dock to the last ship. Two cranes were loading heavy boxes containing rifles, explosives, radio equipment, medicine, food, and drinkable water. The holds also contained a stranger item: hats with mosquito netting to protect their heads from irritating bites. Since it was an unmistakable sign of what kind of terrain they could expect for the landing, the boxes were hermetically sealed. The CIA had organized production of several thousand of these peculiar items of clothing in the greatest secrecy. José Ramón walked toward the prow. He wanted to know the name of the ship that would be taking them to Cuba's coast: the *Houston*. "Must be American," he commented to his comrades nearby. But José Ramón was wrong; the *Houston* was the property of Eduardo García and sons, the owners of García Lines S.A., a shipping company that made trips between Havana and ports in the United States and Central America. The CIA had leased five ships from Eduardo García to transport the troops. Two of them, the *Río Escondido* and the *Houston*, would never return from the adventure. They would both sink off the coast of the Bay of Pigs.

On the *Houston*'s prow, portside, and starboard, .50-caliber machine guns had been set up, evidently to defend against possible attacks from enemy planes and to fire on the coast.

José Ramón's squad was ordered to stay on the dock. He set his knapsack on a post and lay down, buttoning up his jacket to the collar. The temperature had gone down. He nodded off. A little after 3 a.m., the order was given to board ship. José Ramón was struck by the spectacle on deck. The 2nd and 5th Battalions had taken up the entire space: the holds in the prow and stern, the lifeboats, the space under the stairs. There was almost no place left. A single look was enough to realize that the merchant ship was not suited to a military operation of the scope they were about to undertake. The men would have to crowd together on deck under the sun, exposed to the wind and weather. Sanitary services for the almost 400 men were inadequate. The cabins had been reserved for the top officers, the only ones to enjoy hot meals on board. The soldiers would have to make do with cold rations in boxes, canned and precooked food, sugar, salt, chocolates and preserves. In addition, there was a problem that posed the risk of a tragedy: drums of gasoline stored in the holds and on almost the entire deck. The men were walking around 45,000 gallons of high-octane gasoline.

A little after dawn, José Ramón was contemplating the sea when a comrade told him that Americans had arrived at the air base and were meeting with the battalion's top leaders. The information was correct.

Sitting on crude wooden benches, the brigade's General Staff and battalion commanders listened to the invasion plan. Colonel Jack Hawkins explained, "The invasion, which should begin today at 5 p.m. with the departure of the brigade from this very dock, is called Operation Pluto, and consists of this force landing on three points of the Bay of Pigs south of Las Villas province: Blue Beach (Girón); Red Beach (Playa Larga); and Green Beach (Caleta Buena), a point 10 kilometers east of Girón. Playa Girón will be the center of the operation, and that is where the headquarters will be. Playa Larga, 34 kilometers northwest, will be the forward command post for the infantry. The paratroopers will be dropped over Horquitas, Yaguaramas and Jocuma near the Covadonga Sugar Mill, and on the road that goes from the Australia Sugar Mill to Playa Larga. Your job will be to attack, occupy, and defend those places." Everyone at the meeting noticed how one of the visitors corrected

Hawkins on certain points and was apparently the highest-ranking person there. This later made them think that the man was Richard Mervin Bissell.

Whether or not he was at the brigade's send-off briefing, Bissell, the brains behind Operation Pluto, must have been euphoric that morning. He was on the verge of achieving his greatest triumph. The CIA's most colossal operation had been his work exclusively from the very start. He had negotiated more than a few hurdles to reach that point, the largest of them being John F. Kennedy's misgivings about the plan to invade Cuba.

Apaprently, Bissell began playing dirty even before Kennedy was elected president. If not, how explain the cable he sent to Trax Base October 31, 1960, just a couple of days before the election? In it Bissell ordered guerrilla training to be cut back, to be replaced by steps to create an amphibious and airborne assault force that could invade and conquer a piece of Cuban territory. Without even consulting President Eisenhower, who nonetheless gave his approval shortly afterward, the CIA director of plans abandoned his strategy of using an insurgent movement to overthrow the Revolution —something he knew was impossible— and created a new and more dangerous strategy: the invasion. Politically, the change was a profound one. Why didn't he wait a few more days to consult with the president-elect? Was he afraid that if Kennedy was elected and not Richard Nixon, the idea of another invasion of a Latin American country would be the direct opposite of the president's expressed political views and inclination? It is still not known whether Dulles and Bissell informed Kennedy of the change in strategy after the election or if he was made to believe the project had been a direct invasion from the start.

More than once in later meetings, the president proposed the variant of dropping men in groups over the country's mountains. It would be less spectacular and less risky for the prestige of the United States in the event of failure. Dulles and Bissell repeatedly argued against the idea.

"It is considered militarily infeasible to infiltrate in small units a force of this size to a single area where it could assemble, receive supplies, and engage in coordinated military action... Smaller scale infiltrations would not produce a psychological effect sufficient to precipitate general uprisings of wide-spread revolt among disaffected elements of Castro's armed forces... The Joint Chiefs of Staff have evaluated the military aspects of the plan for a landing by the Cuban opposition. They have concluded that 'this plan has a fair chance of ultimate success' (that is of detonating a major and ultimately successful revolt against Castro) and that, if ultimate success is not achieved there is every likelihood that the landing can be the means of establishing in favorable terrain a powerful guerrilla force which could be sustained almost indefinitely. The latter outcome would not be (and need not appear as) a serious defeat. It would be the means of exerting continuing pressure on the regime and would be a continuing demonstration of inability of the regime to establish order. It could create an opportunity for an OAS intervention to impose a cease-fire and hold elections."[2]

It is clear the President was misinformed. Up until about a month before, the CIA had a powerful espionage station in the U.S. embassy in Havana. The internal counterrevolution had tried to distort the reality of what was happening in the country. But for the CIA's professionals in the art of obtaining and assessing information, with their vast experience in measuring states of opinon and undeniable realities, it was enough to see just one of those enormous rallies of support for the Revolution to know what was going on. They could not predict a "major uprising." In the same memorandum, and as irrefutable proof that the president was being lied to, Bissell says:

"Any evaluation of the chances of success of the assault force should be realistic about the fighting qualities of the militia. No definitive conclusions can be advanced but it must be remembered that the majority of the militia are not fighters by instinct or background and are not militiamen by their own choice."[3]

Could it be that the CIA and FBI agents and the career diplomats who worked as their agents in the U.S. embassy in Havana —more than 300 of them— didn't know that people joined the militias

---

[2] Memorandum for the president from McGeorge Bundy (February 18, 1961). Opinion of Richard Bissell, Kennedy Library, Bissell, Cuba, February 17, 1961, NSF, Box 35. In *Foreign Relations of the United States, 1961-1963*, vol. X (Washington, D.C., United States Government Printing Office, 1997), pp. 102-3.

[3] Ibid.

voluntarily, subjected to a number of tests to gauge their determination and firmness of support for the Revolution?

Everything seems to indicate that Bissell was not on the Puerto Cabezas dock that morning, but in his office in Quarters Eye, where he soon received a very optimistic report on the brigade from Colonel Jack Hawkins. Like the Marine Corps colonel, the director of plans was probably breathing easier. Moreover, despite Kennedy's public denial that U.S. armed forces would invade the island, if things turned out badly —and he more than anyone else knew they could— he was sure the young, inexperienced, recently sworn-in president would not be able to say no to the hawks of the Pentagon and CIA. He would make the only decision possible for avoiding defeat: an invasion of Cuba. Bissell was an admirer of John Wayne.

José Ramón had just cleaned his M-1 carbine and was looking out at the ocean. The merchant ships *Río Escondido* and *Lake Charles* were nearby. After a while, he went down to the dock and began walking slowly among the crowd. Suddenly he noticed a group of men dressed in civilian and military clothes, all wearing dark glasses and carrying pistols or submachine guns. One stood out. He was wearing a white suit and a felt hat. It was Luis Somoza, chief of the Nicaraguan Army. The group stopped, and José Ramón found himself facing the man in the white suit, M-1 in hand. Other brigade members came up and surrounded him, and Somoza improvised a brief speech. He wished the invaders luck and assured them they would be victorious because they were well-equipped. Everyone applauded. On the way back to the *Houston*, a brigade member who was a former member of the Rebel Army commented, visibly upset, "After having fought one dictator, why applaud this one?" Friction within the brigade between former soldiers and those who had fought Batista had been evident since they started training together. They avoided each other.

Finally, the first ship set sail at 5 p.m. It was the *Atlantic*. Then the *Caribe,* the *Lake Charles,* and the *Río Escondido* cast off. Almost at nightfall, the *Houston* left, followed by the *Bárbara J* and the *Blagar*. The latter carried the assault brigade command. The five ships had set sail carrying 1,242 troops and thousands of tons of war materiel in their holds. Behind them, the *Opratava* and the *La Playa* cast off, both ships belonging to United Fruit. They would remain in the south Caribbean and go to the Bay of Pigs with an additional load of logistics supplies once the beachhead was consolidated. Some of the brigade members went to sleep worried that night because they had not seen any U.S. warships. As San Román later told Haynes Johnson, the men who trained in Guatemala were only participating in the invasion because of the Americans' presence. "They did not trust me or anyone else. They just trusted the Americans."[4]

Their doubts were cleared up at dawn when from the *Houston*, euphoric, they spotted a U.S. Navy destroyer. It had shut off its engines and was obviously waiting for the *Houston* to approach. José Ramón got a pair of binoculars and looked at the warship's registration number. It was destroyer No. 701. Its presence raised troop morale and that day's rations seemed better than the day before.

At 9 a.m., the company captains were summoned to a meeting. Three hours later, they returned to their units and talked to their men. In this somewhat informal way, in the middle of the ocean —where no agent of Fidel Castro's could run and inform— the secret jealously guarded by the CIA was revealed: the place chosen for invading Cuba would be the Bay of Pigs in the Zapata Swamp on Cuba's southern coast. "In the swamps?" Bullari, the squad leader, asked. "We won't have any problems," the E Company captain answered. "It's practically unihabited there and no military forces are in the region. Girón, one of the landing points, is a beach where they are building a tourist resort and it has a landing strip. One company will take over the airport and help the engineers make it operational as soon as possible. Three to five days after our landing, when the beachhead is consolidated, a plane from Miami will land with the Cuban Revolutionary Council, our provisional government. And afterwards, the Americans."

Smiles broke out on some faces. "And will we have to go into the swamps?"

"Not at all," the captain emphasized. "We will land on one of three beaches on the coast, on solid ground, and these cover about forty kilometers. I repeat: it is high and solid ground. The ones who are going to have to go into the swamps are the militia members, if

---

[4] Haynes Johnson: *The Bay of Pigs*. Norton, New York, 1964, p. 76.

they want to get to where we are. It's not going to be easy for them, because the two access roads that go through the swamp from the nearest towns to the coast will have been taken over by the paratroopers."

"So, will they be the first ones to go into battle?" José Ramón asked. "That's the plan, but our American leaders say things are going to go so well for us that we won't stop until we get to Havana. A lot of people are expected to join us."

"And what is our mission?" "Our battalion will be the first to land on Playa Larga, and then the 5th Battalion will follow. Our company, E, will go left until we reach a crossroad and then head north. We will march four kilometers to a village called Pálpite and wait there for the paratrooper platoon to be dropped. Another platoon from the 5th Battalion will advance along the right flank to a village called Soplillar."

That was when the Cubans learned where they were going and what they had to do. It had all been the work of the U.S. government. In a conference about the Bay of Pigs held in the United States in 1996 with U.S. and Cuban-American academics, the latter tried to claim that the invasion had been the result to a certain extent of cooperation between the so-called anti-Castro resistance and the U.S. government. At that point in the discussion, Professor Piero Gleijeses from the School of Advanced International Studies at Johns Hopkins University said, "I think that what Mr. Fernández, Mr. Durán, and Mr. Baloyra [referring to Lino B. Fernández, Alfredo G. Durán and Enrique A. Baloyra] are saying is very interesting and I am very glad to hear this. But I also hope we don't lose track of what really happened.

"The Bay of Pigs operation was not a cooperative arrangement between the United States and the Cuban Resistance. The Cubans who were involved in the Bay of Pigs were U.S. assets... And what they thought is not even relevant. The plans were made by the United States. The leadership was selected by the United States... So when we are talking about the Bay of Pigs, we are talking about U.S. aggression against Cuba..."[5]

---

[5] *Politics of Illusion: The Bay of Pigs Invasion Reexamined* (Boulder: Lynne Rienner Publishers, 1998), p. 72.

It was afternoon, and the men on deck shielded themselves from the sun's rays as best they could. The artillerymen assigned to the .50-caliber machine guns stayed busy, some doing maintenance work and others monitoring the skies. It soon began to get dark.

By 5:30 a.m. on Saturday April 15, most of the men from both battalions were awake. It was cold. About three miles away on the starboard side, they could see destroyer 701. Some of the men tuned in small transistor radios to Radio Swan. The first morning news bulletin was about the supposed crisis of the regime. Radio Swan reported that Che Guevara had been purged, and that during a discussion in the prime minister's office with Fidel, Raúl, Martínez Sánchez, and Núñez Jiménez, Martínez Sánchez had shot Che, wounding him. Those who didn't have radios were informed of the "good news"; morale shot up. Nobody questioned the accuracy of the news broadcast by that radio station for almost a year, and it was easy for listeners to conclude that the regime was falling apart piece by piece; all that was needed was the final blow, and that's what they were there for.

Actually, at that moment Che Guevara was at his command post in Cueva de los Portales in Pinar del Río province, where he had been assigned as military commander. Fidel Castro was at Point One, the national command post for the Revolutionary Armed Forces and militias. However, those facts were not on Radio Swan's morning's newscast. An hour later, a late-breaking news flash shocked the brigade members on board. The radio station was announcing to the world: "at dawn, airplanes from Castro's Air Force bombed the airports of Columbia and San Antonio de los Baños and Antonio Maceo International Airport in Santiago de Cuba." Radio Swan repeated this "news" several times, adding that there were many dead and injured and that the military bases had been practically destroyed. On the *Houston*, as on the other ships, the jubilation was intense. José Ramón tuned back in at mid-morning. The bulletins reporting the bombings of Cuba's airports were still being repeated, but now they were adding that "after firing on Columbia, one of the FAR planes was forced to land at the Miami city airport. It was a B-26 marked with the number 933, and it had numerous bullet holes on its fuselage." The news report claimed they were "pilots from Castro's Air Force who had made the air raid on the previously-mentioned airports," and it was announced that the deserter would make major revelations in the coming hours.

That afternoon, a U.S. immigration official handed out statements to the press from the supposed deserter.

"I am one of the twelve B-26 pilots who stayed in Castro's Air Force after the defection of Pedro Luis Díaz Lanz and the purges that followed. Three of my comrades and I had been planning to escape from Castro's Cuba somehow for months... Yesterday morning, I was assigned to a routine patrol from my base, San Antonio de los Baños, over a section of Pinar del Río and around the Isle of Pines. I told my friends from Camp Libertad and they agreed that we had to act."[6]

The news items were so well put together and the announcers so emphatic that more than a few of the brigade members on board thought it might be true. Others scoffed. They simply didn't believe it. They had seen the B-26 planes painted with Cuban insignia on the Happy Valley tarmac and now they understood why. Somebody suggested they tune in to a Cuban radio station. All of the radio stations were in sync. The Cuban government was denouncing the aggression, saying that the planes came from U.S. bases, and warning the people that this attack could be the prelude to an invasion. The country was mobilizing. And so were the organizers of Operation Pluto; H Hour was approaching Cuba's coast, but the U.S. president could still stop the landing.

"Project chiefs agreed that in event of a policy decision to call off the invasion they would move the troops to sea, tell them that new intelligence made the invasion inadvisable, and divert the force to Vieques Island for demobilization. On 12 April at a meeting with the President it was decided that Mr. Berle world tell Miro Cardona there would be no overt U.S. support of the invasion. The President publicly announced there would be no U.S. support. On 13 April all WH/4 headquarters sections went on 24 hour duty. The Revolutionary Council was assembled in New York and advised that it would be briefed in stages on the military aspects of the project. On 14 April —while the Brigade was heading out to sea— "the

---

[6] Statements by Mario Zúñiga, 2506 pilot, 1961.

Council agreed to go into 'isolation' during the landing phase of the military operation."[7]

At 12 noon, after distributing the boxes of rations, the battalion's officers were summoned to a meeting in the ship's mess hall. They wore high-crowned, wide-brimmed Texan hats in order to stand out from the troops. A real nuisance, a hindrance whose uselessness was demonstrated as soon as they went into battle, although more than a few of the officers decided to wear them. They would not be on the frontlines of combat.

The man sat around a rectangular table in the hall and Hugo Sueiro, chief of the 2nd Battalion, holding the operation plan in his hand, began explaining in detail what the brigade's mission would be after it landed, and what his battalion's mission would be. He opened up enlarged aerial photos and the company and squad leaders studied closely what they were supposed to do after the landing.

The three access roads that crossed the swamp, the canals, and the *bohíos*—all of it was extraordinarily visible in the photos. The map was updated with the smallest details. Sueiro and Erneido Oliva, the brigade's second-in-command, never would have imagined that the same map would soon be helping the revolutionary forces.

"Afterwards, I confiscated a map in Playa Larga that belonged to Erneido Oliva; it was plasticized and updated with aerial photos. It had the road from Playa Larga to Playa Girón, which my map didn't have. My map was old."[8]

Sueiro insisted that no prisoner be mistreated and all prisoners were to be immediately brought before the commanding officers for interrogation. He also emphasized respect for women and cash payments or a signed document from the battalion for all food seized. All working motor vehicles would be requisitioned. Treatment of the civilian population was very important for winning followers. Success would only be possible with the support of the Cuban population. "And what will they do with the prisoners?" someone in the room asked.

[7] *Inspector General's Survey of the Cuban Operation. October 1961.* Report by CIA General Inspector Lyman Kirpatrik. Document declassified by the U.S. government.

[8] Testimony of José Ramón Fernández, vice president of the Council of Ministers, 1990. Author's archives.

"That's the business of the G-2 and the people from Operation 40," Sueiro quickly answered. Nobody else responded. Actually, the men at the meeting knew very little about the mysterious Operation 40. They had heard about it in early March, when sixty-three men who arrived at Trax Base were housed in a barracks isolated from the rest of the troops. Vicente León León, a former Army colonel who had been an assistant to President Carlos Prío, was their leader. The recruits soon learned that these men were the ones who investigated the recruits who showed up at the Front's offices in Miami.

Their main leader, Joaquín Sanjenís, had remained in Miami. He was supposed to fly directly to the liberated zones and take charge of civilian intelligence. During their stay of a little over a month on Trax Base, two dozen of these Operation 40 troops were transferred to the G-2 section, which was supposed to be in charge of interrogating prisoners during battle. The rest were to travel on the last ship of the convoy, the *Atlantic*. They would be the last to land once the beachhead had been secured. Twenty-seven of them would be divided into nine three-man teams. They would have the mission of doing reconnaissance in the area beyond the lines of fire, to try to find the revolutionary forces, determine the weapons they possessed, the number of troops, their morale, their supplies, and the access routes they were using.

To carry out their missions, these teams would be dressed as civilians or militia members and would carry radios for maintaining contact with the rearguard. Another twelve members of this group would interrogate the civilian population to get information on cities near the battlefield, single out military and civilian military leaders, locate barracks, police and power stations, telephone offices, and banking agencies.

Finally, another twenty men organized into ten teams would get things going in cities taken over by the brigade. They would seize public and State Security records and take charge of military and civilian prisoners who supported the regime, physically eliminating them. They would consider these prisoners' level of commitment to the government after obtaining the necessary information from them.

This last, select group did not land; it stayed aboard the *Atlantic* and retreated. On the morning of April 17, under attack by the Revolutionary Air Force, the ship raised anchor and headed out to sea. The captain made his decision without consulting, but he promised to return at nightfall. He did not. He appeared on the morning of April 18, very far from the Cuban coast. Vicente León was one of the men who did land and died in battle. From the beginning, the future members of Operation 40 had included the counterintelligence section from the operations base in Miami. These men had been carefully selected by the CIA and trained as case officers to form a future Cuban intelligence service. They were charged with finding, training, and leading agents.

According to CIA Inspector General Lyman Kirkpatrick, at the time of the invasion the Miami base had thirty-one agents in Cuba who reported every day. They directed operations on the island, some of them successful.

"One of its most helpful services was reporting on meetings of FRD committees and other anti-Castro groups and on political maneuvering within the FRD hierarchy. It also helped in recruiting for the strike force at a time when the political leaders were sabotaging the effort. Security and counterintelligence teams" —Operation 40—"were also trained for integration with the strike force. These had the primary mission of securing vital records and documents during the invasion and a secondary mission of assisting in establishing and maintaining martial law. The service also carried on radio monitoring and conducted interrogations and debriefings."[9]

The members of Operation 40 who were captured made sure they hid their real mission. A single invader who was a member of the brigade's command revealed almost everything about the group's composition and mission but was silent about giving prisoners the third degree or physically eliminating them.[10]

As the meeting was about to end, the 2nd Battalion's leader emphasized again how the civilian population should be treated and added that the ships would be carrying some 3,000 rifles to distribute to those who joined the invaders.

[9] *Inspector General's Survey of the Cuban Operation. October 1961.* Report by CIA General Inspector Lyman Kirpatrik. Document declassified by the U.S. government.

[10] José Raúl Varona González, head of Brigade 2506's G-2, gave an extensive account of Operation 40. Author's archives.

When the meeting was over, the battalion's supply clerk burst in with a case of cold beer. It was also distributed to the troops. "We'll drink the next one in Havana," someone in the room commented and everyone laughed. When they went back out on deck, they found the troops in a good mood. On the horizon, they could see two U.S. warships sailing toward Cuba.

At lunchtime the men began to complain again about the precooked, cold food. Some were irritated about how the officers had hot food cooked on board. They complained so much that the brigade's second-in-command, Erneido Oliva, and the captain of the *Houston*, Luis Morse, were obliged to give orders for food to be cooked for all the troops the next day.

The ban on smoking, constantly violated, was emphasized. At nightfall a shot rang out and for a few minutes confusion reigned. It turned out that a member of the 2nd Battalion was cleaning his gun and it went off accidentally, wounding him in the leg. He was quickly taken to the mess hall and examined. It was stressed that they should be careful while cleaning their weapons. But the suspicion that it had been intentional stuck in some people's minds. They were confident in their victory, in support from the United States, and in the regime's imminent collapse. But the fact that they were so close to Cuba —which almost all of them had left over the past two years in the midst of a veritable revolutionary tide— was enough to set anyone's nerves on edge.

This was not the first accident on board. On the *Atlantic*, an artilleryman's 50-caliber machine gun accidentally went off during a drill, killing one invader instantly and injuring another.

When things were back to normal on the *Houston* again, it was evening and everyone settled down to sleep. José Ramón woke up with a start early in the morning. The ship had shut off its engines and many of the men on deck were looking out to sea with surprise. A powerful light blinded them. A few minutes went by, and the light made a circle off the stern. Then it was turned off and was lost in the darkness. The *Houston* continued on its path as the men speculated, but very few of them got it right. It was a submarine that was escorting the invading fleet. It had approached to pick up the wounded man.

At dawn on Sunday, April 16, the invaders on the *Houston* held their small radios close as they listened to Radio Swan. That morning, they heard news about fierce, victorious battles by the anti-Castro guerrilla fighters in the Escambray, bombs that had gone off in recent days in Havana, sabotage throughout the island, new uprisings in Oriente and Pinar del Río, and a large number of people killed in bombings the day before. The radio station exhorted the Cuban people over and over to rise up against Fidel Castro's regime and announced that freedom was near. "Gentlemen, if we take too long to get there, we will be able to land in the port of Havana instead of the swamp."

That comment by a soldier did not impress those who were able to hear it. Very few questioned the accuracy of the news, but some of them would have liked to hear that another invading force had landed from another direction, far from the swamp. They would feel more relaxed. Actually, the CIA had organized an operation in Oriente to create a diversion and confuse Fidel Castro; at that moment, this battalion would have been in combat near Baracoa. But invading Oriente would have been an extremely dangerous mission at that point.

On the morning of April 16, Oriente province was being defended by a considerable militia force and Rebel Army soldiers who were on maximum combat readiness.

Earlier that month, Commander Raúl Castro, minister of the Revolutionary Armed Forces, had been in Oriente. He also had been appointed military commander of the province. On April 16, he and his general staff made another detailed review of defense plans for that vast region. The most vulnerable points were the coastal zone between Nicaro and Pilón, and the area around the U.S. naval base at Guantánamo.

Commander Eddy Suñol had been assigned to defend that territory, and several reinforced units with land and anti-aircraft artillery were placed under his command. Another possible place for the landing was Baracoa, which was reinforced with three battalions. A group of battalions deployed in Mangos de Baraguá under the command of Captain Senén Casas could move north or south.

Fidel Castro, in recalling the situation in Oriente at the time, noted:

"On the evening of April 14, Raúl was in Oriente. They have the troops distributed, they have the regions organized, everything. They even have some planes in the Santiago de Cuba airport... Then they called me here in Havana and informed me that in the area of Baracoa a group of ships and a possible landing were observed... Using Baracoa's forces, measures were taken to repel the landing... Now, that operation would not have mobilized a single soldier from west to east, because there were enough men in Oriente, in those mountain areas, farmers who were organized and armed. So any force that would have landed there would have failed and would have had no objective. Of course, a landing would have gotten our attention, our interest, but it would not have had any military consequence because there were enough resources in Oriente to defeat an invasion."[11]

Fidel Castro's reference to the group of ships spotted near Baracoa turned out to be well-founded. It was a CIA operation code-named Mars, aimed at making the Cuban government believe that the invasion had finally happened.

"I concentrated on training to be part of an invasion force commanded by Nino Díaz... They had trained us in the camp north of Lake Pontchartrain until late April 1961, when we left by boat for Cuba. We left from the Algiers naval base on the Mississippi River, in New Orleans. There were 160 of us. The boat was called the *Santa Ana* and we sailed under a Costa Rican flag."[12]

On April 14, the same day the Assault Brigade set sail from Puerto Cabezas, the *Santa Ana*, with its 168 men, waited for dark to land on a beach near Imías, several dozen kilometers from the Guantánamo naval base. The important mission of the *Santa Ana* invaders was to go into combat as soon as the landing took place and make enough noise to force Fidel Castro to move trops to that province. Then, two days later, he would be surprised by the Bay of Pigs.

At nightfall, the *Santa Ana* got within four miles of the coast. A speedboat was lowered and it headed quickly and silently for the coast. "We were dressed in olive-green uniforms like the ones used by the Cuban Army...We approached Mocambo Beach, which is next to Imías. I went on a reconnaisaince patrol on the night of April 13."[13]

[11] Quintín Pino Machado: *La batalla de Playa a Girón*, Editorial Ciencias Sociales, La Habana, 1983, p. 284.
[12] Statements by Enrique *Kike* Fernández Ruiz de la Torre. Archives of the Ministry of the Interior.
[13] Ibid.

At that point, there was an exchange of communication between the CIA agent in charge of the operation, who was in the captain's cabin of the ship, battalion leader Higinio Díaz Ane, and the reconnaissance team.

The team repeatedly reported many lights, which they presumed were from military forces. The CIA agent, who used the pseudonym of Curly, insisted they find an appropriate landing site. The explorers soon returned, confirming the presence of military forces. The battalion chief said the landing should be suspended. Curly objected angrily (he didn't have to go ashore) and after an argument, it was decided to postpone the landing until the following night. The explorers were right. The presence of the *Santa Ana* and the speedboat prowling near the coast had not gone unnoticed.

"Raúl instructed him (Commander Eddy Suñol) to place an antiaircraft battery near the coast and to open fire with one of those weapons[14] in case of a landing. I remember clearly that Raúl warned Suñol not to fire until the mercenaries had landed. He repeated that two or three times."[15]

The airport bombings at dawn the next day did not dispel the fears of the invaders aboard the *Santa Ana* but it did raise their morale. None of them doubted they would be victorious and they were anxious for it.

That night the explorers silently made their way to the coast again.

"The second night, the intermediate speedboat taking us to shore broke down. When it hit the reefs, the propeller was wrecked. Another boat had to come pick us up. In the middle of that situation, we heard trucks and jeeps passing by."[16]

"They're waiting for us," one of the battallion's officers commented to Nino Díaz, who stood up to the pressure from the CIA official to land. Finally, the ship headed out to sea.

At midnight on Sunday April 16, the *Houston* slowly entered the Bay of Pigs. There was absolute silence on board, broken only by

---

[14] Antiaircraft battery with four-barreled heavy machine guns, known popularly as *cuatro bocas* ["four mouths"] Each battery had six guns, for a total of twenty-four rapid-fire barrels of 12.7-mm. ammunition.

[15] Testimony of Más Martín, Miguel A. Sánchez: *Girón no fue solo en abril,* Editorial Orbe, Havana, 1979, p. 107.

[16] Statements by Enrique " Kike" Fernández Ruiz de la Torre. Document cited.

the sound of the ship's engines and the waves lapping. All of its lights had been turned off except for a small one on the bridge.

A little after 1 a.m. the ladders were hung and José Ramón checked his equipment one last time. Eight outboard-motor speedboats were released from their moorings and cranes in the prow and stern lifted the vessels up, setting them into the calm waters. The ship rocked gently and a soft breeze blew through the tense atmosphere. The ship's antiaircraft artillerymen were in combat position, scrutinizing the skies and the coast. The artillerymen on the escort ship, the *Barbara J*, were also in position. After a while, the first men from the 2nd Battalion climbed down into the speedboats. José Ramón settled into the prow and looked out at the shore, clutching his M-3 submachine gun. The darkness was impenetrable, but about a mile away toward the coast, he could see a green light. It was the signal placed by the frogmen. José Ramón thought they would occupy the beach without combat. It looked deserted. He was not wrong. There were no combat units at Playa Larga to defend it.

In the first week of April, Commander Fidel Castro and other Rebel Army leaders had toured construction sites on the Zapata Peninsula. As he walked over the Playa Girón breakwater he said, "This is an ideal place for a landing."[17] Fidel ordered the transfer of a battalion from Cienfuegos to the Australia Sugar Mill, thirty kilometers from Playa Larga and seventy from Playa Girón. This unit would be responsible for defending the coast between Playa Larga and Caleta del Rosario, a point between the two beaches. He ordered another battalion to be placed in Playa Girón. Due to shortcomings in organization and communications, this order was not carried out.

Remembering those days, Fidel Castro said, "I had ordered the placement of a battalion at the site of the landing three or four days earlier. But at that time, everything was in its very early stages; we still didn't have a general staff."

Therefore, on the night of the landing, Playa Girón was being defended by a half dozen charcoal makers, militia members who were on guard duty. They each had Czech-made M-52 semiautomatic rifles and sixty rounds of ammunition. The militia

[17] Testimony of Abraham Maciques, development director of the Zapata Peninsula at the time.

leader, Mariano Mustelier, had a Czech-made submachine gun and ninety rounds.

In Playa Larga, the other landing point where the *Houston*'s first speedboat was about to arrive, there was just one observation post that night. It was covered by a five-man squad from the 339th Battalion and under the command of militia member José Ramón González Suco.

"The battalion arrived at the Australia Sugar Mill on April 8 or 10, and if I remember correctly, they sent me with four men from my squad to Playa Larga. They chose me because I knew how to run the Motorola shortwave radio that was there. I had been there in January working on tourism construction sites, and I used that radio, which belonged to the Ministry of Construction, to request sand, cement, and so forth when the project director needed it. That beach was a paradise. When we took over the radio, the operator —who was leaving for time off with the rest of the workers— warned me not to keep it on all the time because the voltage was defective. So we would turn it on every thirty minutes to communicate with the battalion and give our report. The only weapons we had, which were the only ones in the area, were five Czech submachine guns with eighty rounds each and a VZ machine gun with bipod and 200 rounds for belt or box magazines. We really liked seeing it work with the belt—it was like something out of a movie… That Sunday afternoon, one of the battalion's companies arrived. They had been cutting burned sugar cane, and all of the men were covered with soot. They went to the beach and went swimming and then went back to the Australia Sugar Mill. If they had stayed, those people would not have landed. At least, we would have been able to hold them off until the rest of the battalion arrived. But they left. They'd just come to swim at the beach… Quintana had the VZ; he was a very strong guy, but kind of slow. I asked him if he knew how to use it. He told me he did, but he started fooling around with it, and it accidentally went off a few times. So I called over the radio and asked the battalion chief to send someone to teach us. El Chino came and gave us instructions… A little after midnight, the man who was doing guard duty on the beach saw a shape and reported it to me. They had told me that a Navy cruiser would be putting into port in Caletón, a little further to the right. It was a very dark night, and you couldn't see anything. Then I heard the sound of a motor. I told my people that I would order the cruiser to halt and that they should stay behind with the VZ. A few minutes later I saw it, and I could see perfectly that there was a man with his foot on the prow. He had a rifle. I raised my submachine gun and yelled, 'Halt!' and fired into the air. They answered with a burst of M-3 fire. Just imagine, when I fired again with my Czech submachine gun, which has a much smaller caliber, it was as if I was firing with a toy. The VZ opened fire but right away it got jammed. After the battle I found out that the VZ belts are crap. They're more effective with boxes. But the guys wanted it to be like in the movies."[18]

From the *Houston*, they opened fire on the coast. Between approximately 2 a.m. and 6 a.m., some 5,000 machine-gun rounds were fired.

The five militia members could not offer any resistance, but they were able to communicate to the battalion's command that they were under attack. Later they took refuge in one of the construction sites, where they were taken prisoner the next morning.

Fidel Castro knew that an invasion was being prepared. The airport bombings had convinced him of its imminence. But he did not know how many men would land and most importantly, he didn't know where.

The CIA had managed to keep the landing site a secret. Suco's testimony is eloquent.

---

[18] Testimony of José Ramón González Suco, militia member, 1991. Author's archives.

The CIA did not fool Fidel Castro

On October 7, 1960, at the United Nations, Cuban Foreign Minister Raúl Roa denounced preparations for the invasion. "...Since late August and early September, Guatemalan troops and barges have been massing off that country's Atlantic Coast. On Helvetia Farm, located in the municipality of El Palmar adjacent to the departments of Retalhuleu and Quetzaltenango in the western part of the country, recently acquired by Roberto Alejos, the brother of the Guatemalan ambassador to the United States, Carlos Alejos, and members of the family provided for by the palatial court, numerous exiles and adventure-seekers are receiving special training under the command of U.S. military personnel. The total number of foreigners is 185, of which forty-five are Americans. At that farm, a concrete landing strip has been built with underground hangars, and a road to the Pacific Coast is being built. Monitoring devices have been installed. The access roads to the Helvetia Farm are being guarded by Guatemalan soldiers. The foreign elements are not allowed to have contact with the local population... Bombers with Cuban insignia have been seen at the La Aurora airport. There is a public rumor that they have the double mission of being available to attack Cuba or to simulate Cuban aggression against Guatemala."

This revelation by Roa at the UN has either been barely acknowledged or ignored by U.S. and Cuban-American historians who have addressed the issue. Some of them say the first leak about the camps was provided by journalist Paul P. Kennedy in a long article —in the tone of an adventure story— he wrote about Trax

155

Base. Others say the issue was blown open by an article in the Guatemalan newspaper *La Hora* on October 30, 1960, when journalist Clemente Barroquín revealed that a plan to invade Cuba was under way in the mountains of Retalhuleu, "Prepared not by our country, which is so poor and so disorganized, but for all practical purposes by the United States."

Cuba had made its revelations at the UN weeks before these articles were published.

By that time, maintaining secrecy around the Cubans' camps in Guatemala was not a priority for the CIA. Its main concern was keeping U.S. government involvement in the project under wraps, as well as the magnitude of the operation and the day, hour, and place of the invasion. While it was not very credible, the FRD carried out a vast amount of work internationally to make itself look like the force behind the matter. More than a few people had doubts about this, but nobody was in a position to disprove it.

The CIA could not hide its participation for very long. It became impossible to maintain the secret of the training camps with their U.S. instructors and personnel, guarded by hundreds of Guatemalan troops, with the constant coming and going of men and military equipment and planes landing and taking off from the jungle region, surrounded by thousands of peasant homes. According to one intelligence proverb, "You can't hide a hippopotamus with a handkerchief." Nor is it easy to hide a hippopotamus when it must move from one place to another in Miami, go for medical exams, leave the family and disappear mysteriously at night; or, a short time later, when letters begin to arrive that are censored but give hints about the hippo's absence.

"But what harm could it do for Cubans to talk in Miami or New York, if that existed, compared to the talk among thousands of coffee workers who were around our camp in the Guatemalan mountains as they were taking home a miserable 40 cents a day for their work. This base was chosen by American government officials, just a mountain range west of the Pan-American Highway. Where was the Cuban air base? The place, which, just like all the others, was not chosen by the Cubans, was right in the town of Retalhuleu, with some 4,000 inhabitants of dubious political inclinations: not much of a secret base for a secret operation... And besides, when in history was it possible to hide from the enemy the massive preparation of a conventional direct attack? Was General Eisenhower able to hide from Hitler preparations for the invasion of Europe during World War II?"[1]

Some of the Cuban-American invaders and writers on the issue claim there were undercover Cuban State Security agents on Trax Base. The most-often cited account refers to Benigno Pérez Vivanco, a recruit selected to be the leader of an infiltration team, as being a G-2 agent. In his book, *Shadow Warrior*, Félix Rodríguez Mendigutía says, "Even though precautions had been taken when the primary selections were made, at least one Castro spy, for example, made it into the Grey teams. His name was Benigno Pérez. We knew him to be a former lieutenant in Castro's armed forces who, like many of his fellow officers, had defected to the U.S.

"Pérez was a hardworking individual. I remember seeing him as a small man who drove trucks and bulldozers, a cigar seemingly clenched permanently between his teeth. But one thing about him made me wary: the guy would never look you in the face. When you spoke to him he'd avert his eyes, as if he was ashamed of something. He was older than most of us, and I wondered why he was selected for the Grey teams. At the time I guessed it was because they believed he'd still have good contacts in Cuba as a former Castro officer.

"I was happy when he was finally assigned to someone else's unit —I would have refused to have him on mine simply because I had a queasy feeling in my gut whenever Pérez's name was mentioned. But it wasn't so good for the guys he worked with, because Pérez didn't have good contacts in Cuba, but great contacts— many of them members of Castro's secret police —and every one of his fellow team members was captured. Today, Benigno Pérez lives the good life in Cuba as a high-ranking officer of the DGI..."[2]

Benigno Pérez Vivanco had fought against the Fulgencio Batista dictatorship as part of the Second National Front of the Escambray, led by Eloy Gutiérrez Menoyo, and because of his participation in eight battles he was promoted to captain. After the triumph of the

[1] José Pérez San Román: *Respuesta:La verdad sobre Girón*, p. 27.
[2] Félix Rodríguez: work cited., pp. 63-64.

Revolution, Menoyo demoted him to first lieutenant, arguing that he needed to keep the higher post reserved for someone else. Benigno complained to Commander Camilo Cienfuegos, who upon learning that Benigno had been a heavy equipment operator, assigned him to the Isle of Pines development zone. In July 1960, due to disagreements with his supervisor, Benigno left for the United States with several friends. He got a job there driving a forklift for the United Fruit Company. In August, he was recruited by the FRD and he went to Guatemala, where he helped build the landing strip at the Rayo air base in Retalhuleu.

Soon, he was a favorite of the Filipino colonel, Valeriano Vallejo, and the leader of the American instructors, Carl. "I would go everywhere with Vallejo and with Carl. They really trusted me. I got along well with all of the personnel, except those who had been in the old Army and were supporters of Batista. I didn't have any problems with any of them, but they were not my friends. I had fought against the dictatorship and it was not easy for me to understand how some of these people were now my comrades. And there were a lot of Batista supporters in the camp."[3]

In late November, with the original teams now dissolved and Assault Brigade 2506 in the process of being created, eighty-two men were chosen to continue training in irregular warfare and enter secretly into Cuba for training and for coordinating actions by underground groups in support of the invasion. Benigno left the base with the rest of the men chosen and shortly afterward, started rigorous training again in the jungles of Panama.

He secretly entered Cuba on the northern Havana coast on March 22 as head of the Inca Team. The team was carrying seventeen tons of weapons and explosives for underground organizations. After a number of incidents, Benigno Pérez and his radio operator went into hiding in apartment 6-B of the Almar Building in Miramar.

Throughout April, he provided explosives training for three underground groups and acted as advisor for several successful sabotage actions in the capital. On April 21, after week of heavy raids to round up conspirators and two days after Brigade 2506 was defeated, Benigno and his radio operator, Rafael García Rubio, returned to the apartment where they were hiding. It was

[3] Testimony of Benigno Pérez Vivanco. Author's archives.

about 6 a.m. They had spent the night in a motel with two women to avoid being discovered in the pre-dawn, the most dangerous time of the night. They did not realize that their movements had caught the attention of neighbors who were part of the Committees for the Defense of the Revolution (CDR) in that building. Under instructions of State Security, the CDR members were closely monitoring the two men.

Shortly after 6 a.m., having been notified that the two suspects had returned, four State Security agents went to the building. Two of them remained at the main entrance and the other two went up to the apartment. These men had been on the job for a week and were exhausted. Before opening his door, Marcial Arufe peeked through the screen. He saw an unfamiliar face, unshaven and wearing an olive-green cap. He asked Benigno and Garcia to escape by using the freight elevator. A couple of minutes later as they were going down to the lobby, the two heard an exchange of shots. They didn't make it to the street; they were stopped at the door. At State Security offices, Benigno saw some of his old comrades from the guerrilla struggle against Batista. They were astonished to see him there, arrested for being a terrorist and counterrevolutionary.

He was sentenced to death by firing squad, but his sentence was commuted to thirty years in prison. Fourteen years later, he was released on parole and got married.

Benigno Pérez now lives in Matanzas province and works as a sugarcane combine operator for an agricultural cooperative.

The truth is Cuban State Security never penetrated the CIA's operation or its camps in Guatemala.

The first information on the existence of these bases emerged in the Guatemalan media and in public protests. Several revelations and statements were made by the Guatemalan Labor Party as early as June 1960. Law students and others who were members of the Salvador Orozco Circle in Quetzaltenango made public statements that had an impact at the Central University of Guatemala City. The matter was taken to Parliament, and several deputies appealed to the government, issuing public letters of denunciation. The matter of the camps hit the streets. A student demonstration protesting the presence of the anti-Fidelista Cubans who were being trained in their country ended in a rally in front of the U.S. embassy in late October 1960. Revelations by Colonel Carlos A. Paz Tejeda regarding military camps and bases on Guatemalan territory were published in a full-page article by the Guatemalan newspaper *Prensa Libre*, with a daily press run of 30,000. That took the issue to the barracks.

Meanwhile, in the offices of Section M (intelligence) in Cuba, the press reports from Guatemala were piling up. There were letters from supporters of the Revolution and even from residents of Miami and New York, and some reports from Cuban State Security agents. They all had one thing in common: they revealed the invasion plan, the existence of the camps, and the places where they were located. Nothing more. It is evident that these reports included information prepared in Quarters Eye by CIA agents assigned to disinformation operations aimed at confusing and disorienting Fidel Castro.

As early as September 30, a State Security agent who had infiltrated a conspiratorial branch of the MRR (Revolutionary Recovery Movement) in Havana, told the agent who worked with to him, "This report is the most important of all, because of the magnitude of the things raised in it, which will determine aborting the Yankee embassy's plan. On October 15, all of the teams will arrive at the following points: Sagua de Tánamo, north of Las Villas and Sierra de los Órganos. They will be brought on Yankee Air Force planes piloted by seventy Cubans. They will try to reinforce and create new fronts. The general attack, in other words the landing and bombing, involves seventy planes, and the commando attack will be exactly on October 25 in the morning. Beginning October 1, the attacks and sabotage will start."[4]

Nothing happened. Only one air operation was carried out by the Brigade 2506 air force. It was in October and consisted of dropping a load of military supplies over the Escambray Mountains south of Las Villas.

It is evident that Raúl Roa's statements at the UN on October 7, 1960, were thoroughly analyzed by Richard Bissell and his top collaborators and used to put out further disinformation.

Hence the cable that Cuban intelligence received from Mexico on October 30, just three weeks after the Cuban foreign minister's

---

[4] Archives of the Ministry of the Interior.

revelations in the UN: "Our friends in Guatemala inform us of the transfer of 6,000 men from the Helvetia farm to Nicaragua."[5] Another report to Cuban State Security authorities, dated December 29, 1960, said, "With respect to your question to us about whether we have a concrete report on the mercenaries who left in thirteen ships on October 27/60, we can tell you that in December 1960 we received a report in this section dated 26/11/60 that says the following:

"It has been verified that some 6,000 troops were moved in the following manner:

"a) Only foreign mercenaries were sent to Nicaragua on October 27 (particularly Cubans, Salvadorans, Hondurans, etc.).

"b) Another group was led to a camp on the Chinajá airfield, where they were seen in the days that followed.

"c) The Guatemalan troops that are included in the total remained at the Helvetia farm and later another contingent of approximately 500 regular troops was sent to that farm. Quite a few Americans also are at Helvetia.

"d) The agricultural workers and farmers enlisted in this army were demobilized, returning to their agricultural work, but closely monitored. It is assumed that this is a temporary situation for them.

"Everything else is still the same at the Helvetia base and nearby farms: there is always a total of 150 planes (without specifying what kind), which coincides with what Idígoras told the FAG pilots on October 13, 1960.

"The ones who remain camped out there are training only in parachute jumps, using a very large transport plane; other aspects of training are considered finished.

"In addition, on October 30, 1960, a cable was received from Mexico in which our friends in Guatemala inform us of the transfer of 6,000 men from the Helvetia farm to Nicaragua.

"It is certain that this transfer was carried out from Puerto Barrios. From previous reports, we have knowledge of the presence of thirteen vessels without registration or flags in Puerto Barrios.[6]

---

5 In late October on the Trax Base, recruits for the future brigade numbered no more than 600. Obviously, the CIA multiplied that by ten. MININT archives.

6 Archives of the Ministry of the Interior.

The disinformation leaps out at you. No movements had taken place and the Brigade's real forces were significantly smaller. In Cuba, State Security analyzed all the information and drew its own conclusions. Reported troop movements and figures on mercenaries, planes and ships were regarded with caution, while it was further confirmed that the camps and invasion plans existed.

In January 1961, as a response to public revelations about the camps and the conflict it had created in the Guatemalan Congress, that country's government used a wily subterfuge: it invited the press and several opposition congress members to visit the alleged training centers so they could see for themselves that there were no Cubans. Brigade pilot Eduardo Ferrer remembers the day of the visit as follows: "In early January, we were told that the next day a group of fifty reporters from all over the Americas and Europe were coming to Rayo. Their purpose was to report the truth about the base to the outside world...

"The flight bringing the newsmen to Rayo was due to arrive at precisely 11:00 AM. By 9:00 AM there was no one at the base. Very early that morning, we had received orders to pack our knapsacks and canteens and proceed three kilometers into the jungle. We spent the morning in hiding. To justify the existence of the base, a detachment of Guatemalan soldiers was brought in. Four hours later, a scout found us and reported that the Constellation, with all newsmen aboard, had departed on its return trip with a 'no-news cargo.' We stumbled back to Rayo, having covered six kilometers of steaming Central American jungle".[7]

Evidently, the CIA used certain Cuban embassies in the region for their operation, particularly the one in Costa Rica. Along with the real friends of Cuba who were around the embassies at the time, there were others who were unquestionably on the CIA's payroll. Apparently, one of them penetrated the Cuban Embassy in Costa Rica in early January 1961.

"It was learned here that the nerve centers of these types of activities were in Nicaragua and Guatemala, and given that we

[7] Eduardo Ferrer *Operación Puma.*, International Aviation Consultants, INC., 1975, p. 112.

didn't have relations with either of those countries, we had to place an agent in Costa Rica. I remember that I arrived on December 24. They were waiting to have dinner with me... One day, in January 1961, when I arrived at the embassy, I went in through a corner entrance and I saw a guy come out. He was a typical dandy, dressed in white and wearing two-tone shoes, and well, because of his appearance, he reminded me of a homosexual from my hometown. So I asked Wilfredo González, who was the attaché who worked with me, 'Hey, who is that man?' González told me that he was bringing information about plans for attacks against Cuba, and that he wanted to see the ambassador.

"So I asked him what he had told the guy. He had told him the ambassador wasn't there. I told him, 'Go get him, and tell him the commercial attaché will see him!' And so the man comes. He sits down in front of me and tells me that he didn't care much about Mr. Kennedy, or Mr. Castro, or whoever; that what he cared about was the dough. He wanted $500 for the information. Ah! For all of these cases, the ambassador had told me that if they came to sell information, not to give them a cent...

"The man tells me that his little girl is sick, so I say to him, listen, I can't give you the $500. Take this $30 to get some food for your daughter. So he sits there and he says to me, 'I know how to be a man, too, and I'm going to give you the information for nothing.' So we arranged to meet in Morazán Park. There, he gave us a document, a white, unmarked envelope, and when we got home, we steamed it open. And when we unsealed it, it was in code. So I said to Wilfredo, 'We've got to see that man again!'

"When I saw him, I told him, 'Damn, man, I don't have the code!' So he left and came back with the code. It was the same code that existed during the time of Batista and used by the Department of State, which is now the Ministry of Foreign Affairs. How does a contact not only have coded information, but the code for deciphering the message? The most elemental security measure indicated that it wasn't possible. In short, the information said, 'Landing team... weapons... material resources... military... date: February 24; and landing site: Bay of Pigs.' That was in January 1961. The day arrived and nothing happened. There were comrades here who saw the information as illogical based on their belief that a swamp was not conducive to carrying out an invasion. The informant made contact again in Mexico and delivered more information. After Girón, the man was gone, he disappeared...[8]

It has now been irrefutably confirmed that in January 1961, the invasion was set to take place in the city of Trinidad. Evidently, at that time the Bay of Pigs information was supposed to confuse Fidel Castro. But he did not fall into the trap.

On January 24, the Bay of Pigs was undefended, while a powerful military force was stationed in the Escambray north of the city of Trinidad, and the coasts were closely monitored. The Bay of Pigs would be brought up again, this time in the press, identified as the final destination for the landing of an anti-Castro group from Costa Rica.

On March 2, 1961, when the CIA still had Trinidad as Brigade 2506's objective, the *Diario de Costa Rica*, in its regular edition, reported the revelations made in San Jose by Costa Rican congress members Marcial Aguiluz and Enrique Obregón Valverde. The two men presented photostat copies of a letter dated February 24 in which Cuban counterrevolutionaries Orlando Núñez Pérez and José Miguel Tarafa, delegates of the Democratic Revolutionary Front, reported on their efforts to organize training bases in Costa Rica. Aguiluz and Valverde added that these Cubans were using three farms: Playa Hermosa in Limón province; La Cañera, between Guaipites and Rosanna, and another near the Sixacla River close to Panama.

The newspaper article noted, "At this time, a group of Cubans and Costa Ricans who have trained in a location ten minutes from the Matina stop on Limón-San Jose railroad line have a dock prepared for ships sailing toward the Bay of Pigs (Cuba). For their invasion, they have the convenience of sailing down the river on the *Don Fabio*. In order to appreciate the authenticity of this report, we are publishing part of a message from one of the San Jose leaders to the person in Puerto Limón who is the chief or commander of the group."

Shortly after that, another cable from Costa Rica cleared up any doubts about the revelations published in the *Diario de Costa Rica*.

"It was in early March. The author of *Mamita Yunai*, Carlos Luis Falla, 'Carlufa,' as his friends called him, was a hunter. Then there

---

[8] Testimony of Major Héctor Gallo (Retired).

was a report in the press saying that they are getting prepared in Tortuguero. That is a lake and hunting area. So, this man goes from the hunt to the lake in Tortuguero and personally carries out visual intelligence activities. Then to the embassy, and he tells me that I can be sure that there is none of that there.[9]

The CIA and Pentagon experts did not select the Bay of Pigs until March 14. It went from being the location used by the CIA to confuse Fidel Castro to the final destination of Assault Brigade 2506. As a result, the CIA had carried out a brilliant disinformation operation without setting out to do so. However, Fidel Castro did not allow himself to be led into what had been a trap until March 14.

In late March and early April the revolutionary leadership decided to send home the more than 50,000 militia members stationed in the Escambray. Only one of the seventy-plus battalions was mobilized to defend the Bay of Pigs coast. They were equipped with light weapons and had little military training. Only one platoon and a five-man squad were stationed on two points along the coastline, while the majority of the battalion was sent to the Australia Sugar Mill, twenty-nine and sixty-seven kilometers away, respectively, from Playa Larga and Playa Girón. Top priority in defending the coast was given to Casilda, the port near Trinidad, and the area around it.

A long confidential report for the leader of the Revolution was drawn up by Cuba's G-2 on the mercenary camps and bases in Guatemala, Nicaragua, and Florida and sent to State Security offices April 7, 1961. It had been prepared January 12, and it confirmed the existence of the camps in Guatemala and figures on military forces, but multiplied by ten. In one paragraph, the main source apparently tried to insist on the authenticity of the information. It reads, "On the Helvetia farm there are 600 tents divided into two camps of 300 tents each. A person in one of these tents said that each tent contains an average of ten men, for a total of 6,000 mercenaries."

[9] Ibid.

The recruits on Trax Base slept in barracks, not tents. Havana continued getting the same old disinformation about the number of future invaders.

According to the same report, the enemy air force had jets and B-29 bombers, flying superfortresses. While the Brigade 2506 air force did not have any B-26 bombers, there was no question that it did have planes for bombing military targets. The Cuban government, for its part, stepped up its preparation of antiaircraft artillery courses.

The report also included a summary of information that had appeared in the international media, including in the United States, about the camps and invasion preparations, which added to the information that Havana was receiving from other sources. These news articles mostly from U.S. and British sources have become a source of controversy over the years. Some claim the invasion plan was being telegraphed to Fidel Castro, and others say, correctly, that the Revolution's leader did not learn anything new from the U.S. media. One of the last pages of the long report reads, "As may be observed, this information from U.S. correspondents that provoked an international scandal contributes very little information about the mercenary bases in Guatemala, about which this G-2 information department already had complete information, and which is related in the first part of this report. These activities were appropriately denounced by the government and its representative to the UN, Dr. Raúl Roa."[10]

The report's final words refer to the mercenary activities in Florida. Once again, these demonstrate the CIA's disinformation activities: "It is well-known that Tony Varona's FRD has a camp with 1,400 mercenaries... In total, we can say that there are some 5,000 mercenaries receiving training in different parts of the United States... Mercenaries have been transferred from these training camps in Florida to Guatemala and Swan Island in U.S. Army transport planes and in various civilian cargo planes. Swan Island is being used as a transit station where the mercenaries remain for several days and are then transferred to the Guantánamo naval base... The first group taken to Guantánamo was 150 men who traveled on October

[10] Report prepared for Fidel Castro by State Security on January 12, 1961. Document declassified during the academic conference titled "Girón, 40 Years Later."

24 on the *Burman*, a U.S. Navy warship under the command of Captain Joseph McDonald. Since that date, groups of 150 men have left every week with weapons, ammunition, medicine, and food... The mercenaries in Guantánamo who wear olive-green camouflage uniforms with brown and white markings, like the ones used by the Marine Corps in World War II, are the best troops and have the best weapons."

These final pages of the confidential report sum up one of the CIA's disinformation priorities: making Fidel Castro believe that the invasion would happen at several different points, not just one. "The plan is to send small, commando-type expeditions to different points of the island, timing them to coincide with attacks and sabotage in the cities. These expeditions will leave from Florida, some adjacent cays, and possibly from Swan Island. As the landings take place, the mercenaries camped on the Guantánamo naval base will head for the Sierra Maestra, to use it as an operations base and attack various cities in Oriente province, backed by the invasion forces coming from Swan Island and Guatemala."

After confirming the Bay of Pigs invasion and the landing in Baracoa of a battalion commanded by Higinio Díaz, the CIA hoped Fidel would hesitate before moving his best forces and resources that he was using to defend the capital. They were confident that he would wait for the additional landings. Maybe that is why Brigade 2506 was prepared to face the military forces that came from Santa Clara, more than 200 kilometers from the Bay of Pigs. Most of the invaders were deployed northwest and east of Playa Girón, where the roads from Santa Clara and Cienfuegos converged.

But none of that happened. Eyewitnesses who were at Point One recount how, early in the morning of the 17th, after the reports of the landing at Girón and Playa Larga, Fidel told officers meeting there that the invaders had to be defeated immediately. Without hesitating for an instant, he ordered forces to be mobilized to repel the attack. He was convinced it was the main landing.

The CIA had kept the secret of the place chosen for the invasion, but it had not been able to fool Fidel Castro.

Mission: Paralyze Havana

A long bell rang on all five floors to announce the store was about to close. The central air conditioning system shut off and the temperature inside the enormous building began to rise. Fifty-nine percent of the indoor lighting was turned off, and the elevators came to a halt on the ground floor. The doormen did not allow any more customers in but did not disturb the almost 300 still inside. Any employees who were not helping customers got ready to leave. People who were still browsing through some of the store's nineteen departments, looking at fabrics, dinnerware, basketry, furniture, silver and gold items, records, kitchen utensils, shoes, and hundreds of other items of varying quality and price, or who were waiting their turn to sit down in the cafeteria, could no longer buy anything. In five minutes, the place was practically empty. It was 6 p.m. on April 13, 1961.

Carlos González Vidal rang up his last sale, left the records department and walked quickly toward the fabrics department. His face was flushed, and he seemed to be concentrating and extremely restrained. He raised his hand to his chest, brushing his fingers against the gold Caridad del Cobre medal. Three women employees were still in the fabrics department, one of the store's largest. They did not find anything strange about Carlos being there. He was friendly and jovial. If there was anything that tarnished his character, it was his increasing hostility toward the Revolution. But with his coworkers he was attentive, talkative, and easy going. In recent days, he had helped them at closing time. He closed several sliding doors

169

between the shelves of fabrics to protect them from dust and talked about record sales. "Every day there's less coming in from the United States."

After he put the partitions into place, Carlos was alone. He pulled out a pack of Eden cigarettes from a small pouch and bit one end until he felt the zinc liner break. Actually, it was an incendiary device.

A week earlier, Mario Pombo Matamoros, a leader in the retail industry of a counterrevolutionary group called the Revolutionary People's Movement (MRP), had held a meeting in a house at 156 Paseo to finalize the details of the largest sabotage action carried out by his group: the destruction of the El Encanto Department Store. Afterwards, he discussed the plan with Carlos González, who agreed to carry it out, but on the condition that they immediately get him to the United States.

Early in the morning of April 13, a telephone call roused him from bed. A little while later, he met an MRP liaison, Arturo Martínez Pagalday, in the street. Martínez handed him two incendiary devices and told him to place them in a vulnerable part of the store. That was why Carlos was now in the fabrics department, an ideal place to start a major fire.

He slid one of the packs between two rolls of cloth and went back out into the aisle. He went a few more steps and went behind another set of shelves, repeating his action. He felt safe. He had asked his liaison if the bombs were American, and Mario Pombo had affirmed that with his head: "Someone from over there gave them to me. They have the combustion power of a hundred Molotov cocktails." Mario wasn't lying. Special agent Jorge "Cawy" Comellas, a member of one of the infiltration teams, had given him the devices and explained how to use them.

A few minutes later, Carlos left the store. He got into a car a couple of hundred meters away.

"And?" the driver asked. "I placed them," Carlos answered, without being able to overcome a growing sense of anxiety. He would only calm down once he was far away from Cuba tomorrow night, he thought. The car headed for the Malecón seaside highway, turned left, and disappeared in the direction of the North Shore beaches outside the city.

An explosion went off in the El Encanto, followed by another, setting off a fire in the fabrics department. The smoke began pouring out the cracks of doors and windows. Firefighters aided by hundreds of volunteers worked until dawn pouring tons of water on the burning building, holding the long hoses over their heads and coming to the aid of those who had inhaled smoke. Hundreds more carried merchandise out of the basements or threw buckets of water on the windows of neighboring buildings so they wouldn't blow. But as dawn approached, Cuba's largest department store no longer existed. Where it had stood hours earlier there was nothing but a pile of charred iron bars, bricks and wood. A few days later, the remains of a female employee were pulled from the rubble.

Nobody there asked what had caused the disaster; everybody knew. A CIA agent in Florida charged with sending explosives to Cuba had a favorite saying he used to repeat to his Cuban agents: "With one of these explosives, a single man can cause a terrible commotion in a big city." It was proven true. And one of the Miami CIA station's priorities was sending weapons and explosives to the island, along with agents to train others how to use them.

"Although the invasion preparations were absorbing most of the project's energies and funds, WH/4 Branch was still attempting to nourish the underground. There were six successful boat operations, carrying men and materials,[1] in February and 13 in March, and two successful air drops in March. Infiltration of agents was continuing. As of 15 February Miami Base reported the following numbers and types of agents in Cuba: Counterintelligence, 20; positive intelligence, 5; propaganda, 2; paramilitary, 4. As of 15 March the base reported that these numbers had risen, respectively, to 21, 11, 9, and 6.

"By the invasion date the personnel strength of Miami Base had grown to 160. The intensity of activity there during the latter months of the operation is indicated by the record of a day picked at random —it happened to be 9 February— when 21 case officers spent 140 man hours in personal contact with 125 Cubans.[2]

---

[1] "Materials" refers to the incendiary devices like those that reduced El Encanto to ashes.

[2] *Inspector General's Survey of the Cuban Operation*. October 1961. Report by CIA General Inspector Lyman Kirkpatrick. Document declassified by the U.S. government.

"El Encanto was very pretty and very elegant but old. It had been built at the end of the last century and remodeled and expanded several times. That was why it completely collapsed. The fabric created a lot of smoke, and because it was completely enclosed, the smoke covered everything. Total losses were estimated at 20 million pesos. It was the largest store in the country, and had 930 employees. It was the next day that we discovered that Fe del Valle was missing. After investigating, I came to the conclusion that she had gone up to the fourth floor to the Federation of Cuban Women's office, where the organization kept its funds. She had to go up the escalator, which was stopped. When she got up there and tried to come back down, the smoke that began filling that floor made it hard for her to go down the escalator. Maybe she couldn't find it on that floor full of shelves and increasingly flooded with smoke. There was no other way to go down; the emergency stairs were behind the elevators, and that area had been immediately covered in smoke. That was how Fe del Valle became trapped.

"We immediately began the investigation; we were in the middle of it when the airports were bombed. Then the arrests of counterrevolutionaries began. I was part of State Security operations. So I found out that Carlos González was there, under arrest. I had joined State Security right before that. Previously, I had been an El Encanto employee, and I knew a lot of people there, including Carlos. I had argued with him several times about politics. Well, I asked to see his file and that's how I found out they had arrested him on Baracoa Beach at about midnight while he was sending out signals to sea with a flashlight. It was an unlucky coincidence for Carlos that Pena, the leader of a militia company guarding that part of the coast, was also an El Encanto employee, and he recognized him (Carlos) right away. Well, they sent him to 5th and 14th, where he was kept under investigation. He was surprised when he saw me. He didn't know I was in Security. They had confiscated his two weeks' wages, and it wasn't payday yet. When I asked him how that was possible, he said he had asked for an advance. That wasn't usual or very logical. I began to get suspicious.

"I had been told that they'd seized fifty machine guns in the Tikoa Club, and even though that turned out to be a lie, I knew that the Tikoa was owned by a relative of Carlos. So I told him pointblank: 'You're involved in the matter of the machine guns that they seized at the Tikoa.' 'I certainly am not,' he quickly answered, without stopping to think. I asked my colleague who was taking notes to leave the room. When we were alone, I looked him straight in the face and said, 'You did have something to do with the fire.' He started crying. A while later, he composed himself and confessed. He said that they had given him the devices at 2 p.m. and described to me in detail how he did it."[3]

It's possible that Carlos González could not get over his amazement. On the beach where he was hiding, he had been arrested by a militia member who was an El Encanto employee like himself. In State Security, he had been interrogated by another worker, also a store employee. It seemed like everybody in Cuba knew each other.

The knowledge possessed by the population and State Security about counterrevolutionaries would be a decisive factor in paralyzing clandestine activities in the country.

Destruction of the store represented a high point in subversive activities, but by then counterrevolutionary organizations had been hit so hard that they were in no position to provide their anticipated support to the invasion. In the three previous months, the underground movement had been intensely active in order to make itself felt. A brief overview of news reports gives us a sampling —although perhaps a poor one— of what was happening at the time.

On February 5 in the Ciro Redondo neighborhood of the city of Bayamo, a bomb had gone off in the hands of a worker who had found it, seriously injuring him and five children. That same day, a plane flew over Havana and dropped pamphlets inciting students to go on strike. The next day, hundreds of students from private Catholic schools, almost all of them children of the Cuban bourgeoisie, went out on strike under a slogan broadcast over Radio Swan: "Let the books fall until the tyrant falls." Revolutionary students responded to the strike and it failed.

[3] Testimony of Colonel Oscar Gámez, 1994.

On February 7, the roof of a car fell almost fifty meters from where it was parked in the University of Havana's Cadenas Plaza. A bomb had exploded inside the car. On February 8, a man was put on trial for masterminding the sabotage of tobacco warehouses at 108 Dragones in the capital, causing substantial losses and injuries to twelve people. On the 13th, a counterrevolutionary named Bienvenido Infante Suárez was caught by a group of neighbors just as he was about to place a bomb in the utilities office at Amistad and Barcelona streets; a bomb, a grenade, and a pistol were seized from him. The next day, fourteen members of the MRR —seven of whom belonged to armed groups in the Sagua la Grande mountain region— were arrested. Weapons and armbands with the initials MRRFRD were confiscated from them.

On February 19 an unknown plane dropped thousands of fliers on the heavily populated neighborhoods of Marianao and Regla, inciting people to commit sabotage.

On February 26, as the invasion details were being decided in Washington, the counterrevolutionary movement on the island did everything possible to make itself felt. Meanwhile, without losing track of events, Fidel Castro joined in voluntary labor for the third Sunday in a row, cutting sugarcane for more than six hours. Afterward he sat under a tree to talk with the cooperative's members about the diversification of production and then he had lunch with them. That same day, the *Miami News* published a front-page story under the banner headline, "RUSSIANS BUILD BASE IN CUBA." And reporter Hal Hendrix —who worked for David Atlee Phillips, in charge of the psychological warfare plan at Quarters Eye— claimed that he had received information from Cuba on microfilm to the effect that 300 soldiers had been assigned to guard the base built by the Russians and fifteen soldiers had been executed for protesting a visit by Russian officials. Hendrix was emulating Radio Swan.

On February 28, a fourteen-year-old militia member, Pedro Morejón, was killed from behind by a group of counterrevolutionaries. His body appeared near the river that goes through the village of San Pedro de Mayabón. Four days later another militia member, Lázaro García Granados, was also killed. At about 3 p.m. that same day, a bomb went off at the end of recess at the Nobel Academy, a private school under the Commerce Department. The impact destroyed the walls of three classrooms and doors, chairs, and windows. Seven students were hurt. One of them, sixteen years old, lost her left eye. On March 1, a plane dropped thousands of counterrevolutionary pamphlets over Matanzas, and some 5,000 people gathered and burned them in bonfires. Seventeen kilometers from the city, what was apparently the same plane dropped napalm on sugar cane fields; meanwhile, three bombs went off in the capital. On March 7, a bomb went off in the parking lot of the luxurious Habana Libre Hotel.

Twenty-year-old José María Méndez Marrero was about to park his motorcycle in front of the Sumesa shopping center in Altahabana when a powerful explosion threw him into the air. He was dead by the time he hit the sidewalk. In Campo Florido, a bomb placed in an electrical transformer left the town of Guanabo in darkness. At the Ministry of Labor, a female militia member found a bomb in one of the bathrooms; it was deactivated a few minutes later by another worker. Light planes from the north flew over Camagüey, Pinar del Río, and Artemisa, dropping counterrevolutionary pamphlets. Supporters of the Revolution collected them and publicly burned them.

Carlos Rodríguez Borbolla was a worker in a paper warehouse on Francos and Santa María streets. He was a militia member, and on the night of March 6 he was on guard duty at his workplace. A car stopped in front of the entrance. One of its occupants asked him for directions, and when Carlos got closer, the man hit him in the head. Then the car's occupants stabbed him and burned the warehouse.

On March 8, a bomb went off at 12th and 19th streets in the heavily populated Vedado neighborhood.

On the 11th, a bomb placed in the Vibora Park utility towers caused a blackout for several hours in Víbora, Vedado, Marianao, and Plaza de la Revolución. That same day, Raúl Silvio Vega died after four months of agony. He had been shot from a passing car as he was heading for the Militia Leadership School in Matanzas.

At 3:30 a.m. on March 14, a gunboat opened fire with machine guns and heavy guns on the nationalized oil refinery in Punta Gorda, at the entrance to Santiago de Cuba Bay.[4]

That same day, another bomb caused power outages in several parts of downtown Havana, while fires burned in two of the popular "Ten Cents" stores, one on Monte and Suárez streets and the other on Obispo. Both terrorist acts had been carried out simultaneously using incendiary devices. "They look like pocket cigarette cases, and are filled with highly flammable gelatin. Two percussion caps are added to both sides," explained a warning published in the press.

On March 21 at 11 p.m., a powerful bomb went off in a car parked on 15th Street between 2nd and 4th in Vedado in front of a building where the Federation of Cuban Women was holding a pro-Revolution event. Two people were blown apart by the explosion. Another bomb went off at the corner of San Lázaro and the Malecón, causing panic among pedestrians.

The sabotage and terrorism were answered with improvised acts of mass repudiation and exhortations for the Committees for the Defense of the Revolution (CDRs) to redouble their vigilance. That organization, structured at a block-by-block level in the cities and by farm and landholding in the countryside, had a total of 104,000 committees throughout the country by the end of March.

On March 31, President Kennedy invited Senator James William Fulbright, chairman of the Senate Committee on Foreign Relations, to spend Easter weekend with him in Palm Beach.

President Kennedy was a Catholic, too. When he received the invitation, Fulbright wrote a memorandum that he gave the president when he boarded the plane that would take them south, near Cuba. After analyzing all the pros and cons —for the United States— of each possible course of action with respect to Cuba, Fulbright said, "The prospect must also be faced that an invasion of Cuba by exiles

---

[4] Years later it was learned that the attack had been carried out from aboard the Landing Craft Vehicle *Blagar*, which offered its protection weeks later as the flagship for the Brigade 2506 naval fleet.

would encounter formidable resistance which the exiles, by themselves, might not be able to overcome."[5]

That same day, authorities foiled a plot to assassinate Commander Fidel Castro as he was entering his offices on 11th Street in Vedado.

On April 1, newspapers reported the arrest of a group of counterrevolutionaries. These individuals actually had been arrested on March 24. State Security had dealt a heavy blow to Triple A, one of the organizations that was originally part of the FRD. The Triple A had prepared an attack on the Soviet Union's first ambassador in Cuba, and was responsible for dozens of acts of sabotage and terrorism, including burning down a major mattress factory in the capital. Radio equipment was seized from them.

That week, authorities dismantled another subversive group, led by Roberto Herrera del Rial, who owned the Diamar tailor shop in downtown Havana. Herrera was part of the leadership of the Christian Democratic Movement and was a member of the National Insurrectional Front (FIN), another CIA attempt to unify the smaller underground organizations. In Herrera's tailor shop, blue denim shirts like the ones used by militia members were made as well as Rebel Army and police uniforms, all of which were provided to other underground organizations to be worn while carrying out subversive actions.

On March 29, a warehouse located at 210 32nd Street in Vedado was found full of weapons and explosives belonging to the Student Revolutionary Directorate (DRE): incendiary devices, grenades, weapons of varying caliber, dynamite, fuses and percussion caps. The large store of weapons came from shipments the CIA had made from Florida. The DRE, an organization with few members —according to testimony, they numbered less than 500 men but almost 100 of these were setting bombs. They were mostly religious militants who were strongly and dogmatically anticommunist.

"...The materials he was responsible for were used by other comrades, according to procedures Damián himself ordered. His system was to take the necessary materials to a public place and make the delivery there, and when there was too much material, it was returned to him and he kept it for the next action."[6]

---

[5] *Fulbright of Arkansas: The Public Positions of a Private Thinker*, Robert Luce: McKay, Washington D.C., 1963.
[6] Statements by Virgilio Campanería Ángel to State Security. MININT archives.

On April 17, while Brigade 2506 was disembarking at the Bay of Pigs, Hans G. Ebner, then considered the DRE's national military coordinator, hastily hid the last materials that the organization possessed in the cistern of the Mechanical Engineering building at Santo Tomás de Villanueva Catholic University: six time bombs, detonators, napalm, several dozen C-4 explosives, and half a dozen olive-green uniforms. More than a few DRE militants had been educated and encouraged to conspire by the priests who ran Catholic schools.

On April 3, Roberto Sierra Barrios, a twenty-four-year-old militia member who worked at a small carpentry shop, was preparing to take the bus in front of the *Verde Olivo* and *Vanidades* printing plants when an explosion threw him into the air. He died later at the hospital. The next day, the young man's mother and wife told reporters that the terrorists should be shot.

Two days later at 5 p.m., a fire broke out in the warehouse at the Camilo Cienfuegos sugar mill, formerly Hershey's. Losses amounted to 279,000 one-hundred-pound sacks of sugar.

On April 7, Carlos Manuel Calvo Martínez, a member of MRR, placed a bomb in the doorway of the El Encanto department store, destroying the windows of nearby stores. Calvo was arrested.

On April 11, after a citizen's report, authorities seized a .30-caliber machine gun, bazooka, four M-3s, six Garand M-1s, field radio equipment, explosives, and abundant ammunition at a house on the highway northeast of the capital. Twenty counterrevolutionaries were arrested.

On April 12, another terrorist, José Ramón Rodríguez Borges, was arrested near the same store, El Encanto. He had two bombs and detonators hidden in a bag.

On April 13, while trying to put out a fire started by counterrevolutionaries in a sugarcane field, four farmers were burned to death. That same night in the capital, the counterrevolutionary movement reduced the country's largest department store to ashes.

One of the heaviest blows dealt to the CIA in the country came on March 18 when several of its top agents were arrested.

"On the afternoon of March 18 a climactic meeting was held in a pastel yellow home on sleepy Calle Once in suburban Miramar.

Humberto Sorí Marín, Rafael Hanscom, and Roger González hunched over a refectory table with six others... Chain-smoking Camels as usual, Sorí Marín pointed his bony finger at targets on spread-out street maps.

"Several blocks away a militia unit on routine patrol stopped in front of a house and knocked on the door. The nervous woman occupant bolted out the back door and ran to the yellow house on Calle Once, which was owned by friends. But the patrol spotted her and smashed its way in. Sorí Marín drew his pistol but was chopped down by a militiaman's snub-nosed Czech machine gun and badly wounded. The others raised their hands."[7]

Actually, it was not a routine patrol nor was it a coincidence.

"I went to the previously mentioned address with two other agents. In the rush, they gave me the wrong house number. Instead of 110, they gave me 108. I got there, and told the two men with me to cover the back. As I was knocking on the door, I looked over at the house next door, and through the dining-room window I saw a group of men meeting around a table. I realized that those were the people. Then they answered the door at No. 108 and a woman came out. I asked her who lived next door, and she said some friends of hers, and that she just happened to be going over there. I let her go, but I suspected she was mixed up in things. I situated myself behind her and advanced while signaling my two colleagues to move toward the neighboring house. I let the woman knock on the door and when they opened it, I pushed her aside, pulled out my gun, and entered the house. I really surprised them. There were seven men. I ordered them not to move and then the other two agents got there. We searched them and disarmed them. Sorí Marín kept saying to me over and over that he was a G-2 agent, and when I looked away for a second, he took off running. I went after him for more than 200 meters, practically to the coast. After shooting into the air several times, I fired at his legs and hit him in the buttocks."[8]

Eleven counterrevolutionaries were arrested at the house, including an organizer of the underground movement on the island, a top leader of the MRR, and a key CIA agent in Cuba, Rogelio

---

[7] Warren Hinckle and William W. Turner, *The Fish Is Red: The Story of the Secret War against Castro* (New York: Harper & Row, 1981), pp. 72-73.

[8] Testimony of Colonel José Luis Domínguez. 1995.

González Corzo. He had been operating for almost two years under the pseudonym of Francisco, a name that appeared over and over in hundreds of Cuban State Security reports. When he was arrested he showed a fake ID with the name of Harold Boves Castillo. Also arrested was Rafael Díaz Hanscom, national coordinator of the United Revolutionary Front, which had been recently created by the CIA as a coordinating group for the different counterrevolutionary organizations.

That night, two more counterrevolutionaries were arrested after they knocked on the door of the house marked 108 and a G-2 agent answered.

Several days later, Captain Federico Mora and a group of combatants were searching around Celimar Beach, where conspirators had buried a cache of weapons and explosives after entering the country from Florida. A neighbor told them that several nights earlier the lights of a nightclub there had been turned on and off several times. Mora realized what that meant. Immediately, he arrested the club's owner. Soon after that, they dug up eleven jute sacks and thirteen duffle bags of nitro-starch, a highly powerful explosive; sixteen cans of safety matches; thirteen rolls of fuse; ten boxes of incendiary grenades; twenty-five fragmentation grenades; ten .45-caliber pistols, six M-1 carbines, eight M-3 machine guns appropriate for urban combat, and abundant ammunition. One of the sacks was bursting with pamphlets urging sabotage and providing instructions. Another contained 120 incendiary devices that looked like cigarette cases. Two similar devices were used to reduce Cuba's largest department store to ashes two weeks later.

In the days leading up to the invasion, the various underground organizations carried out terrorist acts of some significance, although they were few compared to the CIA's plans. The destruction of the El Encanto department store was the largest, the culmination, but ironically, it signaled the beginning of the end of any organized resistance, at least while the battle was taking place. "Our mission was to paralyze Havana."[9] But in Cuba, nothing was being done too late.

On April 15, after the airport bombings, files containing information on many counterrevolutionary conspirators in Cuba were given to

[9] Testimony of Bebo Acosta. Documentary *Girón, ¿derrota o traición?*

180

State Security agents, who were charged with arresting them. Hugh Thomas says in his book *Cuba: the Pursuit of Freedom* that some 2,500 CIA agents or collaborators were arrested. The neutralization of the internal counterrevolution was actually more all-encompassing. The most active counterrevolutionaries were singled out. In a few hours, Cuba's G-2 headquarters on Fifth Avenue and 14th Street and several neighboring houses quickly filled up with detainees. Soon, there were some 1,000 conspirators and collaborators under arrest. Authorities then made use of the 5,000-seat Blanquita Theatre and the 15,000-seat Ciudad Deportiva sports complex, but they did not fill it up. The operation's organizers realized that it had gotten out of control because of the initiative taken by the Revolution's supporters. The number of people arrested was more than what State Security had in its files. On April 8 authorities began taking steps to halt this situation. Only detainees who were brought to detention centers with the passwords "Cuco" or "Cuca" were accepted. Catholic priests and nuns involved in counterrevolutionary activities were not disturbed and remained in their churches and convents, although they were monitored. The total number of detainees in the capital was about 20,000. These arrests took place without any deaths or injuries among the counterrevolutionaries; that was not the case for State Security agents, who suffered one death and one injury. Much has been written about these mass detentions, which took place at an exceptionally dangerous time for the Cuban nation. It was not an unjustified or new measure, although mistakes were made. When the Japanese attacked Pearl Harbor, the U.S. government arrested 100,000 Japanese people and their descendants who lived in the United States and placed them in preventive custody in heavily guarded camps. It has now been shown that almost none of them —to avoid making an absolute statement— were conspiring on behalf of Japan. And the Cubans who were arrested began to be released as soon as the invasion was defeated.

Statements made later by top counterrevolutionary agents corroborated the effectiveness of the neutralization campaign and blows dealt to the counterrevolution right before the invasion. "By the time Girón happened, the unit was disorganized and everything ended with the massive flight of top leaders and the heads of different groups and organizations. The few of us leaders who remained were arrested and I am the last one of that whole episode."[10]

"By April 17 Omar and I were no longer at Aurora's house. We were at the house of Dinorah Cárdenas on 6th Street, where we were arrested on the morning of April 20 after the militia came to search the house. We were in the G-2 for thirteen days and in La Cabaña for six more until they released us on the morning of May 9. While we were under arrest, we used our fake IDs... They never interrogated us, except for preliminary questioning at the Civic Plaza when we were arrested. We got out of La Cabaña on April 9 and on April 11 we were given asylum at the Venezuelan Embassy.[11]

Some argue that Girón gave the Cuban government a pretext to liquidate the so-called internal resistance, justifying this claim by adding on zeros: they talk about 3,000 armed insurgents in the Escambray, adding that each had 100 collaborators, raising the figure to 300,000 in those mountains alone. They claim that during Girón, the number of detainees rose to 150,000, and 200,000 people were later given asylum. They talk about 60,000 political prisoners (saying 6,000 alone were from the MRR, representing ten percent) and of 50,000 conspirators in the capital. And to top it all off, they add some of these figures to supposedly official reports from the revolutionary government.

Some cite official figures, but out of context, such as the comment that "the Cuban government refers to the existence of 179 different rebel groups in the mountains, the plains and the cities." But what they keep very much under wraps is that the figure refers to the total number of groups that existed over approximately five years of internal counterrevolution. They also fail to mention how after July 1961, insurgents in the mountains formed groups of no more than ten to fifteen individuals to avoid persecution. Nor do they say that in the cities, there was a proliferation of organizations with tiny

---

[10] Statements by Octavio Barroso Gómez to State Security. Archives of the Ministry of the Interior.

[11] Statements by Juan Manuel Guillot Castellanos, national military coordinator of the MRR. Archives of the Ministry of the Interior.

memberships, as Howard Hunt says in his book, *Give Us This Day*. As part of the CIA operation, Hunt oversaw the counterrevolutionary politicians. Referring to one of the FRD's five counterrevolutionary organizations —therefore one of the main ones— he commented, "whose Montecristi movement seemed to be limited to blood relatives".[12]

Along the same lines, Wayne Smith, a political official and assistant to the U.S. ambassador in Cuba until relations were broken off on January 3, 1961, stated,

"We were in contact with the opposition, the resistance. At least some of the organizations, in our view, were quite cohesive and effective. Our conclusion, however, was that the internal resistance never had the capability of overthrowing the government, nor was it likely to [ever] have that capability, even in the long term. In that sense, our conclusion at the embassy was that time was certainly on the side of the government, which was beginning to consolidate its power, and it was, as Jim just said, establishing its link with the Soviet Union—it was beginning to receive Soviet military assistance and its militia were being trained...And if you traveled around the island and talked to people like we did and in fact we even helped a dozen opposition members, you could get the impression that 'Jeez, there are a lot of people here, and maybe they have the capability of affecting the course of government, and even, with time, defeating it.'"[13]

The Cuban capital, where the CIA had set out to create a strong opposition movement to completely destabilize the government through a wave of sabotage and terror, remained tranquil, alert, and loyal to the Revolution. It was the same in the rest of the country.

After Operation Jaula, which had ended two weeks earlier, the calm in the Escambray was broken only by occasional skirmishes. The insurgents who had managed to evade the cordon tried to reestablish their contacts. The only notable event in support of the invasion occurred on the morning of the landing. A dozen members from a cooperative on the Las Delicias Farm in the foothills of the

---

[12] Howard Hunt: *Give Us This Day*, pp. 61-62.
[13] Politics of Illusion: *The Bay of Pigs Invasion Reexamined*, p. 17.

Escambray joined the armed insurgency with their militia rifles. Almost all of them belonged to their workplace militia. Their leader, Medardo León Jiménez, had secretly been in contact for several months with the top insurgent leader, Osvaldo Ramírez. In order to get more weapons for the uprising, León told other conspirators to join the militia.

There were no active counterrevolutionary forces in the Sierra Maestra except for a small group led by the young Alberto Muller, the top leader of the Student Revolutionary Directorate (DRE). Two weeks earlier on April 4, Muller and two dozen Catholic students met at the Caridad del Cobre Sanctuary near the city of Santiago de Cuba, and with the help of the church's priests, formed an armed group several days later in the Manzanillo area of the Sierra Maestra. Muller had radio equipment and a radio operator and was able to coordinate a previously planned air drop of weapons, ammunition, and explosives for his troops. However, it didn't happen. What Muller didn't know was that the Brigade's air force had been transferred to Happy Valley Base and air drops had been suspended. Because of that bloodshed was avoided; the insurgents had no military training. On April 21, two days after the Battle of Girón was over, Muller's group had its first clash with a Rebel Army patrol. Several insurgents were captured and the rest scattered. In the following days, almost the entire group was captured, including its chief, Alberto Muller. Four machine guns were seized from them along with an equal number of grenades, radio equipment, a large amount of medicine and clothing, several cases of books and propaganda and hundreds of armbands for identifying members of the five columns they had planned to create.

At the time of his arrest, Alberto Muller held the rank of commander.

On the other end of the island in the Los Órganos Mountains of Pinar del Río, the reality on Sunday, April 16 was quite different from what was being broadcast on Radio Swan. In Loma del Toro, about thirty men commanded by an unknown former Army lieutenant, Esteban Márquez Novo, tried desperately to break the militias' cordon. Clashes were occurring during those days and a week after the invasion's defeat the group was completely annihilated. Márquez Novo escaped and was given asylum in a Latin American embassy. A year later he secretly returned to Pinar del Río. He was now a CIA agent and was able to build the largest espionage ring that ever operated on Cuban territory: the Western United Front (FUO).

Another group of insurgents run by counterrevolutionary organizations was still in the mountains, but was insignificant. They were more interested in winning a place for themselves in what they thought would be the future government than in fighting the Revolution.

One of the most intransigent underground organizations, Anti-Communist Civic Action (ACA), made up mostly of pro-Batista former soldiers, had been eliminated just three weeks earlier after being penetrated by State Security. Cuban authorities intercepted a letter in which CIA agent and U.S. National Guard commander Howard Frederick Anderson, who had lived in Cuba for thirteen years, told his bosses in Washington that ACA "knows what it has in its hands, and truly has great organization and manpower." He closed his letter by sending effusive greetings to Clarence —the CIA agent in charge— and Jimmy, and "a big hug for Art." After being arrested, Anderson confessed that Art was the pseudonym of a Mr. Avignon, a CIA agent who had been based in the U.S. Embassy in Havana until diplomatic relations were broken off between the two countries.

Anderson had successfully coordinated several operations to bring weapons and explosives into the country in the months leading up to the invasion. One of the last deliveries had been made on the high seas on February 23, 1961 and consisted of eight tons of weapons: fifty-four Thompson machine guns, six bazookas, four 61-mm mortars, two anti-tank cannons, 574 grenades, sixteen BAR automatic rifles, three .30-caliber machine guns, and 152 Springfield rifles. Five barrels of gelatin dynamite, napalm, and other incendiary materials remained on the CIA's ship, the *Rex*, because they were too heavy to load onto the counterrevolutionary organization's tuna-fishing boat.

The head of State Security in Pinar del Río at the time, Rebel Army Captain Antonio Llibre Artigas, remembers those days.

"We were working on several very important cases before the invasion. Apparently, the CIA was prioritizing certain provinces near Havana. Pinar del Río has coastal areas with very good conditions for landing troops. One of those cases, perhaps the most important, was the one involving Anti-Communist Civic Action, created by former soldiers and mostly made up of that type of individual. And a very important part was played in that group by an American, Howard Frederick Anderson, whom we detected almost by accident and mainly because we had an infiltrated agent who was a shrewd, brilliant man with a photographic memory.

"The main conspirator took him to make some contacts, and at a given moment, they left him in front of the Coney Island amusement park, and the conspirator crossed over to talk to a man. Our agent saw him from far off and described him to us. That was the beginning. Afterwards, they delivered a letter to him so that, after making contact with the *Rex* on the high seas during an arms infiltration operation, he would deliver it to the captain. Of course, we photographed the letter and we were struck by two things: one was the familiarity with which the author addressed several Americans who evidently were based in the United States, and the other was the signature, which said 'Lee.' Anderson was extremely confident; well, he had good reason. The conspirators were ex-military, men you could trust. They had picked up weapons on the high seas and brought them in later by way of the Pinar del Río coast and buried them in safe places. At least, that's what we had made them think. That is why the American got overconfident and risked writing the letter. Actually, we were completely involved in the entire activity, to the extent that the men who went out to the *Rex* to pick up the weapons were all ours. But we couldn't identify the author of the letters. Of course, it was a "nickname." Howard did not seem to be involved. But we were on the right track. They had serious plans for an uprising, evidently in support of the invasion, including uprisings outside of Pinar del Río and in Las Villas and Oriente.

"While we were working on the case, we arrested Howard because we had seen him having contact with the main defendant. But it was not because we knew that he was the most important [individual]; except for those letters, he had a very good cover.

186

Because he was an American, and it was such a delicate matter, I participated in the search of his house. I remember that I was looking through photographs and saw one of a yacht called the *Lee*. For us, that was conclusive. Afterwards, the main defendants cleared up everything for us about Howard's central participation in the conspiracy. Once he was arrested, we talked with him and placed that tremendous responsibility on him. We asked him to publicly reveal everything the CIA was doing against Cuba. He told us that if he did, he would do a lot of damage to his government. We reasoned with him, always very respectfully. And there came a moment when he seemed willing [to talk]; then came the order to facilitate a meeting between him and a representative of his government. After that meeting, held in private, he clammed up and didn't talk any more.[14]

There were more CIA operations to bring in weapons, ammunition, and explosives into Pinar del Río than any other province. Three decades later, quite a few of these shipments are still buried where they were hidden. Most likely, the counterrevolutionary agents who hid them don't remember where they are buried. But many other conspirators, especially in the capital, were holding tons of C-4 explosives in the days before the invasion. However, Cuban State Security and the Committees for the Defense of the Revolution prevented them from doing anything with those explosives.

Evidently, the counterrevolution's agents and activists inflated reports about the actions they carried out: sabotage, attacks. Richard Bissell gives an exaggerated account in his memoirs of the figures and outcome; where an ordinary fire took place, he talks about total destruction. And there is not a single mention of any reactions to these deeds: the rallies to repudiate and condemn the crimes and sabotage; public burnings of the fliers dropped from planes; revolutionary fervor; greater vigilance and reaffirmations of support for the revolutionary government. Likewise, the underground organizations put out distorted reports about the degree of popular support for Fidel, which fit in perfectly with the plans of the main organizers of the anti-Cuba operation.

---

[14] Howard Frederick Anderson was found guilty and sentenced to the death penalty by the court that tried him.

Now we have a highway

"A lot of women die in childbirth," Victorino thought as he sat under a tree. "Basilia Blanco began giving birth and it took a long time. She lost a lot of blood. They went to Covadonga for a doctor, but he didn't want to come. So her husband went to the Rural Guard and they took her to the doctor, but she was already dead. And the children also die after they're born." Victorino Sierra thought about two of his children who had died, one from gastroenteritis. The other was a two-year-old girl. "The Covadonga doctor said it was meningitis," he murmured. "Quintina Sierra's two-year-old son died. The little boy got plugged up; he couldn't vomit or poop. Encarnación went into labor, and four days later they took her to Caleta Buena and from there to Cienfuegos. That's where she died. The same thing happened with América; she was half-dead by the time they took her to Aguada. It was the same with Palmira too, but the veins of her legs burst while she was on the ranch, and she was dead by the time her husband got back with help. The baby died inside her belly. Yes, a lot of women die in childbirth."

Victorino looked up suddenly at the oven a few feet away from him. He thought he had heard a small explosion. His face tightened. There was another explosion, more powerful, telling him that its covering of earth had slipped away in some spot, allowing oxygen inside and causing the fire to flare up. Victorino got up to cover the opening with more dirt. He grabbed a rough ladder, leaned it against the oven and carefully climbed each rung. One false step and his foot —scantily clad in a cloth espadrille— would sink into the thin dirt crust, which was heated to a temperature of more than 100 degrees. A few seconds later, Victorino settled back down under the carob tree.

He had begun building the oven a month ago. First he found a place in the forest. Then he and his eleven-year-old son cleared the area of brush and stones, and pushed down any half-buried rocks. They covered the ground with dry branches and twigs and burned them. Finally, they sprinkled cinders from other ovens. They scratched grooves going out in different directions from the spot. That gave them the foundation for the oven. They exchanged their machetes for short axes and began cutting down trees in the surrounding mountains, dragging them using poles five to six feet long. The lumber in that area was not the best, but at least it wasn't the hated, poor-quality wood known as *soplillo*.

When Victorino was very young, his father built him a "donkey." It was a piece of lumber that held thirty kilograms of firewood. A piece of rope was tied to it and looped under the arms, across the back and over the forehead. That was how they brought firewood from the mountain to the oven, over increasingly longer distances. That's what they called "bringing in firewood by donkey." But there was no donkey. The donkey was the person dragging the wood. And that was Victorino's only toy as a child.

That was how they built the oven, in the form of a circle, one block of wood next to the other, slightly sloped, one layer over the other. Then they covered it with a layer of branches and a layer of dirt. The opening at the top was left uncovered, and they inserted burning coals until they were sure that the green firewood had caught fire. Then they covered the opening and made small holes all around for the oven to "breathe." The color of the smoke showed them how the wood was burning. If the fire became stronger on the south side, the holes on that side had to be covered and the holes on the north side had to be opened. A round-the-clock vigil started to make sure the oven didn't blow up. If the main opening was left uncovered by accident and not closed on time, the oven could turn into a volcano. That was why Victorino had been in the mountains for twelve days watching over the oven, relieved for spells by his son, but he didn't trust him enough yet to leave him alone with the oven all night.

In the rainy season when water levels rose in the swamp, Victorino and his son would get up at 4 a.m., drink coffee, fill a can with candied guava, salt pork and hard crackers and board a "bongo," or barge. Pushing off with poles Venetian-style, they traveled far down the channel toward the cays where precious hardwood could still be found. Once they arrived at the forest, they would jump off the barge and push it from behind, the water reaching waist- and chest-high. Sometimes they would slip in the sinkholes.

Several hours later they would arrive at the chosen cay. That was when the wood-cutting began. After felling a tree, Victorino and his son would climb onto it and use their axes to level off its sides. If the lumber was for making railroad ties, they would cut a four-sided board the way a carpenter would with a saw. They would drag it to their barge and go back and cut another. They would keep working until they had ten or fifteen. They would also cut down *bolo* trees to use for posts in tobacco-curing sheds, *ocuje* trees for drying sheds and other precious woods for making furniture, but these were becoming more and more scarce. After several hours of exhausting work, they would stop to "snack": a piece of salt pork with crackers and then the guava to kill the repugnant taste of the pork and avoid indigestion. Once the barge was loaded with wood, Victorino and his son would push it back toward the channel. On the bank, Victorino would take the rope tied to the barge's prow and sling it around his chest, pulling hard until the heavily-laden craft slowly began to move. His son stayed a few feet behind, using the pole to keep the barge away from the banks of the channel. It would be almost nightfall by the time father and son, completely exhausted, got back to their shanty, where Victorino's wife had a meager dinner waiting.

As he gulped down a small portion of corn flour and water with sugar, Victorino thought about how much he would charge for the load. He knew the aches and pains wouldn't let him sleep that night. In a corner of the shanty, his son pulled out chiggers stuck in the soles of his feet. If he didn't, they would dig in and the itching would be unbearable.

The owner of the *chucho*, the place where charcoal and wood were bought and sold, paid him fifty centavos for each piece of lumber. The foreman gave him a voucher to use in the store owned by the same man who owned the land, the mountain and the *chu-*

cho, and Victorino would buy enough to keep surviving: salt, sugar, coffee, lard, salt pork, crackers, guava, rice and beans.

Victorino Sierra was a charcoal maker, and charcoal makers don't talk very much. The solitude and silence imposed by their rough work and the deep waters and lush vegetation of their surroundings made the swamp a realm of silence. He liked being alone, sitting under a tree and watching the oven. He would give free rein to his thoughts and memories of the past. "The hurricane of 1952, now that was a real hurricane. It didn't leave anything standing, but there were no deaths because it happened during the day. We stayed inside a hut, and after a while the wind tore it away. The hurricane carried away boxes full of charcoal and wood as if they were leaves. It wasn't that bad, after all, because the Cuban people showed they don't forget about those who are down on their luck. They collected food and clothing to send to us, but not all of it got here. They say the mayor of Augada profited from it. We got a blanket. Another gesture that wasn't too bad was when the millionaire Castellanos sent food, thrown from his plane. Bah! He probably did that in some kind of a fit, because when he became owner of the San Blas Sugar Mill, he kicked out all the families, all forty of them. All of those people had to leave for the coast. People live even worse off there, and that's saying a lot. Which could be worse, here or there? I think people are worse off anywhere in the swamp." Victorino Sierra was right. Anywhere in the swamp was worse.

Victorino's father was an undocumented immigrant from Galicia. That was why he went to live in Zapata Swamp, the most inhospitable place in the country, where the vegetation looked as if it had died at the dawn of civilization. Nobody would come looking for him there.

"The swamp apparently originated from the branching-off of rivers like the Hanábana, which ran south, and others like the Hatiguanico, whose courses ran west. These rivers ran over a layer of limestone with basins, sinkholes, and caves that functioned as a drainage system for rainwater and other rivers. When the basins filled up with too much sediment, the drainage would be blocked, the waters would accumulate, and enormous lagoons would be created, such as the Tesoro. Instead of flowing out into Cochinos Bay, the Hanábana River's waters spread all over the swamp, and the upper course of the Hatiguanico River was covered in mud."[1]

Zapata Swamp is located in southern part of Matanzas province bordering central Cuba and includes Cochinos Bay (Bay of Pigs). Cienfuegos Bay is to the east; the Havana-Matanzas plains are to the north and Broa Cove and the Gulf of Batabanó are to the west. Long channels that cross the swamp like arms were dug by the charcoal makers for transporting lumber and charcoal. The region is divided into three zones: Zapata Swamp itself, the West Zapata Swamp, which covers southern Matanzas province and part of La Habana, and East Zapata Swamp, which covers the area east of Cochinos Bay.

In the Cochinos Bay inlet, the mangrove forest–covered swamplands recede, and a coralline strip emerges with beautiful beaches and sparse vegetation. This strip of solid ground, separated from the rest of the island by a swamp area that extends twelve kilometers north and six east, was the place chosen by the strategists of the CIA and Pentagon for the invasion of Cuba. But they were not the first to discover its exceptional natural qualities. These coasts used to provide safe haven for pirates, and the most notorious, Gilberto Girón, set up camp on the beach that now bears his name.

Zapata Swamp's flora includes more than nine hundred species of native plants, including a hundred that are native to Cuba alone. Its fauna are striking both in the diversity and in the number that are native only to Cuba. Mammals like the conga, carabalí, and dwarf hutia and local species of birds like the Zapata Wren, Santo Tomás Gallinule, and Zapata Sparrow enrich the magnificent landscape of this vast territory, which spreads over 4,520 square kilometers.

Without any doubt, however, the highest expression of the swamp's mysterious charms is the crocodile. He is the king, fearsome and silent like his most powerful enemy: the charcoal maker. The Cuban crocodile (crocodylus rhombifer) is native to the island and lives in a freshwater habitat. The American crocodile also lives in Zapata Swamp but prefers the coasts and salt water.

[1] Antonio Núñez Jiménez: Ob. cit., p.123.

The crocodile is a patient animal, like the charcoal maker. He lies in wait for his prey, immobile for hours. When the hutia finally comes down from its tree and approaches the marsh's edge to drink, the crocodile moves with surprising agility and traps it in powerful jaws. The charcoal maker has always been a coveted prey for the crocodile, and more than a few men have lost their lives in its teeth.

The Cuban crocodile is stubborn and capricious. The American crocodile is cowardly and flees when confronted. To hunt either of them, human beings learned from the animal's habits. They tie a piece of hutia, or better yet pork, to a post buried in the swampy ground underwater, and rising a meter into the air. The animal comes to the bait, stops, balances on its tail and leaps. The crocodile hunter lying in wait lassoes the beast with a rope tied to a stick. He pulls it onto his barge and ties it up. Once on solid ground, he turns it over onto its back.

If the crocodile manages to get away with the meat, the hunter follows its tracks among the crushed jonquil and twisted leaves emerging from the dense waters. He trails the animal to its cave, and then sinks his barge pole into the water until he touches the crocodile. If the crocodile doesn't move, the hunter immerses his arm into the water until he touches it. That's how he knows what side the head is on, and he waits patiently until the animal emerges to breathe and then lassoes it. Some crocodiles prefer to drown than to stick their head out and be captured.

The work of the crocodile hunter requires cool-headedness, patience, daring, and courage. Below, Núñez Jiménez recounts Fidel's first encounter with a crocodile-hunter, in 1959.

"On one of the frequent marches with Fidel between the swamp and the *diente de perro* (dogtooth limestone rock) south of Tesoro Lagoon, we met Zapata Swamp resident Francisco Alzugaray, better known as Kico.

"Kico was in the mud, pulling on a rope so hard he looked like he was going to explode. When he saw us, he greeted the prime minister without letting go of the rope and said, 'Here I am, pulling on this animal.' 'And what animal is that?' Fidel asked. 'Listen, this is one scary crocodile, but I'm going to get him out. Everybody here donates their money for the Agrarian Reform. I don't have any money, but I'm going to give this crocodile to INRA (National Institute of Agrarian Reform).'

"A few minutes later, Kico was able to pull the animal's head out of the mud. He had the rope tied around its neck, and as we watched, he tied its mouth with a piece of rope and threw it into his boat. Fidel was interested in Kico and his profession. 'It would be a good idea for a future Tesoro Lagoon tourist center to have a crocodile farm. Kico, do you think you could help us catch some crocodiles to start the farm?' And before Kico could answer, he added, 'It's true that crocodiles have been disappearing from the swamp, but it's also true that by building a farm, we can save the Cuban species, use it for tourism and use its skin.' Kico became enthusiastic. Starting that same day, he began searching all over the swamp for crocodiles for a farm.[2]

"Some time later when the farm was almost ready, we went back to the swamp with Fidel. We were welcomed by Rolando Escardó, who went from being a poet to the head of the Zapata Regional Agrarian Development Zone. Escardó complained about Kico's behavior, saying he sometimes got drunk. Fidel, very tired from his nonstop work in Havana, was only able to say, 'And how would you expect a man to behave when he's never left these swamps and hunts crocodiles for a living?'"[3]

Tesoro Lagoon may be Zapata Swamp's most precious natural treasure. Its sixteen square kilometers could impress and captivate the most urbane city dweller. Ducks, cormorants, ibises, and herons spread their wings in the marshland brush. Lotuses and swamp lilies float on the lagoon's still waters. Carnations and lush orchids flourish in this gigantic natural habitat. In the swamp's lagoons and marshes the crocodile reigns together with turtles, trout, Cuban cichlid, and one of the oldest fish in the world: the manjuari. Its body calls to mind prehistoric times, when the differences between fish and reptiles were still blurry. The manjuari's snout looks like a crocodile's while its body is covered by extremely hard armor instead of scales.

On May 25, 1959, Victorino Sierra was thinking about something else as he sat at the foot of his oven. The landowners —who also owned the *chuchos* and the stores— had ordered a halt to all

---

[2] Today, at the entrance to the canal that leads to the Tesoro Lagoon Tourist Center, there is a crocodile farm with some 4,000 of those animals.
[3] Antonio Núñez Jiménez: Ob. cit., p.142.

wood-cutting. Victorino didn't know why. He was worried, because it was the first time in his life that the owners had stopped the woodcutting that made them rich. He did not personally know the owners because they lived in the capital or in Cienfuegos; however, nobody questioned the decision because it had been reported by the foremen, who represented the owners.

For several months Victorino Sierra had been hearing rumors and then he heard the news on a small battery-operated radio in the village that Batista had fled and Fidel was now in power. Later, Alejo "El Moro," who had gone to Aguada de Pasajeros, brought back a newspaper, and Victorino and the others saw the face of the "bearded one" from the Sierra. But that bearded man meant nothing to Victorino, even though Alejo —who was a man of very few words— now talked non-stop about Fidel whenever anybody mentioned his name.

Victorino just listened. Nothing had changed in Zapata Swamp, although some people were saying that they had seen the bearded man flying over Tesoro Lagoon in a helicopter. But if the owners had stopped the cutting, there was nothing the *Comandante* could do, because the owners had always been the ones who ran things in Cuba.

That is what Victorino was thinking about —as well as his hunger— when he heard a strange sound. First he looked at the oven and then at the sky. Yes, that flying critter was the helicopter that he had seen two or three times flying over the swamp. "It's going to land in Cayo Ramona," Victorino said to himself and in a burst of energy, he ran toward the village.

"In May, the owners stopped all work. They did it to turn the charcoal makers against the Revolution, to blame the Revolution. There was hunger, because when nobody bought lumber or charcoal there were no vouchers. I went to Aguada and talked with the revolutionary authorities there. They took me in a small plane to Santa Clara, where I explained what was going on and I returned to Zapata Swamp. A week later, on May 25, I saw a helicopter circling over the village. I came out running, shoeless and shirtless. Then I saw him. It was Fidel. I was hugging him before he could step out of the helicopter. Fidel asked me, 'Do you know Alejo El Moro?' 'That's me.' 'What's going on here?' I realized they had told him what I had reported in Santa Clara. Well, I told him about the situation. I remember that when I finished, I said to him that there was nothing to eat. 'We're going to resolve that,' he answered. I stayed next to him, but he was surrounded by everyone from the village, men, women and children. It was tremendous! He explained to us that they were going to give each family one hundred pesos to deal with the problem for the time being, and that I should take a census and go to Havana to get the money. He organized the first cooperative right there. A sack of charcoal had always weighed thirteen arrobas, and the bosses paid ninety-five cents for it. The firewood was twenty-five cents for every hundred arrobas, thirty if it was júcaro or llana wood. A firewood quota had to be met in order to buy things at the company store. I talked to Fidel about all of that. I remember I told him that not even priests came to Zapata Swamp. A priest would come once a year to do a mass baptism of everybody and then leave.

"Fidel told me that he wanted to go to Girón and he asked for my help, so I got hold of an old '46 Chevrolet pickup and we headed for the beach. Pedrito Miret —that's what Fidel called him— and Núñez Jiménez were with him. The pilot Díaz Lanz, who later became a traitor, flew back to the Australia Sugar Mill in the helicopter to fuel it. Fidel had told him to come back and pick him up at 5 p.m. on Girón Beach. After we got to the beach, we got a little bit of food together between the few of us charcoal makers who were there.[4]

Manuel Alvariño, a Zapata Swamp native who lived nearby, was with Fidel that day. His account, repeated and talked about many times afterward, is a good piece of the storytelling so popular in Cuba's countryside.

"He had lunch at Aniceto's house. They made him white beans with the only pig's foot that could be scrounged up. When the plate of beans was placed on the table, the little pig's foot was pointing at Fidel. So Pedrito Miret said, 'Look, Fidel, we need to try to fix the world,' and he turned the plate around so that the foot was pointing at him instead. Fidel turned the plate back around, so that the foot was pointing at him again and said, 'Look, Pedrito, better leave the world the way it is.'"

[4] Testimony of Alejo "El Moro," charcoal maker, 1990. Author's archives.

One of Alvariño's daughters, Xiomara, watched the scene from a window without really understanding who that man was, but she was beginning to feel an unusual admiration for him. She would see him again, but in Havana a year later. It would be when she graduated as a sewer. Hundreds of young women from Zapata Swamp went to school in the capital in the following years.

"At about 5 p.m., he began looking up at the sky," Alejo ("El Moro") continued. "And after a while, he says to me, 'Moro, if the helicopter has been in an accident, how are you going to get me out of here?' 'In the same truck,' I answer him. 'No, I'm not talking about Cayo Ramona, I'm talking about getting out, going to Covadonga.' 'Comandante, I'll go to Covadonga and get word out.'

"He stayed for the night because the helicopter actually had been in an accident. I organized guard duty to protect Fidel. I told the charcoal makers there who had machetes to cut clubs for those who didn't, and for everybody to protect the *Comandante*. To surround the house and not let a mouse get past. Nobody slept that night; everybody was protecting Fidel with their machetes and sticks."

In Cayo Ramona that night, Victorino Sierra was counting out loud. "Fidel said from thirteen arrobas to ten arrobas a sack to humanize the work. From ninety-five cents to three pesos a sack." Victorino spent the whole night counting. He had been elected by the village charcoal makers as administrator of the swamp's first cooperative. At this hour, his son was watching over the oven. Victorino smiled.

In Girón, Fidel had said something that seemed crazy to quite a few of the charcoal makers who listened attentively. Girón would be at the end of a highway that would go out from the Covadonga Sugar Mill on the other side of the swamp, making it easier to transport charcoal and wood and improving living conditions for people who lived in the swamp. The road would replace the only means of transport in the entire region: a: narrow gauge railroad built to take out sugarcane from the farms on solid ground. It went out from the Covadonga and Australia sugar mills. The rail car went out once a day, and it was the only line of communication when the swamp's water level rose in the rainy season. It frequently derailed, making the line useless for several days. When that happened, the only way to get a sick person out was on a stretcher all the way to the sugar mill more than thirty kilometers away.

This new road, the first evidence of progress, would also put an end to almost a century of isolation, loneliness, pain, and death. Moreover, without proposing to do so, Fidel had already dealt a mortal blow to the invasion that would later be planned by the U.S. rulers. It was over those new access roads, three in total—two crossing the swamp from the northwest and northeast to the southern coast and one running along the coast—that the militia battalions would advance with their armored vehicles and artillery. Without those roads, it would have been extremely difficult to cross the swamp and reach the beachhead. Commenting on that years later, Fidel told filmmaker Gaetano Pagano, who directed the feature-length film *History Will Absolve Me* for Swedish television, "They landed in a place where they were able to hold on for a while because it was very difficult to reach. The access roads cross several kilometers of swampland where military maneuvers are impossible. That made it a sort of Pass of Thermopylae."

The Revolution did not stop at building these access roads. They were the foundations of what later became a project that was more than a dream; it was the awakening from the nightmare. Fourteen cooperatives were created, and prices for charcoal, wood, and crocodile were quickly raised. Instead of an average of one peso a day, charcoal workers began earning ten. Members of the cooperative were given the right to benefit from the Association of People's Stores, which sold food and clothing at cost and on credit. INRA packed these stores with merchandise. For the first time, the charcoal makers wore shoes, dressed and ate like human beings. Weekly and yearly holidays and other labor and social rights were established. The hunger and misery that had seemed like insurmountable, permanent realities for the charcoal makers disappeared in one fell swoop.

Construction on the only hospital in the area had begun in 1952 in the village of Cayo Ramona after a hurricane, announced with great fanfare in the press as an initiative of the First Lady. In 1959, it was being used as a pig farm, but the work to complete it was done in a few months. During the invasion, it was occupied by the invaders and used as a field hospital. More than thirty years later, that hospital in the heart of the Zapata Swamp is providing general medical care, minor surgery, and acupuncture, and features a maternity home for pregnant women. There are also twelve family-doctor offices in the area. Infant mortality in Zapata Swamp is zero.

Three months before the invasion, a brigade of voluntary teachers arrived at the swamp. In almost every village, schools were built with dirt floors, thatched roofs, and walls, and with palm-board desks. For the first time the thousands of children who lived in the Zapata Peninsula began receiving elementary education and learning about the importance of the national flag waving over their schools. Water filters, lessons in hygiene to prevent illnesses, scholarships, rural transport, health services—all of these were new terms that quickly became part of daily life in the Zapata Swamp. That other swamp, the source of Cuba's most dramatic stories and the inspiration for the nation's first feature-length film, *Mégano,* was buried forever in the marshes.

At the time of the invasion, 300 peasant children from Zapata Swamp were enrolled in school in the capital, and another group of young people had gone from the city to the swamp to teach adults how to read and write. Several dozen children from the Zapata Swamp were in scholarship programs to become craftsmen.

In Soplillar, a settlement near Girón, a little girl named Nemesia Rodríguez was visiting the new village store with her mother and was dazzled by a pair of white shoes. Her mother said those kind of shoes weren't useful in the swamp because of the mud. Finally after some begging, her mother —who had enough money for the first time— bought her the shoes.

Nemesia enjoyed listening to the stories of birds that her neighbor Pelao used to tell. Pelao was one of the poorest charcoal makers in the area and maybe that is why he would take refuge in the mountains to watch the birds. Then he would talk about them with people in the village.

"The Florida duck emigrates to escape the cold fronts. That is why it leaves before December. The flamingos have the biggest population —there are thousands of them. They are large birds with big feet. They're always around. The *carpintero churroso* ("dirty woodpecker") is always rolling around in the mud, which is why its name is well-earned. There are four species of woodpeckers in the swamp: the green one, the dirty one, the scapular, and the jabao. Anybody who tells you different doesn't know anything about birds in the swamp. Oh! The ferminia is not the smallest bird; that's a lie. The smallest bird is the fly hummingbird. Although the long-necked sparrow hawk is also very tiny and is the prettiest."

On December 24, 1959, Christmas Eve, Pelao had no idea that the country's prime minister would soon be having dinner with him. But it was not in the presidential palace or a mansion in the capital; the head of government would be having dinner with him and his family without any protocol in his dilapidated *bohío*.

"I was shaving next to a tree, and then I saw the helicopter flying low and I saw him jump out," Pelao recalls. "There I was with my razor in hand. Núñez Jiménez came up to me. I didn't know who he was. He asked me if it was all right to have dinner at my house and said there were fourteen of them. I said yes. He didn't tell me Fidel was coming. When Fidel got there a little while later in the helicopter, I was looking for a sack of charcoal. He asked me a thousand questions, (such as) whether I earned a little or a lot. The cooperative had been created, and the swamp had started to change. He asked me if I had worked a lot under the previous government. I told him I had. He told me that he was there to spend Christmas Eve with me. He brought a pig and a half, but we didn't touch it; just the tail was eaten, and that was Fidel, because he really likes pig's tail. He brought beer, malt and soft drinks for the kids. He was really content. I remember that he said to me, 'You all are going to see how buses from Havana are going to come here.' I thought he was nuts. But I'll have you know that on Christmas Eve of 1960, the road was finished and buses were coming in from Havana. At the time of the invasion, one of my sons was learning about ceramics in Havana. Some of the good ceramists who are working now in the Boca de la Laguna del Tesoro shop were kids sent by Fidel to study in Havana. Rita Longa was the one who taught them about ceramics."

As long as she lives, Pelao's youngest daughter will remember that Christmas Eve with Fidel. "I was a little girl, but I remember it very well. I sat down next to Fidel and drank malts and soft drinks. The wife of Núñez Jiménez gave me a present of white socks. After dinner, a local farmer came by playing his guitar. I still remember the *déci-ma* (ballad) that he sang that night to Fidel:

Ya tenemos carretera
gracias a Dios y a Fidel,
ya no muere la mujer
de parto por donde quiera.

Now we have a road
thanks to God and to Fidel,
women no longer die
from childbirth anymore.

Con tu valor sin igual
Gracia, Fidel, Comandante,
tú fuiste quien nos libraste
de aquel látigo infernal.

With your matchless valor
Thank you, Fidel, Commander,
you were the one who freed us
from that infernal scourge.

Assault Brigade 2506 landed just a few kilometers from that *bohío* in the village of Soplillar.

"Gentlemen, the time has come!"

The news quickly spread through Happy Valley base that a pre-mission session would be held. Emotions were at a peak. Everyone was tense. It was 10 a.m. on April 13 when the new base supervisor, Gar, Reid Doster,[1] and the other supervisors called together the B-26 pilots to talk about flight operations. The pilots sat waiting silently, expectantly. Finally, with his voice booming through the wooden building, Gar announced, "Gentlemen, the time has come!"[2]

Two hours later, the pilots were put into security isolation. They had received a detailed explanation of their mission: to destroy the combat aircraft the Cuban air force had on the ground. Because of the precarious state of Cuba's planes, this did not seem like an impossible or even difficult task.

The CIA had prepared a thorough intelligence report based on technical espionage carried out by its U-2 spy planes and agents in Cuba. Gar read the report out loud to the pilots.

"The air force is completely disorganized and has an extremely low operational capacity. Since the drastic purge carried out by Castro in June 1959, the air force has been left without qualified pilots and without specialists trained in maintenance and communications. The air force does not have any organized squadrons, nor conventional flights or units, depending, on the

[1] General George Reid Doster.
[2] Eduardo Ferrer. *Operation Puma*. P. 138.

contrary, on individual deployments, controlled and dispatched from headquarters in Havana. Most of the planes are antiquated and inoperative, due to inadequate maintenance and a lack of spare parts. The few planes that are operative are considered capable of taking off, but not entirely in combat condition. The combat effectiveness of the air force is almost non-existent; it has a limited capability of preventive warning for opposing maritime and airborne units and could carry out pursuit attacks against lightly-armed invaders, but in terms it is limited to troop and material transport, machine-gun attacks by planes in flight and visual patrols."[3]

The report was quite accurate. No doubt the CIA had good informants with access to the Cuban air force, in addition to deserters who had gone recently to the United States. The Cubans had low operational capacity, a shortage of trained pilots and mechanics, no squadrons, and antiquated airplanes with no spare parts.

The few planes that could take off were not completely suitable for battle. But one aspect had been left out by the CIA's analysts: the combat morale of the few revolutionary pilots Cuba had. This was not a minor error; it was fundamental. Forgetfulness, carelessness, or the inability to appreciate such a factor was an unpardonable error by experts who routinely provided assessments of enemy forces. The human factor is extremely important in war; more often than not it is decisive. That was evident throughout the seventy combat missions flown in three days of battle by the ten Cuban pilots, several of them with very little training. They numbered the equivalent of 16 percent of the Brigade 2506 air force.

Without question, the Brigade 2506 air force was superior to Cuba's. It had three times as many fighter planes, not including its two- and four-engine aircraft, all in perfect mechanical condition and with sufficient spare parts, different types of weapons, and plenty of ammunition. It had six times as many pilots, not to mention the vital aspect of training. This advantage over the Cuban air force would become even greater after three of Cuba's fighter planes were destroyed on the ground by the April 15 bombings.

In the briefing on the morning of April 13, General Doster insisted on two other extremely important aspects. First, there was the element of surprise, which had to be used to the maximum

[3] Operation Pluto plan. Archives of the Ministry of the Interior.

because it wouldn't exist for subsequent attacks. Second, they would be flying planes painted to look exactly like those of the Cuban air force. That way, the element of surprise would work for them right up until they opened fire. The B-26 pilots were delighted. They knew they were about to commit a criminal act, but their success was assured. Perhaps what some of them did not know was that the U.S. government, in all its cunning, was about to commit a gross violation of the Geneva Conventions on the laws of war. If the mercenary pilots were captured, they could be executed on the spot.

This type of procedure was not unknown to CIA and U.S. Armed Forces officials. In the Battle of the Ardennes during World War II, U.S. forces captured several dozen Germans dressed in U.S. Army uniforms who spoke perfect English. These Germans had infiltrated the U.S. rearguard and caused material and human damages. All of them were executed.

April 1961 was not far off from the twentieth anniversary of Japan's surprise attack on Pearl Harbor, which so outraged the U.S. government and people. The U.S. rulers appeared not only to have forgotten that attack —in which the Japanese flew planes painted with U.S. insignia— but to be bent on outdoing it. At the funeral for the victims of the April 15 airport bombings in Cuba, Fidel Castro noted: "If the attack on Pearl Harbor was seen by the people of the United States as a crime and as a treacherous and cowardly act, our people have the right to consider yesterday's imperialist attack as an act twice as criminal, twice as wily and twice as treacherous."[4]

The mercenary air force's superiority in planes, pilots, and other resources compensated for the difficulty of operating from the far-off base of Happy Valley, located in Puerto Cabezas, on Nicaragua's Caribbean coast. It was about 580 miles from the landing site and two hours and fifty minutes' flying time in a B-26 bomber. These bombers, however, were able fly their missions with a full load of machine guns, bombs, and rockets. They could fly over Cuban territory for an hour or more depending on how much fuel they used. In order to remain over the battlefield as long as possible, their tail gunners had been replaced with extra fuel tanks. "Unofficially"

---

[4] Fidel Castro: Speech on April 16, 1961, at the intersection of 12th and 23rd streets in Vedado.

and for emergencies, they could use the airport in Grand Cayman, which was British territory and had facilities that included a radio beacon halfway to Cuba.

Before naming the pilots who would bomb Cuba's airports, Gar asked for a volunteer for a very important mission. Mario Zúñiga soon left the room with an American supervisor. He had a solo mission.

Two days later, on April 15 at 2 a.m., eight B-26 bombers —half the Brigade 2506 squadron— took off from Happy Valley. They would drop a devastating 20,800 pounds of TNT, 64 five-inch rockets, and fire 20,040 .50-caliber bullets on Cuba's military installations. All of that to destroy a little more than a dozen combat planes.

As they neared the island, they took three different routes. The group of three bombers called "Puma" attacked the Ciudad Libertad airfield east of Havana. According to U-2 spy-plane photographs, many vehicles parked there were loaded with bombs and weaponry, including ammunition for the four-barreled "cuatro bocas" antiaircraft guns. The "Linda" group, also made up of three bombers, headed south of Havana to the San Antonio de los Baños air base, where there were five B-26 bombers, three T-33s, and three Sea Furies, several of them out of commission. The "Gorila" group attacked the port of Antonio Maceo in the city of Santiago de Cuba on Cuba's western tip. According to intelligence, that was the location of a T-33, a B-26, two Sea Furies, and the only PBY (hydroplane) in Cuba.

A few minutes before 6 a.m., the three attacks were carried out simultaneously. In Ciudad Libertad, Puma II piloted by Daniel Fernández Mon with Gastón Pérez as navigator was hit by antiaircraft fire and retreated with its left engine spewing smoke. When it reached the coast, it exploded in a ball of fire and fell into the sea. Puma I was hit on its right engine but was able to leave the battlefield and fly directly to the Boca Chica naval air station in Key West, Florida, where it made an emergency landing. Gorila II made it back to Happy Valley seriously damaged.

Without waiting for initial reports on the outcome of the mission, David Atlee Phillips ordered Radio Swan to broadcast the first news of the bombings. The report's tone was triumphalist, consistent with the radio station's style.

Despite the total surprise of the attack and the fact that the mercenary bombers were painted with Cuban insignia, the antiaircraft gun operators in San Antonio began firing at the first B-26 as soon as it attacked. The Cuban soldiers had been following the enemy's maneuvers, but they thought the planes were from Santiago.

Some of the Cuban air force pilots were asleep at home and others were in barracks far away from the airfields, but two of them were able to make it to their planes and take off.

In Ciudad Libertad, the antiaircraft fire was so heavy that some of the enemy pilots emptied their magazines before they got to the base. This was witnessed by several dozen people in the area. Fifty-three people were injured. Seven were killed, including militia member Eduardo García Delgado, who, as he felt his life slipping away, wrote the name "Fidel" on a door with his own blood.

It was at the Santiago de Cuba airport where the attack most surprised the Cubans. This was because, inexplicably, the only antiaircraft artillery unit able to respond to the attack was the one on duty. The other units had been disassembled for maintenance. That error was not repeated. Military facilities were left relatively unscathed, and none of the airports lost operational capacity.

The main target of the attack was Cuba's airplanes, and the following were destroyed:

T-33	1
B-26	2
F-47	1 (out of commission)
C-47	1
AT-6	1
DC-3	1
PBY (Catalina)	1
Beechcraft	1

The document "Sequence of Events (D2 to D+2)," declassified by the CIA, says:

"Initial pilot reports indicated that 50% of Castro's offensive air was destroyed at Campo Libertad, 75% to 80% aircraft destruction at San Antonio at los Banos, and that the destruction at Santiago included 2 B-26's, 1 DC-8, 1 Lodestar, and 1 T-33 or Sea Fury. Subsequent photographic studies and interpretations indicated considerably less damage."

A report quoted in the book by Brigade 2506 pilot Eduardo Ferrer does not differ too much from information provided by Cuban authorities:

T-33	1
B-26	3 (two of these partially deactivated in San Antonio)
Sea Fury	1
F-47	2
C-47	2
T-6	1
DC-3	1
PBY (Catalina)	1[5]

It has been confirmed that the invading pilots did not destroy any of the Sea Fury fighter planes. In his book, Ferrer refers to "a Sea Fury in a hangar of the Moa Bay Mining Company." Clearly, he did not see that plane because it did not exist. Likewise, two B-26s were destroyed, not three.

After the April 15 attacks, the Cuban air force had eleven combat planes that flew during the three days of battle: three T-33s, four Sea Furies, and four B-26s. At no point were all of them in flying condition at the same time. Other planes were available, but only eleven were in flying condition. In other words, the April 15 attacks resulted in a 22 percent loss in Cuba's fighter planes. The mercenaries would have to destroy the other 78 percent in order to take control of the air.

So much has been written and argued about why there were no more air attacks —which some say were planned for dawn on D-1, others say they were planned for D-Day, and yet others say both— and so many facts are left out, that this point is worth further consideration.

[5] Eduardo Ferrer: *Operation Puma*, p. 161.

First, some statements regarding the eight mercenary B-26s that participated in the April 15 attacks:

"The brigade's small air force was not permitted to use all of its air power against Castro's airports in the surprise attack of April 15."[6]

If the Brigade's Air Force was "small," how describe the Cuban air force on that morning of April 15? The Brigade's B-26 squadron was made up of sixteen bombers in perfect condition. Some writers say they numbered seventeen, and one U.S. instructor refers in his memoirs to twenty-three.

The original plan for April 15 included attacks on two more airports, but this was ruled out after it was confirmed that those no fighter planes were located at those airports. These were the San Julián air base in Pinar del Rio and the Managua military base. If they had been included in the attacks, the mercenaries would have had to use an additional six of their planes, leaving only two back on the base. Evidently, the U.S. officials who planned the attacks thought this ratio of planes per target would ensure a successful mission.

On the other hand, a formation of three B-26 bombers in the air would be confusing for the Cuban antiaircraft soldiers, making them think the planes were from their own air force, which is exactly what happened. As a result, they did not start firing at the planes until after the attack began. If there had been five or six invading planes, the artillerymen would have known they were the enemy right away, because they all knew it was impossible for Cuba's air force to fly that many planes at the same time. The element of surprise for the attack would have been considerably diminished. The air traffic controller at the San Antonio de los Baños airport, Diocles Bello Rosabal, was reading *Bohemia* magazine when he spotted the bombers, but he ignored them and continued reading. He did not sound the alarm until after the attack had begun. He admitted, "If I had seen more planes, I would have jumped out of my chair in a flash."[7]

---

[6] Enrique Ros: *Playa Girón, la verdadera historia.* Ediciones Universal, Miami, Florida, 1994.
[7] Testimony of Diocles Bello Rosabal. Archives of the Ministry of the Interior.

That extra time would have allowed the two Cuban pilots, Bourzac and Fernández, to take off in their Sea Fury and T-33 a few minutes earlier, before the attackers were able to leave.

On the other hand, if all sixteen of the of Brigade 2506 airplanes had participated in the attack on the three airports, it would have been impossible or much less possible to provide air cover for their battalions that were about to disembark at Playa Girón. Three of the eight enemy planes were hit by antiaircraft fire (one was shot down and two damaged), representing a 37 percent loss. If the entire squadron had participated, losses would have been greater and subsequent missions endangered. It is worth noting that to provide air cover for the landing, the Brigade's air force had to send approximately two planes every hour to the battlefield and they would return to base almost seven hours later. That is why it was essential to have as many planes freed up as possible.

No doubt the most controversial aspect was that no further air assaults were carried out. We are not attempting to deny how important it was to the CIA's plans to completely destroy Cuba's air force. "If only one Cuban combat plane escapes destruction and interdicts the field, the operation would be seriously handicapped."[8] Further on in the same memorandum, written by General Lyman Lemnitzer it says, "If surprise is not achieved, it is most likely that the air mission will fail. As a consequence, one or more of Castro's combat aircraft will likely be available for use against the invasion force, and an aircraft armed with .50-caliber machine guns could sink all or most of the invasion force."[9] In hindsight, this could be seen as an exaggeration by Lemnitzer, because ships are sunk with missiles or bombs, not machine guns. In the seventeenth meeting of the Taylor Commission, General Lemnitzer offered a further assessment. "The D-Day strikes were regarded as critical.... I've seen the effects of napalm on aircraft when they're parked close together; also fragmentation bombs."

There is no doubt that General Lemnitzer had seen the effects of such attacks. But that is not what would have happened on April 17

[8] Memorandum From the Joint Chiefs of Staff General Lyman L. Lemnitzer to Secretary of Defense McNamara JCSM-146-61 Washington, March 10, 1961 (Point 3) "Evaluation of the CIA Cuban Volunteer Task Force."
[9] Ibid.

if a second air attack had been carried out. Long before April 15, Fidel Castro had been preparing to prevent that kind of disaster. "In March, we were visited by the Commander in Chief at the San Antonio base. He called a meeting there on the ramp with all the pilots and technicians and personally ordered all of us to keep the few planes we had *dispersed*[10] and to take care of them because we would surely use them in battle."[11]

This dispersion of combat planes, one of the steps taken to protect Cuba's airports, was decisive to the fact that the planes were barely damaged by the April 15 attacks. If a second air assault had been carried out on the morning of April 17, there would have been less damage to the Cuban air force and more to the invaders' air force. According to quite a few U.S. and Cuban-American writers, the cancellation of that second bombing determined the failure of the invasion.

Let's take a look.

That same morning of April 15, Commander Fidel Castro observed the damage inflicted on Ciudad Libertad and San Antonio de los Baños. He had seen the attack on the first airport early that morning from Point One, the General Staff headquarters in the capital.

"We were at the General Staff headquarters, waiting for news, when at 6:00 a.m. a B-26 flew by very low. Almost immediately, a few moments later, we felt the explosion of bombs and antiaircraft fire. We looked out and saw that it was a bombing attack, of a military character, on Ciudad Libertad, over the location of the Artillery School, over the airfields. Another B-26 came right away."[12]

That morning when he went to San Antonio de los Baños, Fidel talked to the pilots. "'All right, men,' he said to Captain Carreras and the others. 'What did you all do? Did you hide?' The captain answered that two "*Patria o Muerte*" (Homeland or Death) planes had taken off. He explained that they were called *Patria o Muerte* planes because they were able to take off. They were neither in nor out of commission; they simply flew badly or very badly. They flew."[13]

---

[10] Author's emphasis.
[11] Enrique Carreras Rolás, in comments to *Verde Olivo* magazine No. 16, 1976.
[12] Fidel Castro. "Report to the Cuban people on the victory at Playa Girón." Broadcast on Cuban television and radio, April 23, 1961.
[13] Enrique Carreras Rolás, in comments to the magazine *Verde Olivo* in 1973.

Fidel agreed with Carreras that the pilots were sleeping too far from their planes, and was pleased when they and their mechanics decided to remain on alert under the wings of their planes.

That same day, April 15, two new batteries of 12.5-mm. antiaircraft guns arrived at the San Antonio base. Each battery had six units of four heavy machine guns. In other words, these reinforcements added forty-eight antiaircraft heavy machine guns.

Two more units of the same type arrived at Ciudad Libertad. That night, another battery of 37-mm. guns was added to defend the San Antonio air base. They were simply waiting for the second air assault.

"Above all, we thought about the variant of air combat. We were tracking the skies almost constantly for the first enemy plane so that we could sound the alarm and our planes could take off as quickly as possible. The comrades who were with me at the time advised me to sleep peacefully and not to worry. They told me, 'Captain, go to sleep. Remember, you have to rest because tomorrow you'll probably go into action.' But the tension kept me awake. I thought that when the enemy planes came, I would waste time waking up, getting into the cockpit and starting the engine. We placed the Sea Fury that I manned as the pilot on duty near the end of runway 5. Nearby, we prepared a T-33. We did that so that if there were an air assault, I would take off in the T-33 with its two M-3 .50-caliber machine guns to intercept and engage in aerial combat. If there were a landing, I would take off in the Sea Fury, which carried a heavier load of rockets and bombs and was designed for air-to-sea combat. On runway 11, we parked the other Sea Fury with Lieutenant Gustavo Bourzac on standby. We parked a B-26 bomber with Captain Silva Tablada and his crew between the ends of the two runways."[14]

But that was not all. There was an additional element to the preparations to repel Brigade 2506's bombers that would have come

[14] Enrique Carreras Rolás. *Por el dominio del aire: Memorias de un piloto de combate, 1943-1988* (Controlling the Air: Memoirs of a Combat Pilot, 1943-1988) Editora Política, 1995, p. 104.

into play if a second air attack had been approved for the early morning of D-Day. Several hours before dawn on that day, April 17, Fidel Castro confirmed that the mercenaries were going to land at Zapata Swamp. "We ordered a confirmation, verification, because then the news arrived that there were ships at one point, and ships at another point. It then became completely, totally clear with the first men wounded in battle that an invading force was firing heavily with bazookas, recoilless guns, and 50-mm naval artillery at the Zapata Swamp. They were mounting an intense attack on Playa Girón and Playa Larga."[15]

It was 3:30 a.m. If a second air assault had been authorized, the B-26 bombers would have been taking off at about that time from the Puerto Cabezas base to arrive at San Antonio de los Baños at daybreak. In fact, Fidel Castro had a lead time of more than two hours.

As this was happening, Enrique Carreras was sleeping under one of the wings of his Sea Fury 542, with a T-33 nearby. He was woken up to be told that Fidel had called, with orders for the two Sea Furies and a B-26 to bomb the ships in the Bay of Pigs as soon as the sun rose. A little while later, they woke up Bourzac, who had been sleeping under the wing of a Sea Fury 580, and at the end of another runway, they alerted Jacques Lagás, whose cot was under the hulking aluminum hull of B-26 bomber no. 937. The artilleryman and mechanic were sleeping inside the plane. Other pilots remained under the wings of their combat planes. They could take off in a matter of minutes. And that is what they did when the alarm sounded or when the first antiaircraft artillery shots were fired.

At 4:45 a.m., Fidel called the air base again. Shorthand notes taken at Point One recorded the Commander in Chief's instructions: "Fidel orders Silva"—referring to pilot Silva Tablada— "of the Antonio de los Baños air base to carry out his mission with two Sea Furies, a B-26, and a jet; the latter should be readied to defend the base... There are three enemy ships in Punta Perdiz...Take off at 5:20.[16] Attack: first ships and then return to Havana to inform. *The*

---

[15] Remarks by Fidel Castro, April 23, 1962.
[16] Author's emphasis.

jet [should be] ready to defend the base… Silva [should] go all the way into the Bay of Pigs; everything on the beach is the enemy."

At 5:20 a.m., the B-26 piloted by Silva Tablada took off for the Bay of Pigs and two more Sea Furies took off, one from runway 5 and the other from runway 11. One of those planes was piloted by Bourzac, whose primary mission was to defend the airport until dawn. "Commander Curbelo sent for us in Operations. He showed us a map, explained what the situation was, and said we would have to sink the ships. But my mission at dawn first would be to provide air cover for the base… We flew in a circle around the perimeter of the base. Not even we could go past that line into the base. Anything that crossed the line was to be fired on. Meantime, we were waiting, in this circle. If we found out enemy planes were coming, we were already waiting for them in this area far from the base. If we could not intercept them from here to there, we would have to let them enter alone. And then, if they went out"—which would be difficult, but possible—"we would be waiting for them here again."[17]

That is the situation the planes of Brigade 2506 would have faced if the second air assault had been authorized. All of Cuba's antiaircraft batteries, equipped with forty-eight 12.5-mm. heavy machine guns and a battery of 37-mm. guns; two more Sea Fury fighters that were much faster and easier to maneuver than the heavy B-26s, with their heavy guns, machine guns, and rockets ready to open fire; and five more pilots were waiting under the wings of their fighter planes, ready to take off. What would have happened if the second air assault had been authorized? Not three or even five B-26s would have been able to fly over the base. Almost all if not all of them would been brought down, some by antiaircraft fire and others by the Sea Furies or T-33s.

But there is something else. A second air assault *was* authorized and carried out against the San Antonio de los Baños air base, where all of Cuba's fighter aircraft had been moved, according to U-2 spy plane reports. The attack took place on the night of Monday, April 17 (D-Day), with the knowledge that Cuba's planes only flew during the day because the island had no radar.

[17] Víctor Casaus: *Girón en la memoria.* "Testimonio de Gustavo Bourzac" (Testimony of Gustavo Bourzac). Editorial Letras Cubanas, Havana, 1982. pp. 56-57.

In books about the invasion published in the United States, some authors try to play down the magnitude of the second air assault on the Cuban air base, others try to gloss over its true significance, and still others provide unconvincing reasons for its failure. The most unscrupulous omit it entirely, as if it never happened.

"JFK realized that the news from the front portended disaster unless the FAR was knocked out. He gave the go-ahead for an air-to-ground strike. Intelligence reports indicated that the dangerous T-33s were now based at San Antonio de los Baños, much closer to the front than Santiago.

"Six B-26s from Happy Valley arrived over San Antonio at dawn on Tuesday. But the field was obscured by a heavy cloud cover and ground haze. The planes did not have enough fuel to circle until the cover broke. They returned to Happy Valley..."[18]

Authors David Wise and Thomas B. Ross say in their book, *The Invisible Government,* "Exactly three B-26s took off from Happy Valley at 8:00 p.m. Monday, April 17. Their target was the San Antonio de los Baños airfield. The strike was led by Joaquin Varela, despite the fact that he and his co-pilot, Tomas Afont, had flown that morning. Varela was unable to find San Antonio in the dark. Under orders to hit only military targets, he dropped no bombs and returned to Happy Valley. The second plane, piloted by Ignacio Rojas and Esteban Bovo Caras, developed engine trouble and turned back before reaching the target. So did the third plane, piloted by Miguel A. Carro and Eduardo Barea Guinea.

"Two hours later, at 10:00 p.m., two more B-26s took off from Happy Valley. Their crews also had flown earlier that day. Gonzalo Herrera and Angel Lopez were in one bomber. Mario Alvarez Cortina and Salvador Miralles were in the other. They had no more success than the first three planes. Five B-26s had gone out Monday night. All returned, but they inflicted no damage on their targets."[19]

---

[18] Warren Hinckle and William W. Turner, *The Fish Is Red: The Story of the Secret War against Castro.* New York: Harper & Row, 1981, pp. 90-91.

[19] David Wise and Thomas B. Ross: *The Invisible Government.* New York: Random.House, 1964, p. 75.

Eduardo Ferrer was one of the Brigade 2506 pilots. His comments about the attack on the base at San Antonio de los Baños were, "Just after midnight of the 17th two flights of two B-26's took off. Joaquín 'Pupy' Varela and Ignacio Rojas captained the aircraft of the first formation, with Tomás Afont and Esteban Bovo-Carás, as navigators. The commanders of the second flight were Gonzalo Herrera and Mario Cortina, with Angel López and Salvador Miralles as navigators.

"Bad weather had moved in and a blackout had been imposed in the area surrounding San Antonio. This resulted in the crews being unable to locate the target, and the mission was aborted."[20]

In his zeal to play down the event, Ferrer does not even tell readers that a second air attack was carried out, and he struggles to explain why the attacking planes suddenly retreated.

Evidently, these U.S. authors can't agree on why this operation using five planes —one-third of the Brigade 2506 B-26 squadron— failed. They agree on only three things: a second air assault was authorized, it was carried out, and it was a total failure.

Unquestionably, the time chosen for the attack was the best. If it had happened at dawn, we know what they would have come up against. Obviously, the Cuban aircraft would be on the ground because they did not fly at night. In fact, the fact that the attacking planes came as close as they did surprised the Cuban pilots who were on base. Let's look at how four top pilots remember these events.

"We were in the cafeteria," Bourzac said. "I remember the first thing they brought out was a steak that was so big, it couldn't even fit on two plates. It was bigger than a bedsheet. 'Whoever's the hungriest, dig in,' Carreras says. 'I am,' I say, serving myself. 'Quiet, comrades, quiet. Can't you hear that?' 'What's the matter, Prendes?' Carreras asks him. 'Quiet, comrades,' Prendes says again."

It was the sound of airplane engines, and the Cuban pilots knew that none of them were flying. Immediately, they heard the air raid alarm. Del Pino recalled, "You could no longer hear our antiaircraft artillery guns. Those of us who had stayed inside the building started shooting out the lights when we couldn't find the switches. It was like something out of a Western" .

[20] Eduardo Ferrer. *Operation Puma*, p. 205.

Bourzac remembered, "The shots were flying and one light was still on. Everybody had ducked under the tables and the shots kept flying."[21]

"I thought the base was under a nighttime assault by mercenary planes," another pilot, Álvaro Prendes, recalled. "I thought I could hear rockets exploding as they hit the roof; I didn't know that what I was hearing was a .50-caliber antiaircraft gun on the roof. I could feel its shots ringing in my head."[22]

"The air raid alarm sounded and comrades were yelling, 'Plane!' The antiaircraft artillerymen immediately began firing their machine guns and their new .37-mm heavy guns... The sky was filled with thousands of tracers of different calibers. Several minutes of heavy fire passed as almost everyone went into the trenches for protection," Carreras said.

"When the sound of the planes was gone, our antiaircraft battery stopped firing. People calmed down and began commenting on what had just happened."[23]

It was not the bad weather, heavy clouds, fog, or darkness that made it hard for them to find the base (some of the mercenary pilots knew it perfectly; they had worked there before, which was doubtless a reason they were selected for the mission). The real reason was that the base had been reinforced. It was the barrage of shrapnel that covered the sky over San Antonio de los Baños that convinced the mercenary pilots to return to Happy Valley. A number of San Antonio residents remember how some of the bombs from the attacking planes fell on nearby farms, and one of them exploded over a poultry barn.

A second air assault, without the element of surprise, could not have been carried out without a high price being paid by the attackers, with little result. "In fact the first strike designed to be the key, turned out later to have been remarkably ineffective; and there is no reason to believe that Castro's air force, having survived the first and been dispersed into hiding, would have been knocked out by the second".[24]

[21] Testimony of Enrique Carreras, Álvaro Prendes, Rafael del Pino, and Gustavo Bourzac. Quintín Pino Machado, *La batalla de Girón*. p. 105.

[22] Álvaro Prendes. *En el punto rojo de mi kolimado*. La Habana: Ediciones Huracán, 1976. p. 120.

[23] Enrique Carrera Rolás: Op. cit., p.120.

[24] Theodore C Sorensen: *Kennedy*.

Some people say the April 15 bombings (two days before the invasion) were a mistake because they alerted Fidel Castro; they say a surprise attack should have been launched on the airfields the same morning as the landing.

It is worth noting that the bombings of April 15 were not actually what alerted the Cuban government about the imminence of the invasion. If anything, they confirmed its suspicions. For example, basic defense of the airfields had been organized weeks earlier. The 339th Battalion had been stationed at the Australia Sugar Mill since the first week of April, and prior to April 15, a squad had occupied the radio installations at Playa Larga and was reporting to headquarters every thirty minutes. The farmers' militia at Playa Girón stood guard ever y night, and Fidel Castro had watched from Point One headquarters as Ciudad Libertad was bombed. The situation would have been the same had the bombings been carried out April 17, but with one difference: at 3:30 a.m. that day Fidel Castro had confirmed the landing and was taking steps to repel it, including the orders mentioned earlier to the Cuban air force pilots. If the air assaults had taken place on April 17 instead of April 15, the mercenary air force would not have had the element of surprise. Upon arriving at the airfields at dawn, the invaders would have found several planes in the air and the rest of the pilots on maximum alert. Moreover, they would not have been able to use the Brigade's sixteen B-26 bombers, because that would have left the disembarking invasion forces without air cover.

Another, no-less important fact: if the first attack had been made on April 17, the two B-26s and the T-33 that were damaged or destroyed on the April 15 would have been left unscathed, making more aircraft available for the Cubans.

Again, if the first air strike on Cuba's airfields had been carried out at dawn on the day of the invasion, the attacking planes would have encountered Cuba's air force on maximum combat alert from 3:30 a.m. on. In short, those are common rules of war.

The repeated assertion that the invading pilots were guaranteed clear skies is not consistent with their orders or equipment. None of the CIA or Pentagon experts who were professionals in the art of war could have stated such a thing. That does not exclude the possibility that some military officer or another eager to pump up the leaders of Brigade 2506 may have told them that the skies would be clear. According to the Operation Pluto plan, several copies of which were delivered to the Brigade's commanding officers:

"Appendix E (Tactical Air Support) to Operation Pluto Plan.
I. - Situation
a. *Enemy forces.* (*see* appendix A)
b. *Friendly forces.* Once the airfield in the Tactical Air Force target zone has been taken, attacks begin with the purpose of destroying or *neutralizing enemy air*,[25] naval and ground forces.[26]

If it had been certain that no FAR plane would be flying, the above-mentioned order to attack after the landing would have been superfluous.

This aspect of the plan was not carried out. Further on, we'll take a look at the reasons.

Another of the many arguments justifying the invasion's defeat is that the Brigade's failure to destroy Cuba's planes left the invaders defenseless. That is not completely true. The *Blagar* and *Barbara J* escort ships were heavily armed. The *Barbara J* had a 77-mm. recoilless gun, two 57-mm. recoilless guns, several twin 20-mm antiaircraft guns, and six .50-caliber machine guns as well as a 40-mile radar system. Both ships were there to protect the brigade from air attacks and that is what they did heavily, on the morning of the landing.

"We arrived, and imagine our surprise when we saw a convoy of four cargo ships, landing craft, LCU and LCVP assault vessels, an LSD ship, and smaller vessels that were taking their people to shore. The group included two LCI crafts as escorts. As soon as they saw us, they opened heavy fire using the twin guns on revolving turrets mounted to the ships' sides and their six .50-caliber machine guns...

[25] Author's emphasis.
[26] Operation Pluto plan. Archives of the Ministry of the Interior, p.26.

"I continued to climb, followed by thousands of tracers. One of them found their mark; the plane shook and the engine began to fail and spew smoke...

"Prendes had always shown great skill, mastery, and ability with jet planes. As soon as he reached the area, he got his bearings and located the ships several miles down the coast. Near them, he fired rockets at the last ships in the formation, hitting an LCT and setting it adrift. Once the enemy forces recovered from their surprise, they aimed their antiaircraft fire at his jet when he attacked the second time, and they were able to hit him as he climbed with dizzying speed."[27]

"I dive, and this time I see tracers from the enemy's line of fire coming up. They look like they're coming toward me and an optical illusion makes it look like they veer off abruptly at the last minute; the more abrupt, the closer they've come. I also see explosions at my altitude, which tells me cannons are firing too... then I feel the impact, a sharp blow that makes the entire plane shake."[28]

"At that moment Bourzac felt an explosion and the Sea Fury immediately began to break down. The pilot saw blue and red flames coming out of the fuselage... As he returned to base, he was advised to eject and parachute. Bourzac thought, 'But what will I fly then? I won't even have a broom to fly.' He decided to save the plane at the risk of his own life. His landing was the most dramatic of those days.... A bunch of combatants ran toward his plane. The mechanics quickly issued a verdict after examining the Sea Fury: gunshots had completely torn off the brake unit and a section of fuselage."[29]

On the morning of April 17, five of the Cubans' eight working planes were hit. Álvaro Prendes, Gustavo Bourzac, and Enrique Carreras all had to make emergency returns to base. Luis Silva Tablada, who was piloting a B-26, was shot down by antiaircraft fire from the Barbara J and Blagar escort ships.

The effectiveness of the invaders' antiaircraft fire was obvious. They were not defenseless. What the CIA planning experts did not take

[27] Enrique Carreras Rolás. Op. cit., pp. 113-115.
[28] Álvaro Prendes: Op. cit., pp. 105-106.
[29] Álvaro Prendes: Op. cit., p. 113.

into account was the reaction of Cuba's pilots, who risked their lives to bring their damaged planes back to base and who would immediately return to combat.

In contrast, after the *Rio Escondido* was sunk and the *Houston* damaged, the Brigade's escort ships headed back out to sea at full speed. If there is any question about the escort ships' hasty flight, official and little-publicized statements from the military commander of Brigade 2506, José Pérez San Román, are devastating. "Number one: the U.S. officer who was captain of the flagship *Blagar* was forced to retreat from the enemy air assault after two of the small fleet's ships were sunk.

"This officer retreated against my order to hold his position and fight (it is a military principle that the commander of support forces receives his orders from the commander of the supported forces). 'Higher authority,' was his answer to my order. 'I have been ordered to do the opposite,' he said, and the ships headed southward to never return. Because of this retreat by our fleet, the Brigade lost the cover provided by the 75-mm recoilless guns and .50-caliber machine guns mounted on all the ships. Moreover, along with the fleet, which never returned, went thousands of tons of supplies, weapons, principal communications equipment, a hospital, drugs, and essential medical supplies. As if that weren't enough, those ships were also carrying airplane fuel, bombs of all kinds, and ammunition for the guns on our B-26 bombers that would have given us the ability —as according to plan— to operate our planes from the beachhead instead of having to do so from Nicaragua."[30]

Another thing they could have done was to immediately use the Playa Girón airfield, which they occupied as soon as they landed. Once it was dark on April 17, they could have used their C-54 transport aircraft for one or two flights and bring enough supplies to Girón to keep some B-26s in the air, operating from the beachhead runway.

The first and only Brigade plane that landed at the Girón airfield did so at dawn on Wednesday April 19, after the invaders had been practically surrounded. That plane brought ammunition.

[30] José Pérez San Román. *Respuesta: La verdad sobre Girón*, p. 29.

Some investigators assert that that the Girón runway was not in operating condition at the time of the invasion, and that was why it wasn't used. That is completely untrue.

Once again, Commander José Pérez San Román's words are eloquent:

"Number two: another criticism of the CIA involves the incorrect information about the target area turned over to my subordinates and me from their [the CIA's] intelligence archives. It was so incorrect that it included U-2 photos showing the Playa Girón airfield as unfinished and still under construction. This forced us to bring dozens of gasoline-powered chainsaws with us to cut down the trees along the highway so that we could use it for landing our B-26s and C-46s... When we got there, we found that the airfield was completely finished, to the last detail of its control tower. There were no trees along the highway that would have prevented small or medium-size planes from landing."[31]

If the Cuban aircraft had been destroyed; if the U.S. government had not abandoned them to their fate; if the Cuban exiles had participated more; if it had been at Trinidad; if the clandestine movement had been warned; if the diversionary landing had been carried out at Baracoa; if air cover had been provided; if the Brigade had been better-equipped; if there had been a direct intervention...

Apparently, if anything had been done differently, their success would have been assured. They refuse to accept the real reasons for their defeat, which can be found by studying the revolutionary government's reaction to the bombing of its airports and the course of the battle itself.

The April 15 fires had not yet been extinguished when Commander in Chief Fidel Castro addressed the people. After informing them of the attack, he said:

"Our country has been the victim of criminal imperialist aggression in violation of all norms of international law. The Cuban delegation to the United Nations has received instructions to directly accuse the government of the United States of being behind this aggression against Cuba. The order has been given to mobilize all

---

[31] Ibid., p. 32.

combat units of the Rebel Army and Revolutionary National Militias. All commands have been put on a state of alert. If this air attack is the prelude to an invasion, the country will be on a war footing. With an iron fist, it will resist and destroy any force that attempts to land on our soil. The people will be kept fully informed. Every Cuban must occupy their assigned post, whether in a military unit or a workplace, with no interruption in production, the literacy campaign, or a single revolutionary task. Our country will resist any enemy attack firmly and calmly, sure of its victory. Patria o muerte! Venceremos! Fidel Castro Ruz."

The next day, at the funeral for the victims of the air assault and as the invading fleet was approaching our coasts, Fidel ended his speech with these words:

"Compañeros workers and peasants of the homeland: yesterday's attack was the prelude to the mercenaries' aggression… Let us sing the National Anthem… Compañeros, all units need to head toward the site of their respective battalions, in view of the mobilization order to maintain the country in a state of alert…" As we can see, Cuba's victory was based on the mobilization of the entire people, thousands of Rebel Army soldiers, more than half a million militia members, and several million members of the Committees for the Defense of the Revolution; all these forces together made up the overwhelming majority of Cuba's population.

It is undeniable that the Cuban people were experiencing intense moments of patriotism and revolutionary fervor. Support for the Revolution and for its leader Fidel Castro had risen to a level never seen before for any other leader in the hemisphere. And this would be decisive.

After his cordial meeting with Fidel Castro in April of 1959, U.S. vice president Richard M. Nixon had no doubt: the Cuban leader could not be subjected to control. Eleven months later, President Dwight Eisenhower, after a period of "clarification," gave the okay to an operation to overthrow the government of Fidel Castro, just as he had done six years earlier with the democrat Jacobo Arbenz in Guatemala. When John F. Kennedy was installed in the White House and informed in detail by CIA director Allen Dulles, the invasion was an accomplished fact. The command post for the operation was set up in Quarters Eye, a Pentagon barracks staffed by experienced CIA and armed forces specialists.

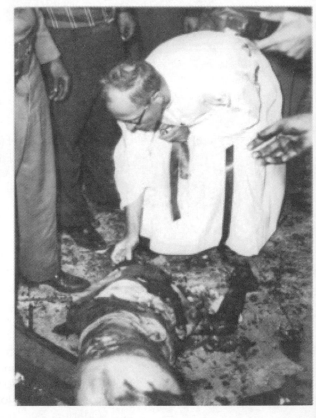

At 3:15 p.m. on Friday, March 4, 1960, the French freighter *La Coubre*, carrying a load of Belgian-made FAL automatic rifles much superior to those used at the time by the U.S. Army, blew up in a Havana dock. The explosion killed one hundred people and injured almost two hundred. Its cause is still a mystery.

The U.S. government had pressured Belgian authorities to stop weapons shipments to the island, and since January of that year, a CIA task force had been waging a clandestine war against the Cuban Revolution.

During the first four months of 1961, the counterrevolutionary underground movement carried out intense efforts to destabilize the Revolution. They had an impact, but the results could not have been more catastrophic for the CIA. The bombs and sabotage failed to intimidate the people. Condemnation was the overwhelming response. Many government opponents were isolated. The people, on the other hand, were psychologically prepared to face and overcome the worst: the invasion.

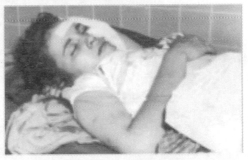

REVOLUCION

La Habana, Sábado, 2 de Abril de 1960

Quema 300 mil arrobas de caña en Matanzas

Cada nuevo golpe que asestan los enemigos de la Patria el pueblo cubano une más y más a este en torno a la Revolución y su máximo líder, el doctor Fidel Castro. Cada zarpazo que lanzan se vuelve contra ellos como un tremendo "boomerang"

Foreign Minister Raúl Roa explains to reporters the shooting down of a small plane from the United States that tried to bomb the Niágara Sugar Mill.

Another small plane shot down, one of those used to drop pamphlets urging people to carry out sabotage and providing instructions on how to do it.

By dawn on April 14, 1961, El Encanto, the country's largest department store, had been reduced to a jumble of twisted wreckage. Losses were estimated at $20 million. A few months earlier, the store had been nationalized. The CIA believed a certain psychological climate had been created. Early the next day, the invasion brigade's tactical air force bombed three of Cuba's airfields as a U.S. Navy fleet escorting the invaders approached the landing area. At the time, nothing pointed to defeat.

The militias of workers, students and farmers became the cornerstone of the Revolution's system of defense. "One, two, three, four, eating shit and wearing out shoes," the counterrevolutionaries would murmur as the militia members went by. For weeks and weeks they marched. Then the weapons arrived, and the sixty-two kilometer march, and—for many—training in the Escambray. The invasion did not catch them by surprise. Nothing was being done too late in Cuba.

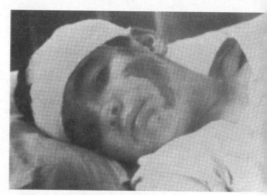

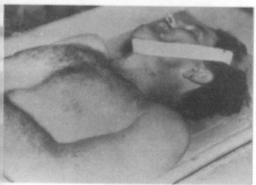

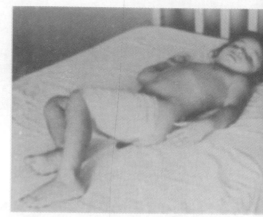

The surprise air raid at dawn on April 15 did not succeed in its objective of destroying the combat planes of the Revolutionary Armed Forces, but it did kill or injure dozens of people. One of those killed, Eduardo García Delgado, wrote Fidel's name with his own blood as he was dying.

On their way back to Happy Valley in Nicaragua, two of the invaders' planes flew over the Isle of Pines and attacked and sunk the Cuban navy ship, the *Baire*. A few hours later, the diplomatic battle began in the United Nations. Foreign Minister Raúl Roa accused the United States and U.S. ambassador Adlai Stevenson asserted his government was not to blame. As proof, Stevenson exhibited a photo that supposedly showed one of the attacking planes, which had landed at Miami International Airport, and whose pilot swore he had taken off in Cuba. Some reporters on the scene discovered the machine guns of the B-26 had not been used for some time. It was another CIA blunder.

After the airfields were bombed, Fidel Castro had no doubt the invasion was imminent and he announced that at the victims' funeral. During his speech, he proclaimed the socialist character of the Revolution. Echoing the words of Abraham Lincoln, he said it was a Revolution of the poor, by the poor, and for the poor.

The only transportation in or out of Zapata Swamp was a small train that often derailed, leaving the area completely isolated. The swamp's inhabitants were poorest in the country. With the Revolution, roads were built, cooperatives were organized, and stores were opened where people could buy all types of goods on credit. Many of the local people began to work in tourism, and the buying power of those who continued making charcoal rose to ten times its former level. Of the nearly one thousand people from the Zapata Swamp who were taken prisoner, only two joined the invaders. They had come from somewhere else and owned a bar in Playa Girón.

Richard Mervin Bissell, director of CIA covert operations and the brains behind different strategies to destroy the Cuban Revolution in 1960 and 1961. After the invasion failed, his name would be invariably associated with the disaster. Below, from left to right, his top collaborators: Navy Colonel Jack Hawkins, the brigade's organizer and military strategist. His disdain for the Cubans was notorious. Colonel Stanley W. Beerli, commander of air operations, and David A. Philips, in charge of propaganda. Philips's mission was to create the appropriate psychological climate among the Cuban people. When the disaster was confirmed, he left Quarters Eye, went home, and vomited. He blamed the president for the invasion's failure and has been mentioned a number of times as a suspect in the assassination of John F. Kennedy. Phillips directed Radio Swan, whose broadcasts into Cuba were described years later as useless.

Texan Grayston Lynch was the first to arrive on the sands of Girón and the first to open fire, slightly wounding a volunteer teacher. He led a group of frogmen charged with marking the best routes for the landing. At Playa Larga, another American carried out an identical mission—Rip Robertson, ("Crocodile"), was known in the CIA because in 1954, during the operation against Jacobo Arbenz in Guatemala, he ordered the bombing of a merchant ship that he thought was Russian but was actually British.

Barracks on Trax Base. Helvetia farm. Guatemala.

Landing strip on Rayo Base. It was built for the operations against Cuba.

B-26 light bomber. The brigade's tactical air force had sixteen of them, in perfect mechanical condition and with plenty of ammunition.

Emblem of the paratroopers. The black bird turned out to be a bad omen.

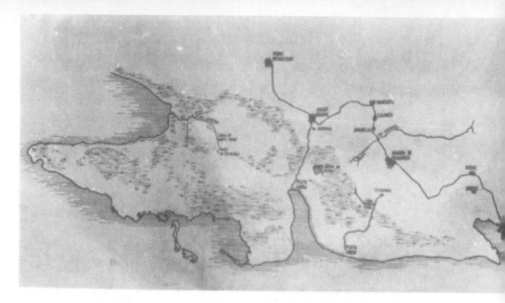

According to the brigade's plan for the operation, the beachhead was to be set up from the area near the Australia Sugar Mill (the paratroop battalion's forward points) to Playa Larga, and from there to Playa Girón along the access road between the two beaches, and ten kilometers to the east. From Girón, it spread to the area near the Covadonga Sugar Mill (paratroop forward points).

View of the Playa Girón tourist resort, where the command post for the brigade was set up, its last stronghold before they were routed. The Assault Brigade landed near the extreme right of the bridge that crosses the inlet.

On the left, one of the five merchant ships that were used to transport the brigade. Their approach to Cuba's coasts did not awaken any suspicion and the hand of the United States remained hidden. On the right, the boats used to land the armored vehicles and other heavy equipment. Below, the boats with outboard motors used to land the troops.

. The truck carrying civilians who were being evacuated received the full impact of the recoilless gun. Immediately, the invaders opened fire. Amparo Ortiz was thrown to the pavement by the blast. Víctor Caballero, (facing page, top), who was hiding on the other side of the access road, climbed up enraged because he thought his family was in the truck. He lowered María Ortíz (middle, bottom photo) from the truck and laid her on the road; she was dead. Dulce María Martín, (first body, bottom photo), after being hit by the bullets, fell on top of her sister's legs. She was bleeding from the nose and mouth. Dulce was 14 years old. Pablo, (left) María García's husband, remembers that a truck full of mercenaries approached at full speed and took the wounded and other survivors to Playa Larga. At the brink of death for several hours without receiving any medical attention, María died in her husband's arms. "Take care of the girls" she said to him before she died. She had been hit by several bullets and had been badly burned. In the unjustified attack, Amparo Ortíz lost her husband (third body, bottom photo), her sister, and her niece.

After sixty-six hours of combat, one hundred and fifty-two people had been killed and more than five hundred wounded. The revolutionaries suffered almost all of their casualties during the advance to drive out the invaders from their positions. More than a few made it to the enemy's barricades.

Gonzalo Rodríguez Mantilla, "Chele," (top photo, this page) stayed next to the telephone at the Covadonga Sugar Mill throughout the three days of battle. After informing Fidel about the landing of "people with spotted clothing on Playa Girón," and the paratroopers he saw being dropped very close to the sugar mill, he asked for weapons. Jose Ramón Suco (facing page, top) was the leader of the five-man squadron on Playa Larga the night of the landing. He was the first militia member to open fire on the invaders. In face of the enemy's superior fire power, they retreated a short time later. Before doing so, Suco had managed to inform the leadership of the battalion at the Australia Sugar Mill that they were under attack. Bambi Martínez (facing page, bottom photo) was a worker at the mill. During the days of the battle, she attended to the injured, both revolutionaries and invaders.

Some of the members of the militia's 123rd Battalion on the buses waved at the planes that were flying overhead. They did not know that in a gross violation of the rules of war, the B-26s of Brigade 2506 were painted with the colors and insignia of the Revolutionary Air Force. Seconds later, shrapnel rained down on the militia members. The viciousness was unimaginable. The pilots, including two Americans, then began to drop napalm bombs on the militia members.

Another factor added to the attackers' impunity: the antiaircraft artillery known as *cuatro bocas* (four-barreled guns) were not close enough to give the militia members protection.

Bill Goodwin was a pilot with the Alabama Air National Guard. He was part of the team of trainers of Brigade 2506's air force. He flew one of the B-26s that shelled and napalmed the 123rd Battalion's troops.

Six of the Revolutionary Air Force's eight combat planes that flew over Playa Larga and Playa Girón on the morning of the landing were hit by the Brigade's antiaircraft fire. Enrique Carreras (top photo, this page) felt his Sea Fury shake and saw smoke coming out of its engine. Álvaro Prendes, (top photo, facing page), realized that the tracers were coming closer and closer; then he felt the impact. Bourzac, (left photo, middle of facing page) felt an explosion and saw blue and red flames stream from the fuselage of his plane. Alberto Fernández felt his plane shake; it had also been hit by the guns of the escort ships *Barbara J.* and *Blagar.* The four made emergency landings, but none of them ejected in their parachutes. They knew that if they lost their planes they wouldn't have even a broom to fly. Soon after that, they flew more missions over the beachhead. Two others met different fates: Luis Silva Tablada (this page, bottom), flying a B-26, and Carlos Ulloa, "El Pollo," (facing page, bottom), flying a Sea Fury, were shot down and crashed into the sea.

Finding himself close to Playa Girón, Commander Efigenio Ameijeiras (top photo, left, in beret), a veteran of the *Granma* landing and of the Sierra Maestra, heard a deafening sound. He looked up at the sky and saw an enormous plane flying overhead; under the militia's fire, it turned around and headed out to sea. It was Manuel Navarro's C-54, which had just taken off from the Girón airfield. Ameijeiras realized this was serious business and "flew" at top speed in his car to the Australia Sugar Mill, where he contacted the commander in chief. Shortly after, he returned to the battle front.

The second in command of the police battalion, Commander Samuel Rodiles (facing page, top), led the vanguard of police officers and militia members who, after battling fiercely and neutralizing an enemy tank with the only bazooka rocket they had left, broke through the defensive perimeter around Girón—with the few troops they had— along the road from Playa Larga to Girón.

Another veteran guerrilla fighter from the Sierra Maestra, Commander Filiberto Olivera Moya (this page, middle) drove out the paratrooper battalion's vanguard troops from Jocuma Curve, preventing them from attacking the Covadonga Sugar Mill. On the morning of April 18, he began crossing the swamp and hours later fought his way into the enemy's beachhead on the Covadonga-San Blas-Playa Girón front. Commander Pedro Miret (facing page, center) arrived at the Covadonga Sugar Mill with a high fever. He commanded several batteries of 122-mm. guns, which he used to harass the enemy until the battle was won.

Commander René de los Santos (facing page, bottom) led the advance from Yaguaramas toward Girón. Captain Emilio Aragonés, "El Gordo," advanced toward San Blas with a tank company. At a forward point known as Helechal, just four kilometers from Girón, Fidel gave the orders for the final assault. When he climbed onto one of the tanks for the march to the front, the troops protested. "No, Fidel! Not you!" Fidel told them he had the same right to fight as anybody else. Finally, he left in the tank.

One day before the landing, Captain José Ramón Fernández (facing page, top; this page, top) was told that on the commander in chief's orders, no matter what happened, he should continue training the militias and Rebel Army cadets. However, on the morning of the invasion, he was one of the first sent to battle. He had no idea then that more than a few members of the Assault Brigade were his former students, including their commander, José Pérez San Román, and second-in-command, Erneido Oliva. The forces under Fernández's command saw the fiercest combat of the battle throughout the night of April 16 and morning of April 17. They were not able to break through the defenses of the invaders, who were helped by the terrain and the weapons Oliva had at his disposal. However, the spirit of the Militia Leaders' School and the Rebel Army's Column no. 1 was such that by dawn the brigade's second-in-command, anticipating another attack, decided to abandon the beach and retreat to Girón. At 5:30 p.m. on April 19, Capt. Fernández entered Playa Girón riding a tank accompanied by Commander Efigenio Ameijeiras and Captain Flavio Bravo.

Captain Artemio Carbó (facing page, bottom) was killed while trying to break through the Girón defensive perimeter. Along a strip of some five hundred meters, thirty-two police and militia combatants were killed and one hundred wounded. Carbó died encouraging his troops until the last minute.

Captain Víctor Dreke (this page, bottom left) was heading for Santa Clara when he heard about the invasion. He asked for permission to fight and led the militia vanguard during three days of combat on the Covadonga-San Blas-Girón front until he was seriously wounded after driving the invaders out of San Blas. Four years later, he accompanied Commander Ernesto Che Guevara in Africa.

"We've got to cut off the heads of these communists!" exclaimed an invader when a jeep driven by Commander Félix Duque (this page, bottom right) suddenly pulled up. Duque had advanced so far that he had reached the brigade's position, but he didn't lose his head. "The best thing for you to do is surrender," he said calmly. He was taken to Girón, and when the invaders were routed, he was taken into a wooded area by his captors, who soon afterward agreed to surrender.

Fidel Castro's escort had no choice but to protect him right on the battlefield. Attempts to convince him it was too dangerous were useless. After being taken prisoner, several of the invaders admitted to him that they had seen him at a very close range but had been so shocked that they did not have the courage to fire at him. Without question, his presence on the battlefield enabled him to lead his forces with such accuracy and spirit that when President Kennedy met with the staff of the invasion operation forty-eight hours after the landing to analyze the situation on the beachhead, the brigade had already been virtually defeated.

J. William Fulbright, chairman of the U.S. Senate Foreign Relations Committee, opposed the invasion and said so to President Kennedy. Allen Dulles (above, left) ignored the senator's views. The Joint Chiefs of Staff approved the final plan for the invasion after changes were made. One way or another, they were all involved with D Day.

José Miró Cardona (this page, top photo, left) was selected by the Americans to lead the provisional government that was to be installed in Cuba after Fidel Castro was overthrown. Antonio Varona, on his right, was a typical politician, a friend of the Mafia who had led the Democratic Revolutionary Front, the FRD, which the U.S. government tried to use as a screen to conceal its role in operations against Cuba. Varona was involved in almost all of the attempts to assassinate Fidel Castro during those years.

"Military technology and the international situation are such that almost any so-called small-scale war may produce a chain reaction in every part of the world…" The strong message from Nikita Khrushchev (this page, center) the day after the landing left no room for doubt. The USSR would not stand with arms crossed.

According to Brigade 2506 chief José Pérez San Román in his book *Respuesta*, in December 1962, during a meeting between President John F. Kennedy and the brigade's general staff, Kennedy told them that one night when he couldn't sleep he had struggled with the prospect of being responsible for the massacre of millions of Germans and Americans in Berlin and for the possibility of World War III. "Sacrificing 1,400 men from the brigade was a lesser evil than West Berlin and World War III," he told them. Whether or not the story is true, the message from the USSR no doubt had an impact. The specter of direct intervention dissipated.

"Are you going to shoot us?" they asked their captors. Soon it was evident that would not happen. More than 85 percent of the brigade's troops were taken prisoner, some of them dozens of kilometers from the landing site after they had wandered around for weeks. The wounded were cared for in Havana's best hospitals. Nine died from suffocation due to negligence in their transportation. Five were executed by firing squad for crimes they had committed previously. All other defeated invaders returned to the United States after twenty months of negotiations and after the Revolution was partially compensated with medicine and food for children.

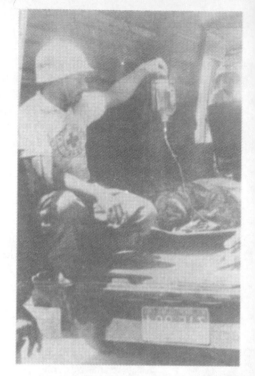

During the battle, the brigade's troops used the most modern and diverse weapons. It wasn't weapons or ammunition that they lacked…

Traces of the battle.

"ANIQUILADOS LOS INVASORES

LA REVOLUCION HA SALIDO

VICTORIOSA", PROCLAMA FIDEL

*Cayó Playa Girón a las
5:30 de ayer. Frustrado
el intento de reembarque*

COMUNICADO NUMERO 6

March 2001. Central figures of the battle meet in Havana forty years later. Americans and Cubans, including five members of Brigade 2506, discussed the operation's details, basic points, and strategy. Toward the close of the discussion, Fidel Castro said, "I am absolutely sure, and I say that here in all frankness, that it was very lucky the invasion failed. It was very lucky for us, and even for the United States, because Vietnam would have happened in Cuba instead of Vietnam."

"An artilleryman in the United Nations"

STATE DEPARTMENT
Telegram received April 16, 1961
Control: 9871
Received: 16 April 1961
7: 33 p.m.

From: New York
To: Secretary of State
No. 2892, April 16, 6 PM
For Secretary and Dulles from Stevenson.

1. Greatly disturbed by clear indications received during day in process developing rebuttal material that bombing incidents in Cuba on Saturday were launched in part at least from outside Cuba.
2. I had definite impression from Barnes[1] when he was here that no action would be taken which could give us political difficulty during current UN debate. This raid, if such it was, if exposed will gravely alter whole atmosphere in G[eneral] A[ssembly]. If Cuba now proves any of planes and pilots came from outside we will face increasingly hostile atmosphere. No one will believe the bombing attacks on Cuba from outside could have been organized without our complicity.

---

[1] Referring to Tracy Barnes, Bissell's assistant.

3. I do not understand how we could let such attack take place two days before debate on Cuban issue in GA. Nor can I understand if we could not prevent such outside attack from taking place at this time why I could not have been warned and provided pre-prepared material with which to defend us. Answers I made to Roa's statements about incident on Saturday were hastily concocted in Department, and revised by me at last minute on assumption this was clear case of attacks by defectors inside Cuba.
4. There is gravest risk of another U-2 disaster in such uncoordinated action.

Stevenson[2]

The telegram from Adlai Stevenson, U.S. ambassador to the UN, caused alarm and unease at the State Department, especially for Secretary of State Dean Rusk, who did not completely agree with the plan to invade Cuba, although he refrained from saying so. At a meeting two days earlier, on April 4, to finalize the details of the plan, the U.S. president asked for a hand vote on whether to go ahead with the invasion. Rusk, like the other officials involved, voted "yes." The idea that they had to get rid of Fidel Castro overrode any misgivings they may have had about the invasion's possibilities of success. Their obsession made them incapable of reasoning objectively. Dean Rusk and his closest collaborators were not exempt. That's why nobody at the State Department imagined that the attack on Cuba would be an item on the UN agenda as early as the same day Cuba's airports were bombed.

That discussion would not have happened on the afternoon of Saturday, April 15, if Cuba's foreign minister had followed the UN's rigorous procedural norms. For several weeks, Cuba had been requesting a point on the General Assembly agenda to discuss its accusations of the latest U.S. aggression. Foreign Minister Raúl Roa was given time to speak on the morning of Monday, April 17. On April 15, there was just one point on the General Assembly's

[2] Kennedy Library, Telegram from Stevenson, April 16, 1961. NSF OF, box 40, Document declassified by U.S. government.

agenda: the situation in the Republic of the Congo. It was a procedural point that would prevent discussion on any other point before the weekend. And on Monday morning, all the headlines would feature the invasion of the "Cuban patriots who, through their own resources and efforts, were in their homeland to liberate Cuba from international communism." Their landing would be a fait accompli, and the attack on the airports would be nothing but a memory. By then, there would be little that Cuba could do in the diplomatic sphere.

That is what the State Department experts thought, but they had overlooked one detail: the man who arrived at the United Nations with quick, decisive steps on the morning of April 15 may have been wearing a suit and tie, but he was not your run-of-the-mill diplomat. He was more like a well-dressed artilleryman, gun in hand, with a perpetual cigarette between his lips. The session began at 10:30. The Assembly president, Frederick H. Boland of Ireland, announced he was giving the floor to the Cuban foreign minister for a point of order.

Roa got up and walked resolutely toward the podium. The U.S. delegates were perplexed. "He can't talk about the bombings; that's a substantive question, not a point of order," they probably tried to reassure themselves. Without wasting any time, Roa denounced the bombings of the airports in Havana, San Antonio de los Baños, and Santiago de Cuba by U.S.-made planes coming from the United States or from Central American satellite countries. "The Cuban delegation accuses..." At that moment, the chairman struck his gavel and exclaimed, "Order!" He warned Roa that he was raising a point of substance, not of order, and was therefore inappropriate. Roa thanked him and returned to the attack, adding that it would be impossible for him to leave the room without formally and officially charging the U.S. imperialist government regarding these events, which were "an extremely serious threat to international peace and security." The General Assembly chairman banged his gavel again and asked Roa to return to his seat. Roa took the microphone again and exclaimed, "I've said it and now I withdraw."

The U.S. delegates must have been speechless. From then on, everything happened so fast that they were still recovering from their surprise as they hurriedly prepared documents —by force, as Adlai Stevenson said— to respond to Cuba's accusations.

After Roa returned to his seat, Soviet representative, Valerian Zorin also asked to speak on a point of order. He said the Cuban ambassador's accusations were very serious and that the matter should be discussed immediately. Boland said they should wait until Monday for a point in the First Committee, Policy and Security, to discuss the Cuban matter. The Soviet representative took the floor again and proposed an emergency meeting of the First Committee rather than waiting until Monday. According to the regulations, the commission's chairman had to consent to an emergency meeting before it could be held. The chairman was the Czech ambassador and he immediately consented. The motion then had to be passed by a two-thirds majority vote of the Assembly. The vote was held and more than two-thirds voted in favor.

The meeting was set for 3 p.m. that day, April 15. Roa was satisfied. He had fired the opening guns of the battle that was about to begin. Brigade 2506 had not yet landed, but the shadow of defeat was already hanging over the State Department.

The meeting began at 3 p.m. The first speaker was Cuba's foreign minister. He listed the articles of the UN Charter that had been violated by the United States in ordering the bombings of Cuba. Following that, Roa said, "Without any doubt, this is the prelude to a large-scale invasion devised, organized, supplied, armed, and financed by the government of the United States of America with the complicity of satellite dictatorships in the Western Hemisphere and the help of traitorous, mercenary Cubans of all kinds, trained on U.S. territory and in Guatemala by Pentagon and Central Intelligence Agency experts. The Cuban revolutionary government officially accuses the government of the United States of North America, before the Policy and Security Committee and international world opinion, of having resorted to the use of force to settle differences with a member state of the United Nations. I would like the representatives to note the cynical efforts of official U.S. propaganda to present a distorted version of the events…"

Ambassador Adlai Stevenson of the United States asked to speak. "I am very happy to see that Doctor Roa has suddenly recovered from his illness.[3] This is the first opportunity I've had to hear Dr. Roa about the sins of the United States and the virtues of Fidel Castro's Cuba, and I should say it is a remarkable experience... I have here a picture of one of those planes. It has the markings of the Castro air force on the tail, which everyone can see for himself. The Cuban star and the initials FAR —Fuerza Aerea Revolucionaria— are clearly visible. I would be very happy to show these pictures to the members of the committee after this statement."

Stevenson then began reading statements from a pilot who had flown to Miami and was hiding his face and refusing to give his name to the media, allegedly for fear of reprisals against his family by the Cuban government. Actually, he was a pilot for Brigade 2506, Mario Zúñiga, the same one who had stepped forward when Gar Teegan—the operations chief—had asked for a volunteer during a meeting before the airport bombings. Stevenson read the statements without knowing that the whole thing was a farce, and quite a crude one, improvised somewhat hastily to hide the hand of the United States in the bombings of Cuba's airports.

"I am one of the twelve B-26 pilots who remained in the Castro air force after the defection of Díaz Lanz and the purges which had followed. Three of my fellow-pilots and I had for months been planning to escape from Cuba. The day before yesterday, I heard that one of the three, Lt. Álvaro Galo, pilot of the FAR B-26 no. 915, had been seen talking to an agent of Ramiro Valdés, the head of the G-2. I warned the other two and we decided that Álvaro Galo, who had always acted like something of a coward, had probably betrayed us. We decided to take action at once. Yesterday morning I had taken off on a routine patrol from my base, San Antonio de los Baños, over a section of Pinar del Rio and around the Isle of Pines. I told my friends at Ciudad Libertad, and they agreed that we had to act. One of them was going to fly to Santiago. The other gave the excuse that he wanted to check his altimeter and they took off from Ciudad Liberta at 6 a.m. I took off at 6:05. Given Álvaro Galo's betrayal, we decided to teach him a lesson, so I flew to San Antonio where his plane was parked and I shot two loads of shrapnel into his plane, as well as three others parked nearby.... My buddies had left earlier to attack the airports that we had agreed to attack. Then,

---

[3] Roa had been very sick with the flu.

being unable because of shortage of fuel to reach the destination agreed upon with my comrades, I had to go to Miami..."

After Stevenson, the Guatemalan representative took the floor to categorically deny that his country had made itself available for the training of forces to attack the Cuban government.

Roa wasted no time. He raised his hand to speak. He was an outstanding, incisive debater. "I should thank the U.S. representative for his pleasure at my 'sudden' recovery of health," he said. He added that it was the first time he had heard Stevenson speak in the UN, although he had read his books. Now he was able to see for himself that there were two Stevensons: before and after being part of the Kennedy administration. Roa noted that anybody could paint Cuba's colors onto an airplane; it was a routine trick used by pirates all over the world.

The U.S. subterfuge began to be questioned the same day after Zúñiga's statements were read out at the UN. The pilot had refused to give his name and had himself photographed with a baseball cap that hid his face, a detail that was noticed by one or two sharp journalists. One of them, Tad Szulc, wrote in a *New York Times* article that it was naïve to assume the Castro government would have any difficulty in immediately discovering the name of any pilot who deserted.

Szulc said certain details of Zúñiga's airplane demonstrated the clumsiness of whoever had dreamed up the lie. For example, the plane showed no sign of having fired recently. To top it off, he noted in his conclusion, "none of us saw the planes that actually bombed the Cuban bases." Reporters asked other uncomfortable questions regarding the other two pilots Zúñiga said had defected and participated in the bombings but were nowhere to be found.

In Havana, at the funeral for the airport bombing victims, Fidel read out news reports about Zúñiga. When he finished reading, he said not even Hollywood would have gone that far. He challenged the United States to present the supposed deserter pilots at the United Nations. By then, Adlai Stevenson knew that he had played a dirty role in the CIA conspiracy. That is why he said in a message to Dean Rusk on the afternoon of Sunday, April 16, "Answers I made to Roa's statements about incident on Saturday were hastily concocted in Department, and revised by me at last minute on assumption that this was clear case of attacks by defectors inside Cuba."

Somehow the discussions at the United Nations on April 16 must have influenced later decisions, especially the rejection of a second air assault on Cuba's bases at dawn on D-Day. This was after photographs taken by U-2 spy planes refuted the pilots' exaggerated reports about the extent of the damage they did to Cuba's airplanes. When Gen. Charles P. Cabell, CIA deputy director and acting director while Dulles was in Puerto Rico—apparently to throw off any suspicions—spoke to Rusk about a second bombing, Rusk said he didn't agree. Among other things, he pointed to the situation in the United Nations, where doubt was being cast on U.S. credibility. A second air attack would be fatal, above all because there would be no way to repeat the pretext of a defection. Who would believe it? On that tragic Sunday afternoon, Rusk, in the presence of Cabell and Bissell, telephoned Kennedy at his weekend home in Glen Ora. By that time the president had read the newspapers and he was upset about the sarcastic coverage of Zúñiga and the two phantom pilots. He listened to the CIA's request for a second air assault and turned it down. Neither Cabell nor Bissell would get on the phone with the president to argue. If the second air attack had been authorized, the position of the United States in the UN would have become even more complicated. And it surely would have been a disaster for the Brigade 2506 air force to enter Cuban air space without the element of surprise; Cuba's airfields had been further reinforced after the April 15 bombings, and Fidel had ordered the air force pilots to take off before dawn and guard their bases by remaining in the air, circling them.

At 10:30 a.m. April 17, discussion resumed in the Policy and Security Committee. Without wasting any time, Roa went on the attack and listed the instances Cuba had gone before international bodies to denounce U.S. aggression. He said on the day of Kennedy's inauguration, Fidel Castro had said in a speech, "Today the new president has spoken. His speech had some positive aspects. We

279

Cubans do not want to prejudge or judge...we know how to wait calmly. We were never invaded by hate; we were never invaded by hysteria, not even when the tremendous danger was hanging over us of a strike by a powerful enemy. What can we say about the prospects for finding peace for our country and for the world? Welcome to that opportunity and welcome to that peace. We know what the new president of the United States is facing. If he starts down an honest path for the good of the world and for his own country, we wish him success. Meanwhile, we will wait for his actions, which are more eloquent than words."

However, as Foreign Minister Roa said in his speech at the UN, "hope evaporated." After presenting further arguments, Roa concluded by saying, "A unanimous clamor is shaking all of Cuba today; it is resounding in our America and reverberating in Asia, Africa, and Europe. My small, heroic country is reenacting the classic struggle between David and Goliath. As a soldier of that noble cause on the battlefront of international relations, allow me to bring that clamor to the stern Areopagus of the United Nations: Homeland or death! We will win!"

In the sessions that followed, speakers included: Stevenson, responding to Roa's accusations; the Soviet ambassador, who said that the invasion could not have been organized without U.S. ships, planes, weapons, and destroyers; the Guinean ambassador, who described the invasion as a cowardly attack on the Cuban people; and the Romanian ambassador, who harshly criticized the U.S. position. Roa asked for the floor again. He sternly answered Stevenson's remarks and announced that former Mexican president Lázaro Cárdenas was in Cuba, having arrived that morning in Havana to risk his life together with the Cuban people. The news created a commotion in the room. In subsequent sessions, speakers included the Romanian representative; the Soviet, who read a message from the prime minister, and the Ecuadoran, who said that his government stood firmly by its position of respect for the self-determination of nations to choose the political system they found most convenient. The Ecuadoran added that the aggression against Cuba had not come out of Cuban territory, but from elsewhere on the planet. He was followed by the Czech representative, and then by the representative of the United Arab Republic, who categorically denounced the aggression against the Cuban people. Then Mali's representative spoke, followed by Mexico's.

Nobody could better sum up what was happening at the United Nations as the battle was taking place in the Ciénaga de Zapata than the U.S. representative:

Telegram received on April 19, 1961
Control: 12110
Received: April 19, 1961 1:35 p.m.
From: New York
To: Secretary of State
No. 2937, April 19, noon
FOR PRESIDENT AND SECRETARY FROM STEVENSON
CUBA

1. Atmosphere in UN, among both our friends and neutrals, is highly unsatisfactory and extremely dangerous to U.S. position throughout world. Sovs and Castro Cubans have been able capture and so far hold moral initiative....
3. So far we have received virtually no support in speeches of others. Immediate approaches in capitals is necessary if Dept desires favorable speeches. Situation so difficult here no one will speak, except those hostile to us, without definite instructions on their govt's policy....
5. Everyone, of course, friend or foe, believes we have engineered this revolution [*euphemistic term for the invasion*] and no amount of denials will change their minds. Our prestige is thus committed, particularly in Latin America. Some states —Communist and «positive neutralists»— are very hostile. Others are uneasy. And those who are for us, especially LA's, are afraid to speak out because they fear internal repercussions of fight in Cuba on their own countries; they pray that this revolt [*another peculiar way of terming the invasion*] will succeed within hours. Also urgently need if possible language to meet universal view that aiding, instigating and organizing from outside is as culpable as intervention in international and inter-American law.

6. Whatever happens now we are in for period of very serious political trouble... From viewpoint U.S. position in world as reflected in UN, overt U.S. intervention in Cuba, after all we have said, would probably be worse than failure present effort...

Stevenson[4]

The United Nations was not the only place outside of Cuba where the Cubans were doing battle and responding to the U.S. aggression. During that same period, a regional baseball tournament was being held in Costa Rica. The day before a game between the Cuban and Guatemalan teams, President Idígoras Fuentes, who had given the CIA permission to use his country's territory to organize Brigade 2506, sent a telegram to the Guatemalan players saying, "HIT THE CUBANS HARD. STOP."

It turned out that the Guatemalan team manager was a friend of Manuel González Guerra, who was leading the Cuban delegation to the event, and he showed him the message. González assembled the Cuban team and informed them of what the Guatemalan president had said. When the game was over, he sent a response by telegram to the Guatemalan government palace that said, "General Idígoras Fuentes. Stop. Cuba 25 Guatemala 0. Stop. Done. Stop. Manuel González Guerra. Stop."

[4] Kennedy Library, Telegram of Stevenson, April 19, 1961. NSF OF, CUBA, Box 40.

The inevitable battle

Jesús Villafuerte Vázquez came back with a bouquet of flowers. He had picked them from the gardens of homes that surrounded the sugar mill. He went into the room where the members of his militia squad slept and placed the flowers on a small table in front of a photo of his girlfriend's smiling face, then filled a glass with *guarapo* (sugar cane juice) and set it next to the flowers. His girlfriend had died exactly one year earlier, April 17, 1960, after falling off a ladder and injuring her head. That tragic day was her eighteenth birthday. The flowers were in memory of her death and the *guarapo* was for her birthday. Jesús remembered her with strong feelings of love. He had taken her photo with him everywhere for the last four months, after being mobilized with his battalion January 5.

Jesús was leader of his squad, which included his father, Ángel Villafuerte. Father and son had participated in the "clean-up of the Escambray" offensive.

In early April of 1961, the militia's 339th Battalion, made up of 528 workers and students from the city of Cienfuegos, were ordered to leave the mountains. The insurgency had been defeated. At the La Campana Farm, the militia members turned in their Belgian-made FAL automatic rifles, which were much superior to the rifles used by the U.S. Army. Later, at the airfield where the militia members assembled to leave for their new destination, they were given Czech-made M-52 semiautomatic rifles, weapons of much lower quality than the FALs they were replacing. The change of weapons considerably reduced the battalion's firepower, and many militia members were cursing it on the morning of April 17.

That night would be the last of Jesús Villafuerte's life. Nine days earlier, after a week of rest, the troops had been summoned to the Asturian Club. "Hey, that's great! We'll be back together," Jesús had said when he found out he would be leading his squad again.

They arrived at the Australia Sugar Mill on April 10. Two days later, a group of five militia members was sent to Playa Larga. Their mission was to set up an observation post and guard the radio installation on that beach, twenty-nine kilometers from the mill. José Ramón González Suco led the group of five. Early in the morning of April 17, he was the one who radioed in that they could see lights and movement on the water. Néstor Ortiz, the radio operator on duty at the mill, delivered the message to the battalion's commander, Captain Cordero. A little while later, Suco sent another message: "A boat is landing and firing at the beach. These people are on top of us. We're going to destroy the radio and head for the trenches."

The message left no room for doubt; Cordero ordered the battalion to form ranks. Jesús came out of his room. Before closing the door, he glanced one more time at his girlfriend's photo. The candle burning in front of it was about to go out.

"My son Jesús was a squad leader in the third platoon of the third company, which Cordero assigned to Playa Larga. There was no transportation for the rest of the troops. We had driven about twenty kilometers when the truck driver, a civilian sugarcane worker, lost his nerve. He said he was running out of gas and wouldn't be able to make it. He suddenly stopped the truck. So Jesús said to him, 'Look, if you can't keep going, my dad knows how to drive a truck and he'll get us to the beach.' But the man kept going. When we got to a curve that was very close to the beach, we got out of the truck and began to spread out."[1] The men were carrying almost no ammunition: sixty or eighty cartridges for each M-52 rifle; ninety for the Czech submachine guns and two hundred for the three BZ machine guns. Some militia members had even less.

[1] Testimony of militia member Ángel Villafuerte Ayala, 1990. Author's archives.

"The platoon was crouched down. 'Count heads, Solís.' 'Twenty-seven, and with you, twenty-eight.' I told the people with the three BZs to remove the cartridge belts and use the magazines. We had two hundred rounds for each BZ and eighty for each rifle —nothing compared to what they used against us. Finally, I told everyone not to fire unless I did. We began advancing over the access road at about midnight. After we had gone a little way, one of the men said to me in a low voice, 'Lieutenant'—I wasn't a lieutenant; the guy must have been nervous— 'some people are coming this way.' We set the BZ on the ground, making a noise. Then we heard one of the people coming toward us say, 'Halt! Who goes there?'

"'The 339th from Cienfuegos,' I answered. 'And you?'

"'E Company from the Second Battalion.'

"'That doesn't exist in Cuba.'

"A mercenary yelled at us from the other flank, 'We're from the Liberation Army! We didn't come to fight you people. Surrender!'

"'Fire!' I yelled.

"There was a hell of a lot of firing. After a while, they stopped shooting and so did we. It became absolutely silent. Then I clearly heard one of them say to another, 'Hey, it feels like a telephone is ringing in my ear.' 'And I'm thirsty.' I heard them say that one of them was wounded and they took him away. Then they started firing again, but this time with heavy machine guns, and we fired back with whatever we had. We'd retreated to the other side of the ditch and were firing from there, but it was very uneven. The Czech rifles fired one shot at a time. I was sure they were coming after us and were going to finish us off, but they didn't dare. We could hear them using their code words: 'Eagle, eagle,' with the answer, 'Black eagle.' 'If you don't say the password fast, I'll shoot you.' You could tell they were nervous. Another one seemed to be saying something over the radio. He said, 'Mr. Officer, sir'—they used the formal address—'Since I've been at this post, you haven't sent us any water or ammunitions or relief. If you don't relieve me, I'll abandon my post.' At least they could ask for that. We didn't have any communications equipment or water and our ammunition was running out."[2]

---

[2] Testimony of militia member Luis "Oriente" Clemente Carralero, 1990. Author's archives.

Jesús Villafuerte Vázquez had ordered his men to space themselves out every ten or fifteen feet. He had placed himself in the middle, next to the BZ operator. His father had shifted positions, and at daybreak Jesús discovered he was right next to him. Jesús didn't reproach him for abandoning his post; he knew the old man wasn't going anywhere. The BZ's ammunition had run out, and now the men were firing sporadically at enemy lines, mostly so the mercenaries would know they were still there. However, it had become daylight, and in the middle of an area cleared by bulldozers, the men of the 339th Battalion made easy targets.

Edgar Butari was a squad leader in the mercenaries' E Company. It was the same squad that included José Ramón Pérez Peña, the former Ten Cent store employee from Camagüey. Butari braced his Garand against his shoulder and began picking off the militia members who were laying flat against the ground about eighty meters away at the foot of the access road.

"Jesús was moving people around, trying to make them into the smallest targets possible. We heard the sound of a truck; it was going straight toward the mercenaries. It didn't have any rails in the back, and we could see several women from where we were. Right then, they shot at it with a large-caliber gun or bazooka. The truck flew into the air."[3]

"We shouted 'aguila' again but we got no answer. The truck was coming closer, so everybody turned their weapons and started shooting and that thing exploded just like that. POW! It jumped in the air and came down in flames. Then we saw there were three women and two girls, little ones, that's all, in the truck, and a couple of militiamen. I don't know how that happened but that's what we got out of it, three women and two girls, killed."[4]

It's hard if not impossible to imagine how the occupants of that truck could have heard that strange password from a hundred feet away where the men of E Company were lying in hiding. The old truck's noisy engine would have made it impossible to hear anyone's

---

[3] Testimony of militia member Ángel Villafuerte Ayala, 1990, Author's archives.
[4] Testimony of invader Mario Abril to journalists David Wise and Thomas B. Ross in *The Invisible Government*, p. 68.

voice. Also, there were no militia members in the truck; they were civilians, and perfectly visible. After all these years, the survivors of that barbarous, unjustified attack have not been able to forget that terrible moment.

"It was midnight when the shooting started. At daybreak, they took us out in a truck. It was my Aunt Amparo Ortiz and her husband, her sister María Ortiz and her husband, Cira María García and her family, my sister Dulce María, and me. All of a sudden, they started shooting from where the INRA sign was. The truck rose up into the air and smashed into the ditch. Dulce María fell onto my legs; she was bleeding from her mouth and nose. I looked over, screaming, and saw Cira María García lying on the road with her husband next to her, and a little further away, María Ortiz was yelling in pain from her burns."[5]

"Víctor Caballero pulled out my sister, who was already dead, and set her on the ground. I was looking for the others. I couldn't see Cira María, because her husband had carried her a few meters away from the road. When I saw her, it was horrible, because the poor thing was badly burned and hurt. I kept looking for my niece, Dulce María Martín, who they killed there; she was fourteen years old. My other niece got banged up when she fell out of the truck, but she wasn't shot. I kept running around and looked for my sister, who was also dead. I kept walking around among the dead and wounded, but I couldn't find my husband.... Then I found him; he was dead. About fifteen minutes later, a truck with mercenaries came and they took us to Playa Larga. I was dazed. I remember I just kept saying I couldn't leave my dead loved ones there."[6]

"Look what you've done to my sister!' I yelled at the mercenaries when they put me into the truck. 'Bring my sister!' One of them told me, 'I'm sorry. She's dead. We're at war.' Then I started crying. I really loved my sister; she was about to turn fifteen years old. She was a Young Rebel in the sixth grade. One of the mercenaries in the truck saw me crying and screaming and tried to give me ten pesos. I don't know why he did that. 'I don't want money, I want my sister!' I yelled at him. They took us to one of the construction sites at Playa

[5] Testimony of Nora Martín of Jagüey Grande, 1990, Author's Archives.
[6] Testimony of Amparo Ortiz, woman charcoal worker, in *Girón no fue solo en abril*, by Miguel A. Sánchez, p.145.

Larga. They asked me to cook and I refused. Amparo was more docile. She started peeling onions. María Ortiz was lying on the ground there. She was dying. They told us they didn't have anything to treat her with there and that their hospital was at Girón. But they didn't take her there."[7]

At Girón, thirty-nine kilometers to the east, a priest named Ismael de Lugo was practicing a speech addressing the Cuban people he was about to read over the mercenaries' radio transmitter. It said:

"The chief of the Assault Brigade's Ecclesiastical Services, Reverend Father Ismael de Lugo, a member of the Capuchin order, addresses the Catholic people of Cuba in his own name and that of his chaplains. Attention! Attention! Cuban Catholics! The liberation forces have landed on Cuba's beaches. We come in the name of God, justice, and democracy, to reestablish the law that has been violated, the freedom that has been trampled, and the religion that has been methodized and slandered. We come not out of hate, but of love. We come to bring peace, even if we must make war to attain it. The Assault Brigade is made up of thousands of Cubans, all of whom are Christians and Catholics. Their morality is the morality of the Crusaders. They are coming to reestablish the principles that our teacher legislated in his Sermon on the Mount.

"Before the landing, they all heard Holy Mass and received the Holy Sacraments. They know why they are fighting and what they are fighting for. They don't want our patron saint, the Black Virgin, Caridad del Cobre, to suffer any more as she contemplates so much ungodliness from her sanctuary, so much secularism, and so much communism. At this time, we need the collaboration of all Catholics in Cuba. We are asking for your prayers for our victory, for divine protection for our soldiers, and for civic cooperation in not coming out of your homes. We are praying to the God of the armies that the battle will be brief so that the least amount possible of fraternal and Cuban blood is shed. Our fight is the fight of those who believe in God against the atheists, of those who believe in spiritual values against materialism. It is the fight of democracy against communism. Ideologies are only defeated with another, superior ideology. And

[7] Testimony of Nora Martín. Author's archives.

the only ideology capable of defeating communist ideology is Christian ideology. That is why we are here, and that is what we are fighting for.

"Cuban Catholics! Our military power is devastating and invincible, but even greater is the power of our morality and our faith in God and in his protection and help. Cuban Catholics! I send an embrace from the Liberation Army to all of your relatives, family, and friends. Soon you will be able to be together. Have faith that victory is ours, because God is with us and the Virgin of Caridad cannot abandon her children.

Catholics! Long live free, democratic, and Catholic Cuba! Long live Christ the King! Long live our glorious patron saint! God bless you.

Father Ismael de Lugo. Chief of Brigade, Ecclesiastical Services."[8]

A few feet away from the still-burning truck, Ángel and Jesús Villafuerte were trying to find protection in the clearing. They couldn't see the men from E Company, but the mercenaries could see them. The mercenaries had taken over a small hill; it was full of holes because a gas station was being built there, and from there they could see both sides of the road perfectly well. The men from José Ramón Peña's squad continued picking off militia members.

"After daybreak, the bullets were hitting really close and they had killed and wounded a number of battalion members. That was when Jesús said, 'Dad, I'm hurt.' I got closer to him and touched him, but I didn't see any wound. I talked to him but he didn't answer. He had collapsed. I turned him over; the bullet had gone through the other side of his body. I gave him a little bit of water and it ran over his face. He was dead. So I stayed there, looking at him without knowing what to do. It occurred to me to put his hat on. I didn't want to believe it. A comrade said to me, 'Don't move. They're picking us off.'"[9]

---

[8] Ismael de Lugo's real name was Fermín Asla Polo and he was a native of the Lugo region of Spain. He had fought in the Spanish Civil War on the side of the Falangist troops. A notebook containing the quoted speech was confiscated from him.

[9] Testimony of Ángel Villafuerte Ayala. Author's archives.

Shortly after that, Ángel was slightly wounded and he was taken to the town of Jagüey Grande. "After I was treated at the hospital, I went to the funeral home to look for my son's body, but he wasn't there. They told me they had sent him to Cienfuegos, because that was where he was from. When I got to Cienfuegos, I went straight to the Pujol Funeral Home, where I worked, but he was not there either. So I went home. When my wife saw me without the boy, she was frightened. I didn't have the courage to tell her the truth. I told her he was wounded. Then I went to Aguada de Pasajeros and he wasn't there, either. I was asking people for rides the whole time. I went back to Jagüey. Jesús was laid out in the funeral home. I called my boss and he sent the hearse. I put dry ice in the coffin and we headed for Cienfuegos. On the way, I thought about how I was going to tell my wife that they had killed our boy. She died a little while later. She never recovered."[10]

For Ángel Villafuerte Ayala, the war ended right then and there. However, without realizing it, he, his son and their comrades had put up resistance that ruined part of the mercenaries' plan. They had prevented E Company from advancing north four kilometers to the town of Pálpite. There, at the edge of Zapata Swamp and at the end of the beachhead, Company E was supposed to join forces with the paratroopers. The mercenaries' 2nd Battalion halted as soon as it clashed with the militia's 339th Battalion. The mercenaries had been told that the majority of the militias would go over to their side. That's why they were surprised when they called for surrender and were answered with "Fire!"

At Girón, the mercenaries did not expect the clash they had with the few militia members who were there, either. The first person who saw the light out over the ocean was Mariano Mustelier, the local militia leader, who was in a jeep that night patrolling the tourist resort construction sites. He was accompanied by Valerio Rodríguez, a thirteen-year-old literacy teacher.

There was something strange about the blinking red light. Mariano thought it was a ship on the way to Cienfuegos that had lost its way in the bay. He got in his jeep and drove east to park in front of the

---

[10] Testimony of Ángel Villafuerte Ayala. Author's archives.

290

ship and signal it with his headlights. The literacy teacher, who thought he had been living a real adventure since arriving at Zapata Swamp two months earlier, immediately jumped out of the vehicle.

"About 100 yards offshore, one of their six red beach marker lights suddenly started blinking.[11] Several of the men scrambled for it. Gray reached it first, covered it up and groped for the switch. It had been carefully taped on 'off.' The blinking, caused by a short, stopped... Fifty yards offshore, he heard a jeep coming. Gray later learned that the jeep had been alerted by the blinking red landing lights... Gray never forgot the loud, long squeaking of the brakes. He raised his head for a look. At that moment the jeep swung around toward the sea, bathing the landing party in its headlights. At once, Gray started firing directly into them. They were the first shots at the Bay of Pigs."[12]

The jeep's headlights exploded, slightly wounding Valerio Rodríguez in the eye. It was symbolically ironic. The first shots of the invasion that was supposed to destroy the Cuban Revolution had been fired by a U.S. officer and the first person wounded was a literacy campaign volunteer who was teaching the local charcoal makers how to read.

Mariano Mustelier made an important decision. He sent a local worker to the Covadonga Sugar Mill thirty kilometers north to sound the alert. That was where the closest telephone was. The Playa Girón radio installation was not working. There was a small detachment of twenty-three local militia members at the beach, most of them charcoal makers armed with M-52 rifles and old Springfields. That night, six of the men were on guard duty as usual at the most important points: the generator, the aqueduct, a small dock for light boats, the airport, a carpentry workshop, and the traffic circle at the entrance to the beach in the north.

As soon as the militia members became aware of the danger, one of them turned off the generator. The others fled for the hills and escaped capture. One of them, Eugenio B. Palma, was killed in the

---

[11] The beach marker lights placed by the frogmen under Grayston Lynch's command were visible from the sea only if they were working properly.
[12] Peter Wyden. *The Bay of Pigs.*

attempt. The invaders quickly occupied a cabin that served as militia headquarters near the tourist resort construction site, seizing a list of Girón's militia members and weapons. They searched all the cabins.

"We were in one of the cabins working on a literacy census when we heard shooting. I went to the window and saw a ball of fire coming from the ocean. A few minutes later, some of the literacy campaign volunteers arrived, including Valerio, who was wounded in one eye. 'It's a landing,' they told us. We stayed in the cabin, and a little while later some men wearing strange uniforms came in and took us prisoner. At dawn, they moved us to the cafeteria, where they were holding a lot of charcoal makers as prisoners—about 300. They separated the men from the women and began interrogating us. They did it in a little room that was next to the cafeteria. 'Where are you from?' they asked me. 'From Bolondrón'. 'And what are you doing here?' 'I'm teaching people how to read and write'. 'Is that why Fidel brought you here?' 'No, no, Fidel didn't bring us; we came because we wanted to.' They took notes on all my answers and proposed that I join them. I said no. 'I'm a teacher. I like to teach. I don't like the army.'"[13]

Manuel Alvariño, the charcoal worker who had taken care of Fidel on May 25, 1959, and who delighted in telling the story of the pig's foot, was not very convincing during his interrogation by the mercenaries' G-2. "They told me they would give me five pesos for each member of my family and that if I joined their army, I could be anything from a soldier to a commander. 'No, I don't like the army,' I answered. 'We have your militia member record here,' they said, showing me the record. So I said, 'Yes, I'm a militia member, but to guard my workplace.'"[14]

About four hundred prisoners yet to be questioned were still in the cafeteria. Most were local residents and a few were construction workers. Only six of them joined the invaders: four of them were former foremen and the other two were Antonio Blanco Sr. and Jr., the father-and-son owners of a bar in Girón.

[13] Testimony of Ana María Hernández Bravo, leader of literacy campaign volunteers at Playa Girón, 1990. Author's archives.
[14] Testimony of Manuel Alvariño, charcoal maker, 1989. Author's archives.

At about 1 a.m., a mechanic from Girón arrived at the Covadonga Sugar Mill with news of the landing. The telephone operator on duty in the office immediately passed the news on to Rebel Army headquarters in Cienfuegos, which notified State Security headquarters in Las Villas province. Through these and other channels, the information made it to Point One in the capital just three hours after the landing had begun.

"At about 2 a.m., the guard on duty woke me up saying the Commander in Chief was calling me over the phone.... At first I didn't understand very well what he was saying. I realized Fidel was asking me if I knew about what had happened; I had no idea, I was half asleep. Then he told me that they had come, but I didn't understand—they had come? Who? What? Then I realized that they had landed.... Fidel told me to get hold of a vehicle. I clearly remember him saying, 'Go to Matanzas at top speed, and take the school's students with you to repel the landing....'

"The Matanzas Militia Leadership School had been organized according to Fidel's instructions to provide courses for a number of workers, specially selected trade union leaders, to train them as officers of the National Revolutionary Militia.... Many of these militia officials are now colonels and some of them are generals of the FAR.... I remember we arrived in Matanzas before dawn; it was still quite dark. At the entrance they were inspecting trucks going by on the highway that were carrying the most incredible products and fruits, including one loaded with chickens.... The students were up, and I still remember the image of people coming out of the lunchroom mugs in hand, having just finished breakfast....

"Discipline and morale were good at the school. I think the school was the best combat unit in Cuba at the time, there's no doubt about it.... I took off, leaving the school to get organized. I went ahead.... I very clearly remember seeing people on the road: a farmer with his cow, another chopping weeds at the side of the road, another on his way to work. People didn't know what was happening...."[15]

Captain José Ramón Fernández didn't know an enemy force had landed. He was far from suspecting that more than a few of the

[15] Testimony of General José Ramón Fernández. Author's archives.

Brigade 2506 cadres he was soon to battle had been his students. Captain Fernández had graduated at the top of his class from the School of Cadets in 1947. Five years later, he completed advanced studies in artillery, and later he perfected them at the Fort Sill Field Artillery School in the United States. He became a professor at the School of Cadets, but on March 10, without abandoning his uniform, he began to conspire against the dictator, Fulgencio Batista. Four years later, on April 3, 1956, he was arrested. Tried for the crime of conspiracy to commit rebellion, he was stripped of his rank and sentenced to four years in prison, but that was interrupted by the victory of the Revolution on January 1, 1959.

Three days after the victory of the Revolution, after returning from the Isle of Pines and arresting General Eulogio Cantillo, whom Batista had left to run the government, José Ramón Fernández gave up all of his responsibilities and went home. On January 12, Fidel summoned him to his office together with other officers who had been imprisoned for conspiring against Batista. During their meeting Fidel gave out a number of assignments, and placed Fernández at the head of the School of Cadets. Fernández did not respond. At the end of the meeting, he explained to Fidel that he did not have anything against the Revolution, for which he had complete sympathy and believed in its projects for change in the country. But his movement had failed, and he felt he didn't deserve the post, that those who had made the Revolution should lead it. Besides, he added, he already had a job in civilian life as the administrator of a sugar mill.

"How much are you making there?" Fidel asked him.

"Eleven hundred pesos a month."

"That's a lot more than what I can pay you." Fidel paced back and forth and added, "You go to your sugar mill, I'll devote myself to writing a book about the Sierra, and to hell with the Revolution!"

Fernández thought for a few seconds and then asked, "Where did you want me to go?"

"In Jagüey, an aid center had been set up. People's morale was good. There was a lot of movement among the people, all with very good attitudes, dressed in their militia uniforms, everyone mobilized.... It was even more palpable at the Australia Sugar Mill. When I got to the mill I saw the administrator and asked him how

294

many militia members were there. 'Seven.' I went to the telephone and reported to the Commander in Chief. I think it was 8 a.m. "What's going on there?" Fidel asked me. "Nothing, I don't know anything, I just got here," I said to him. The rumor started going around that paratroopers were in front of and behind the mill. People began gathering on the east side of the water tank, asking for weapons—about 200 people."[16]

The first troops headed for Yaguaramas and Covadonga, northeast and north of Girón. Commander Juan Almeida, who was leading the Central Army based in Santa Clara, had received orders from Fidel to move the 117th Battalion to the Covadonga Sugar Mill and place it under the orders of Commander Filiberto Olivera Moya. Almeida also instructed Commander René de los Santos to carry out the attack on Playa Girón from the town of Yaguaramas.

"What is my mission, chief?" De los Santos asked.

"Get your people and get to that beach."[17]

Shortly after that, Fidel ordered another force to advance toward the coast in the direction of Cienfuegos-Juraguá-Girón. In fact, the main directives of the offensive to surround the beachhead were established and began to be implemented early in the morning on April 17.

For a better understanding of the battleground, the distances between the main points involved are listed below:

Australia-Pálpite:	25 km
Australia-Playa Larga:	29 km
Playa Larga-Playa Girón:	34 km
Australia-Playa Girón:	68 km
Covadonga-Playa Girón:	30 km
Covadonga-San Blas:	15 km
Yaguaramas-Playa Girón:	44 km
Yaguaramas-San Blas:	29 km

[16] Testimony of General José Ramón Fernández. Author's archives.
[17] Testimony of René de los Santos, in Quintín Pino. *La batalla de Girón.* P.78.

At dawn on the April 17, Brigade 2506 had disembarked 88 percent of its troops. The 3rd, 4th, and 6th battalions and a tank company had landed at Playa Girón. They had occupied the airfield, which was in operational condition to the surprise and joy of the invaders, especially the commanding officers. The 3rd Infantry Battalion, reinforced, moved east to Caleta Buena in the direction of Juraguá. In the north, in the direction of Covadonga and Yaguaramas, the paratrooper battalion's A Company took their positions as planned. The 2nd Infantry Battalion had landed in the west, at Playa Larga. The 5th Battalion, still on the *Houston*, had interrupted its landing when the ship's captain decided to move out to sea and wait for nightfall to return to the bay because of the presence of Cuban air force planes. Now, however, he was returning to Playa Larga after receiving a radioed counterorder from Happy Valley, apparently from the U.S. military chief, Colonel Jack Hawkins, or from Quarters Eye. The order would be fatal for the battalion, but not for the brigade. This force was made up of recruits who had arrived at the Trax Base in the last sixty days and didn't have much training.

One serious difficulty at dawn on that day was that the 2nd Battalion's E Company in Playa Larga had not been able to advance and occupy the village of Pálpite because of resistance from a group of militia members at the edge of the beach.

There was no other combat on any other front of the almost 400 square kilometers of beachhead early on the morning of the landing. However, José Pérez San Román, the Cuban commander of Brigade 2506, sent a message to Quarters Eye saying they had only enough ammunition "for four hours."[18]

Messages like this, which were a distortion of reality and apparently were aimed at trying to force the U.S. armed forces to be more involved, were repeated during the course of the battle. There had been others even earlier. At 3 a.m., a radioed message reporting on the disembarkation of troops from the *Atlantic,* said it had been "under fire." Actually, the disembarkation of troops and weapons in Playa Girón had taken place without any problems

[18] Tomás Diez Acosta. *La guerra encubierta.* Document 19. Sequence of events (D-2 to D+2). De-classified by the U.S. government.

or armed response, simply because there were no revolutionary forces deployed there. The greatest danger was posed by Cuba's air force, although the brigade's shipboard anti-aircraft defense system was seen to be active.

A little before 6 a.m., a squadron of six C-46s and a C-54 carrying paratroopers took off and flew north. The paratroopers who were dropped were carrying a range of weapons, enough to occupy and defend the positions assaulted. Each platoon of twenty-four men had a .30-caliber machine gun; a bazooka; a 60-mm. mortar; a 57-mm. cannon, and three Browning automatic rifles. The men operating the .30-caliber machine gun and the bazooka were armed with M-3 submachine guns, and the others had Garand M-1s, some for sniper use. Each group carried ten boxes of 2,500 rounds for the .30-caliber gun; twelve mortar grenades; six bazooka rockets, and eight 57-mm. rockets. Each paratrooper had 270 rounds of ammunition.

"We overflew the town of Girón, heading northeast along the San Blas road. I pushed the red button activating the light in the rear cabin which would alert the paratroopers to get ready for their jump. About eight miles further down the road, I spotted a jeep with three passengers. As we passed over them, they stopped and begin to fire rifles and pistols at us. A few of the bullets hit the plane but did little damage. I wanted to put as much distance between them and the jeep as possible, so I decided to drop the troops directly over the junction and not a couple of miles before it, as had been planned. When we reached the spot, I pushed the button that lit the green light and rang the signal bell. In less than fifteen seconds all thirty men were in the air.

"I banked eastward, allowing the PDO's, Alberto Pérez and Chiqui Ginebra, time to pick up the static lines and hook up the new ones for unloading the supplies which we then dropped near the men. We had completed the first part of our mission without mishap. I descended to fifty feet and headed back down the road, planning to try to scare off the men in the jeep. We were surprised to see it overturned and smoking, its occupants apparently dead."[19]

[19] Eduardo Ferrer, *Operation Puma*, pp. 176.

Down below, a truck drove over the westernmost access road toward Jagüey Grande. Like Eduardo Ferrer, the B-26 pilots escorting the two transport planes had excellent visibility, enough to see that the passengers hanging onto the sides of the truck were civilians.

"The plane dropped the paratroopers into a field before arriving at San Isidro. Then we saw another plane flying low behind us, almost grazing the highway. My dad told my mom, 'Knock hard so the driver will stop.' Then he pushed my brother and yelled, 'Get down on the ground, that plane is going to land on the highway.' I was sitting on a wooden box of cans of condensed milk and carrying my six-month-old nephew. Then the plane began firing. My mom fell; they had hit her in the belly and in one arm. My grandmother was hit in the spine by a bullet, leaving her disabled. My brother got hit in a leg and an arm. I bent over and my mom opened her eyes. I asked her if she was hurt. She lifted her arm and tried to touch me, but she crumpled. Then my dad took me down from the truck. 'If you don't take mom down, I'm not going. She's alive.' My dad had placed a sheet over her and you couldn't see the wound in her belly. That's why I thought she was alive. Then the wind lifted the sheet and I saw the wound. Everything was coming out. My dad placed me under a júcaro tree. My brother was saying to us, 'If I die, don't just leave me lying there like mom.' A little while later, a militia chief from the town took us down the road and sent us to Jagüey. They had already taken my mom to Jagüey. I wanted to see her, and they took me to the funeral home. I kept remembering how the wind lifted the sheet and I could see her wound. I could see my mom's guts."[20]

The truck that Nemesia's family was riding in was used for a number of years after that. It was a '51 Ford with wood-and-rope railings. Its doors were painted blue, with yellow letters spelling out the word "INRA." There was no way it could have been taken for a military vehicle.

Due to a navigation error, one of the paratrooper B Company platoons was dropped quite far from their target, near the highway

[20] Testimony of Nemesia Rodríguez Montalvo, 1990. Author's archives.
[21] Statements by Galo Astor García, invader. MININT Archives.

between Pálpite and the Australia Sugar Mill. "They dropped us far from where we were supposed to be dropped. I was carrying a Garand and a .45 pistol. We landed about two or three kilometers from the Australia Sugar Mill. Twenty-seven of us from this group gathered on a hill where we left almost all of our weapons, rigged so they would explode if someone tried to take them. We left the cay and ran into sentries on a farm; they wounded one of us. We spread out. When we were captured, we confessed to a lieutenant at the Australia Sugar Mill that we had left the weapons booby-trapped, and the same guy who set them up disarmed the traps."[21]

The other platoon of invaders that was supposed to occupy Pálpite saw people moving around in the village and two vehicles on the highway and decided to wait in the hills nearby. Two trucks were carrying three dozen civilians from Jagüey Grande to Playa Larga under the command of the chief of the military post. A little way down the road, they were intercepted by Abraham Maciques, director of development on the Zapata peninsula, who told them that Playa Larga had been occupied by the invaders and that Fidel was saying Pálpite must not be taken. So they decided ten men should stay in the village.

"We got behind the charcoal ovens and sacks that were there. At close to dawn, a plane came, but we thought it was one of ours. Then it fired a rocket that blew up Cotilo Morejón's stand. The plane passed over three times, we started to call out people's names and when nobody answered, I said to myself, 'They've killed everybody here.' Then we saw the paratroopers being dropped in Sicotes; that's where they dropped the group that was supposed to occupy Pálpite. Then they dropped a big box. We counted twenty-four paratroopers in all. They stayed hidden over there."[22]

The company of paratroopers dropped near the Covadonga Sugar Mill had better luck. They immediately occupied settlements and villages

[22] Testimony of Julio Somoza, resident of Jagüey Grande, 1990. Author's archives.

along the road to Girón and stationed an advance post very close to the Covadonga Sugar Mill, but didn't dare invade the mill itself:

"At about 6 a.m. I heard the ring indicating a long-distance phone call and I picked up the phone:

"Look, because of what's going on there, we're going to establish a direct line with Point One. The password is 'Death to the invader' and the response is 'Venceremos.' Then I heard the unmistakable voice of Fidel.

'Hey, what is it you do there?'

'I'm the telephone operator, Commander.'

'But what else, damn it?'

'I'm a militia member here.'

'Okay. What's going on there?'

'They're invading Playa Girón; they are wearing clothes full of spots. Fidel, man, what we need is for you send us some weapons.'

'And how many of you militia members are there?'

'We have 189 militia members at the mill, but without weapons. We need weapons.' Just then, they told me paratroopers were being dropped. I told Fidel and went to verify. I got to the doorway of the mill's office and managed to see some of them still in the air. Someone yelled to me that he counted twenty-four. I went back to the telephone and picked up the receiver.

'Death to the invader!' It was Fidel.

'Venceremos,' I answered. 'They've dropped twenty-four.'

'How far away?'

'Two kilometers.'

'Let's see.' It sounded like he was in front of a map. 'How far from Covadonga and in what place?'

'Have you been to Covadonga?'

'Yes.'

'Leaving Covadonga by the highway that goes to Playa Girón, on a curve where there's a windmill, there is a clearing there; that's where they were dropped."

'Do you know if they're advancing or retreating?'

'I don't know. It doesn't seem like they're advancing, because there are a few comrades spread out with the few rifles that we have here, firing at them sporadically. Fidel, why don't you send us some weapons?'

'And how many weapons do you have there?'

'We have eleven weapons: eight M-52 rifles, two Springfields, and a Brazilian carbine.

'Damn! If I had those weapons, I'd stand there and not let those people move. The problem with you all is that you've gone yellow.'

'No, man, no! How can we be yellow if we're asking for weapons?'

'Listen, don't complain to me any more about weapons. Arm yourselves with machetes, sticks, and stones, but don't let them take the sugar mill, damn it!'

"Immediately, I told everyone what Fidel was saying. The comrades from the Integrated Revolutionary Organizations (ORI) didn't believe I was talking to Fidel and they came to see me. 'Hey Chele, are you sure that the guy you were talking to was Fidel?' That pissed me off. I picked up the telephone, and Fidel was on the other end of the line.

'Death to the Invader!'

'Venceremos! Listen, Fidel, the comrades from the organizations here don't believe it's you who's giving me instructions.

'Put them on the phone.'

"I heard the guy from the ORI saying 'Yes, Commander. Yes, Commander. Yes, Commander,' and hang up. 'It's Fidel. We have to arm ourselves with machetes, but they can't take the mill.' And he ran out like a shot.

"By about 9 a.m., the people from the mill had equipped themselves with whatever they had. People were in high spirits and very impassioned. Some people went to Cienfuegos to find weapons and then come back. The people were asking for weapons. The forty-some counterrevolutionaries in town had been picked up and taken to Rodas.

"At about 12:30 or 1 p.m., several trucks full of militia members went by. I picked up the telephone.

'Point One. Death to the invader!'

'Venceremos!'

'Fidel, now these sons of bitches are screwed.'

'Why? What's going on now?'

'The troops are going by.'

"It was good for Fidel to hear this, because he knew what it meant."[23]

[23] Testimony of Gonzalo Rodríguez Mantilla, "Chele," a worker at the Covadonga Sugar Mill. 1990. Author's archives.

The 117th Battalion had been placed under the orders of Commander Filiberto Olivera Moya, who was leading the Covadonga Front. The battalion was incomplete. The troops that arrived included two companies and an 85-mm. mortar battery. Olivera ordered the troops to flush out the enemy from Jocuma, the curve in the road four kilometers from the mill. Two of this battalion's companies were advancing on San Blas from the left flank, coming out of Yaguaramas.

In Girón that morning, Manuel Alvariño was standing on a chair in the cafeteria where the prisoners were and looking through the window, giving a blow-by-blow account of the battle taking place in the skies over Girón.

"The little plane is attacking the ship. The ship exploded and the fire almost got the little plane, which is now flying upward, straight as an arrow. One of the big planes is smoking." Tony Blanco, the bar owner who had joined the mercenaries, went to the window saying, 'How are the communists doing?' By the afternoon, their attitude had changed. Several of them came to the cafeteria and said to us, 'You all are in danger here, and there's no reason for you to die. Tomorrow at 6 a.m. everyone here is going to work.' When I went out, one of them said to us, 'Tomorrow you all can move into one of the cabins, because now these houses are going to be for you.' I thought to myself, 'No, for your mother, you son of a bitch!'"[24]

At 1 p.m., one of them came and told us to get up, that he was going to count us and bring us lunch, but they didn't bring anything. The bombs from the air assault on the ships were breaking the windows. Later, they let us go. As we were leaving Girón, they arrested us again. 'We don't have orders to let anyone go.' One of them went for instructions and came back with a 'yes.' 'It's just temporary permission. Tomorrow, you all come back at 6 a.m. Our password is 'Eagle,' and you should answer 'Imperial.' Some of the mercenaries didn't agree, saying, 'If these

[24] Testimony of Manuel Alvariño. Author's archives.

people go now, they're not going to come back tomorrow unless it's with the militia.'"[25]

From his unusual observation post, charcoal maker Manuel Alvariño had seen the Sea Fury fighter plane piloted by Enrique Carreras. Minutes earlier, Carreras had almost been hit by enemy fire from a B-26 following on his tail. Just in time, he made a 180-degree turn and got behind the enemy plane. He opened fire, hitting an engine, and the B-26 quickly flew away, out to sea. It never made it back to Happy Valley or anywhere else. The Sea Fury gained altitude. At 5,000 feet, confident that nobody was following him, Carreras looked down and saw a ship moving in front of Playa Girón. He went down like a shot. A barrage of shrapnel came up to meet him from the heavily armed escort ship *Blagar*. Carreras made it safely through the wall of antiaircraft fire, and when he had the ship in his sight —which was defective, by the way— he fired. The *Rio Escondido* blew up. Apparently, he'd hit it in the right spot.

On a previous mission, Carreras had hit the stern of another enemy ship, the *Houston*, which had run aground on a coral reef at Punta Cazones and was on fire.

The destruction of the *Rio Escondido* signified the loss of 145 tons of ammunition, 38,000 gallons of vehicle fuel and 3,000 gallons of airplane fuel. The *Houston* was carrying 24,160 pounds of food in its holds; potable water; 150 gallons of gasoline; five tons of ammunition for individual weapons; eight tons of powerful explosives; a ton-and-a-half of napalm, and small amounts of pyrotechnic and chemical explosives.[26]

None of the lost cargo was indispensable to Brigade 2506 for the first days of battle after securing the beachhead. Everything they needed for taking the beachhead and defending it was on dry land.

In Playa Larga, Erneido Oliva decided to hold about 150 civilians and two dozen militia members from the 339th Battalion as prisoners.

[25] Testimony of Pedro Flores, charcoal maker, 1990. Author's archives.
[26] Operation Pluto Plan, seized from José Pérez San Román. MININT Archives.

Suco, the leader of the squad from that battalion that had been guarding the radio installation at Playa Larga, recalled, "A literacy worker was resting his head on me, and one of the mercenaries came up and said to him, 'What is that uniform?'

"'The literacy campaign.'

"'Are you a communist?'

"'I'm a *fidelista*,' answered the boy, who was not even fifteen years old. And the mercenary said to him, 'You know all the *fidelistas* are communists.'

"'Oh. Then I'm a communist.'

"'Bastard!' the mercenary said, and he walked away. Every once in a while, one of them would come in and say something. One of them told us that we militia members would be killed that night because we had killed his brother. Guasasa answered him back. He was a famous guy there, a construction worker who was always drunk and very clever. Well, they were commenting there that the mercenaries had taken him prisoner on the beach while he was sleeping off his drunkenness. And he spent almost the entire day waking up and going back to sleep. He woke up when the mercenary was saying this to us, and Guasasa said to another charcoal maker —who he thought was the one being threatened— 'Guajiro, forget about that. The Commander will be here anytime now and this'll all be over.' We all looked at each other. The mercenary looked at him with murder in his eyes.

"I remember an argument between a mercenary and one of his officers. I could hear it from the cafeteria:

"'Isn't this nice.'

"'Report for duty!'

'Ever since I got here, I've been working my ass off over there, and they haven't relieved me. I say 'eagle, eagle,' and nothing, and all of you are over here.'

"'Report for duty! Report for duty!' the officer kept saying to him."[27]

At the Australia Sugar Mill, Capt. José Ramón Fernández had confirmed there were no paratroopers nearby and he was waiting impatiently for the battalion from the Militia Leadership School in Matanzas.

[27] Testimony of José Ramón Gonzáles Suco, militia member, 1990. Author's archives.

304

"There was a broken-down jeep with a captain who turned out to be the commander of the 339th Battalion. I remember he was sitting in the jeep with one or two others. So, I went up to him and asked, 'And who are you?'

"'I'm the commander of the 339th Battalion,' he answered.

"Then I said to him, 'And where are your people?' He answered, 'We've been repelling the landing since dawn.'

"'But where are your people?'

"'All of my people are prisoners or dead,' he said.

"'I asked him, 'What forces are between the mercenaries and those of us here?'

"'There's none.'

"'Okay, so go and get your people.'

"'No, no,' he answered. 'The only ones left are these three here with me.'"[28]

The commander of the 339th Battalion had been exaggerating. At dawn, the troops from that unit, a single company that had been engaged in battle near the entrance to Playa Larga, had retreated. The little ammunition they had was gone, and the snipers of the mercenaries' E Company, 2nd Battalion, had begun picking them off. Six revolutionaries were killed and thirteen wounded.

The men began retreating into the mountains and along the edges of the access road. About fifty of them ran toward Caletón de Buenaventura, about 500 meters west of the beach, where they joined sailors from an SV-3 coastal patrol who had moved their .50-caliber machine gun from their boat to the construction site of a meat processing plant. Later, they and the charcoal makers' families from the Buenaventura Cooperative retreated to another village fifteen kilometers away, Santo Tomás, in the western part of the Zapata Swamp. Just before dawn, two more companies from this battalion found transportation and headed for the battlefield. Shortly after that, they split up after an air raid hit moments before the paratroopers were dropped. Some of the revolutionaries went into the mountains and came out at Soplillar, where they remained. Others retreated to assembly points: the sugar mill and the Los

[28] Testimony of José Ramón Fernández. Author's archives.

Alpes farm near Jagüey. A small group remained with the second-in-command.

Abraham Maciques, director of development at the Zapata Swamp, had spoken with Fidel shortly before dawn. Maciques reported that the 339th Battalion was at the Zapata Swamp. Fidel, aware of how important it was to prevent the enemy from occupying Pálpite, told Maciques to tell the battalion's commander that Pálpite must not fall to the invaders. Maciques got into his jeep and drove down the highway to Playa Larga. "I don't have any bullets," Cordero told him when they found each other. They both got into the jeep and headed back to the sugar mill. On the way there, they came across militia members from Jagüey Grande led by Antero Fernández, a Rebel Army lieutenant and chief of the Jagüey barracks. Maciques told them that paratroopers had been dropped and heavy combat was taking place on the beach. They left a dozen men in Pálpite and continued on to Australia. Fernández rode in a separate vehicle found nearby. Maciques and Cordero went ahead to warn everyone about the magnitude of the invasion and to get reinforcements.

As they were leaving the swamp, shooting broke out. It was the paratrooper platoon that was supposed to be dropped at the north end of the road to block it and prevent anyone going through the swamp to Pálpite. Due to a navigational error, the paratroopers had been dropped about a hundred meters away from the road in a low area and now they were hiding on the mountain of a cay, from where they could observe any movements on the access road. Antero Fernández was shot, apparently hit by sniper fire from the paratroopers. When the men finally arrived at the Australia Sugar Mill, they held a meeting with the head of the 339th Battalion, which Capt. José Ramón Fernández remembers.

Julián Morejón, the battalion's second-in-command, watched as the paratroopers were dropped into a field a few hundred meters from Pálpite. He and a number of militia members retreated; they had no ammunition and they were about to be taken prisoner by the invaders who had just been dropped.

A peculiar situation had been created at that time of the morning on the road from the Australia Sugar Mill to Playa Larga. On the beach, the 2nd Battalion was well-equipped with heavy weapons and waiting for reinforcements that included tanks. Between the beach and Pálpite—about four kilometers—small, scattered groups of militia members from the 339th Battalion were retreating down the access road or taking refuge in the mountains. Others were doing the same in Buenaventura, cut off from their units. More were in Soplillar, east of Pálpite. The ones who had been stationed in Caleta del Rosario had mistaken an enemy tank for a friendly one and were taken prisoner after two of their troops were killed and three wounded.

A platoon of paratroopers was near Pálpite with all of their weapons. Pálpite itself was a no-man's land, a place of nothing but fire from the paratroopers' rifles, machine guns, and mortars. More groups of militia members from the 339th Battalion were between Pálpite and the entrance to Laguna del Tesoro, along with civilians from Jagüey who were fleeing. Right outside the swamp, the other paratrooper platoon was on the mountain of a cay where they could monitor the highway, and lying on the highway was the body of Antero Fernández. None of the few revolutionary forces that were moving on the highway at dawn on the day of the landing were in a position to take on the invaders at Playa Larga—due to lack of ammunition or leadership—or to force out the paratroopers from around Pálpite, or to occupy and hold the strategically important highway. However, the resistance they had put up for three hours until dawn outside of Playa Larga and their impassioned response when the enemy shouted at them to surrender prevented the beachhead from being completely occupied. It implanted uncertainty in the minds of the invaders. Contrary to what they had been told, the militia members were not waiting to join up with them.

That was when a force of 300 men arrived at the Australia Sugar Mill from the 219th Battalion, from Calimete, Amarilla, Manguito, and Zona Rural, and the 223rd from Colón.[29] They had had very little military training and were armed with M-51 semiautomatic rifles with just twenty cartridges per weapon. Capt. Fernández

[29] The battalions from Matanzas province were numbered beginning with 2, from Las Villas with 3, and from Havana with 1.

ordered the commanding officer of these troops, Capt. Conrado Benítez Lores, to advance on the highway at top speed and take Pálpite. The battalion left but it didn't reach Pálpite. On the way there, it was attacked by enemy planes, which killed six and dispersed the troops. Later, Fernández changed his order. Given the strategic importance of this road and the possibility that the invaders might try to block it by dynamiting the drainage ditches, he ordered the battalion to protect it. Soon after that, the troops were reinforced by the 227th Battalion.

At approximately 9 a.m. the Militia Leadership School battalion arrived.

"I told them not to get out of the trucks, and I climbed on top of a truck cabin. I remember I told them that the mercenaries had landed; that the people who wanted to destroy the Revolution were on Cuban soil; that Fidel had given us the mission of repelling the landing; that they were a trained unit; that they could do it, and I ordered them to march on Pálpite....

"In Pálpite a group of the mercenary paratroopers had apparently been dropped somewhat scattered. The unit from the Militia Leadership School occupied Pálpite.... It was approximately noon. A map showed a small airstrip in the town of Soplillar. Immediately I ordered the 5th Company to march on Soplillar and occupy and block the runway.... Then I called Fidel and told him we had taken Pálpite. He said to me, 'We've won the war!' And he was right. The occupation of Pálpite was decisive because it controlled the entrance to the beachhead. In other words, we had established a beachhead within enemy territory."[30]

While one platoon of enemy paratroopers remained hidden in the woods and watched as the Militia Leadership School battalion marched to Pálpite, about ten kilometers south, another enemy platoon, which had remained near the village without occupying it, retreated in face of the militia's advance after a brief exchange of gunfire.

[30] Testimony of José Ramón Fernández. Author's archives.

308

"At dawn, the airplanes fired on the truck we were traveling in, which belonged to Carmelo Hernández. There were thirteen of us from my family and we all ran for the mountain. I was with my wife and my two children, ages six and eight. Then we ran into three paratroopers.

'Where are you all going?' they asked us.

'They told us to leave the village,' I answered.

They allowed us to go, maybe because of what they saw in us and after asking if there were any militia members around. They were going towards Girón. They seemed to be running away. 'These are bad people,' I told my children, 'but you can't say that out loud.' We spent the entire day on the mountain. We saw a plane coming and went to cross the access road. Then we saw a truck coming. It was in first gear; the driver didn't know how to handle it. We thought it was somebody we knew, but no; it was five mercenary paratroopers, one of them on the hood with a machine gun mounted on a bipod. One of them said to me, 'I need you to give me your clothes.' My father looked at him and said, 'Sure, we'll give them to you.' But another one who seemed to be the leader said to the guy who had asked me for my clothes, 'What do you want his clothes for? You people just keep going.' They asked us again if we had seen any militia members. We went back to the mountain. We made camp and prepared several cans of milk with spring water. That's the best stuff there is; I'll never forget it. Maybe it was because I was so hungry. I prepared the thickest milk for the two kids."[31]

Shortly after noon on Monday, April 17, Captain Fernández received the order to march on and occupy Playa Larga. Quickly, he sent a messenger to Pálpite.

"All of the messages were personally delivered by jeep or motorcycle. There wasn't any radio or telephone or anything… Then I confirmed that the mission for the troops from Calimete and Colón was not to advance or retreat, but to guard both sides of the entire road from Australia to Pálpite and all of the drainage ditches, because of that road's importance. I really thought the invaders were going to be more aggressive, and I imagined them in groups with dynamite,

[31] Testimony of Oscar Hernández, charcoal maker, 1990. Author's archives.

blowing places up and trying to penetrate our rearguard, given all the possibilities they had. And I was afraid they would blow up some of these ditches —all of them are made of gravel— and block traffic for a good long time. I was at the command post at the Australia Sugar Mill, with a telephone, maps on the wall and a swinging door. People were coming and going; some of them bringing information, others coming to sound the alarm.... Fidel had told me not to move, to stay next to the telephone there at the Australia Sugar Mill."[32]

The Militia Leadership School battalion of more than 800 troops began its march on foot to Playa Larga, four kilometers south. They marched in two columns, one on each side of the road. It was about 2 p.m. Once again, they were without the protection of antiaircraft artillery because it hadn't arrived yet. Shortly after they began their march, two B-26s appeared overhead. After three consecutive passes, the planes left.

One of the first militia members to fall during that attack was Claudio Argüelles.

A member of the telephone workers' union, he had been invited two weeks earlier to be part of a delegation that would visit the Soviet Union. Argüelles was enrolled in the militia leadership course in Matanzas but had received permission to be absent for two weeks. He was the leader of his militia company and his graduation was assured. His flight to Europe was scheduled for dawn on April 17, but when he heard about the invasion, he changed out of his suit and tie and into his militia uniform and headed for Matanzas. By the time he got to the Militia Leadership School, his battalion had left for the Australia Sugar Mill. He caught up with their caravan on the road and assumed command of his company.

"We were going down the road when we saw two B-26s. There was really a lot of patriotism. Imagine how it affected the troops when we passed through Jagüey Grande and saw the people out in the streets, yelling and singing patriotic songs. They were saying to

[32] Testimony of José Ramón Fernández. Author's archives.

us, 'Give it to 'em good! Clobber them!' That was in the morning. Now we were heading down the road, anxious to take them on. Then the planes flew overhead, and we all waved at them; they had the Cuban flag painted on their tails. On their second pass, they opened fire on us. The access road had drainage ditches, and that was where we took shelter. As they flew over, we shot at them with our FALs and our 7.92-mm. machine guns. Every time the planes came —because they made several passes— we ducked into the ditches, and as they flew over, we came out and fired at them. That's where they killed Claudio Argüelles. A rocket hit him full on. They also killed nineteen-year-old Félix Edén Aguada. When they left, the people regrouped and we continued our march on foot. We still didn't have any antiaircraft artillery and the planes had themselves a feast, but we kept going."[33]

The presence of the planes in the area was reported to the San Antonio de los Baños air base and two T-33s that were flying to Girón were alerted. One of them shot down one of the B-26s and the other was chased by a Sea Fury, managing to escape only with the protection of a U.S. Navy jet.

The militia battalion suffered a dozen casualties, including dead and wounded, and it became evident that without air cover, the march would be difficult, and everyone knew the antiaircraft artillery was about to arrive. The offensive was postponed. Eduardo Ferrer, in a fit of exaggeration, described the air raid as follows: "The bombers made three runs over the convoy, dropping napalm, firing rockets and strafing with deadly accuracy. The Communist casualties exceeded 500 and the road lay strewn with bodies —a scene from the Apocalypse."[34]

According to Ferrer, another air assault left the 123rd Battalion with 900 casualties. He is so unscrupulous that he says he got the number of casualties from a "report published by the enemy."

José Pérez San Román, commander of the mercenary brigade, was not far behind when he said, "According to U.S. government intelligence sources, the communist troops sustained 1,800 dead and 3,000 to 4,000 injuries."[35]

[33] Testimony of Héctor Argilés, militia member, 1990. Author's archives.
[34] Eduardo Ferrer. *Operation Puma*, p.189.
[35] José Pérez San Román: Ob. cit., p. 41.

Not only have they produced abundant theories in their search for scapegoats for their failures, but also in imagining legions of annihilated militia members, roads strewn with bodies, and Apocalyptic scenes. It is as though, after the years gone by and abundant paper and ink, the crushing defeat they suffered had turned into the most spectacular version of *Rambo*.

Total casualties for the revolutionary forces in 66 hours of battle were 156 dead and approximately 300 wounded.

Erneido Oliva, second-in-command of Brigade 2506 and leader of the defense of Playa Larga, realized there was no question after the air attack: the revolutionary forces intended to dislodge the mercenaries from the beach. He reported the situation to San Román and the Second and Third companies of the 4th Battalion were sent in as reinforcements, along with two tanks, a mortar squad, two trucks carrying heavy artillery and several bazookas. Oliva knew he could position all of his artillery, the tanks, the bazookas and the recoilless guns on the road between the Australia Sugar Mill and Pálpite. His defensive positions were excellent. The enemy would have to advance over the narrow access road, which meant only its vanguard could engage in battle. He was convinced that if the vanguard were annihilated, the rest would retreat. At least, that is what military logic indicated.

Holding the same positions, the men of E Company had battled the militia's 339th Battalion since dawn. They were upset because, for one thing, their commanding officers had not gone anywhere near the battle lines.

It was a completely different case with the militia battalions. Their commanding officers on all four fronts had placed themselves in the vanguard during the advance. And there was something else that contributed even more decisively to raising their spirits: Fidel Castro had arrived at the battlefront.

"In Jagüey, he got out of his car in front of a café and had a coffee. The people were saying, 'Now this thing will be settled; Fidel is here.' Then he came here to the sugar mill. While he was touring the place, I went up to him and asked him, 'Commander, how are things going?' And he said to me, 'Don't worry, brother, we're going to end this thing real soon.'"[36]

"Fidel got there between 3 p.m. and 4 p.m. He began to ask me about the situation... At that point, Captain Álvarez Bravo arrived with the antiaircraft artillery. One or two batteries of 85-mm. guns went by with tanks behind them. We took a look around the mill—that's the photo that went around the world and ran on the front pages of newspapers. Local people were there with good revolutionary attitudes. He gave instructions to the artillerymen. I said to him, 'Well, Commander, I want to go with my people...' The morale was good in Pálpite, but there wasn't much organization. The artillery arrived and I started arguing about how to deploy it on the other side of the village. The village was desolate and there was something I'll never forget: on the road to Playa Larga from Australia, on the left side, a house had been burned down. All that was left was the skeleton of an iron bedstead... I watched the offensive being prepared. It was about to get dark and right then, I saw two headlights; Fidel had arrived with his automobiles. Every eight or nine or ten minutes, an enemy grenade was falling there... It wasn't heavy fire from artillery batteries, but they were falling. We began arguing with Fidel. After a while, he selected Commander Borges, a dentist, to go with the 111th Battalion, enter Soplillar and come out at San Blas...[37] And we decided to organize the attack on Playa Larga for midnight. We decided to organize artillery fire in the meantime. Fidel stayed there for about forty minutes; I don't think it was as much as an hour. All of us were pressuring him to leave, for his safety."[38]

The militia battalion, ground artillery, antiaircraft units, and other military forces had been organized a little over six months earlier. They hadn't had sufficient training. The infantry and artillery battalions had passed a two-week course, but neither had gone

[36] Testimony of Dámaso Rodríguez Valdés, general secretary of the union at the Australia Sugar Mill, 1990. Author's archives.
[37] This meant traveling about twenty-four kilometers across the swamp west to east over the northern edge of the beachhead to the intersection of the road that runs from Girón to San Blas.
[38] Testimony of José Ramón Fernández. Rebel Army Lt. Roberto Milián—now a Brigade General (R)—was leading these artillery units. Author's archives.

through the practical exercises necessary before engaging in real combat. Fernández saw that for himself while he was in Pálpite preparing the artillery to attack enemy positions in Playa Larga.

"There was a battery of 120-mm. mortars commanded by a militia officer who had graduated from the first course. So I told him, 'Start firing!' The man waited and waited. Finally, after I ordered him again, he said to me, 'If I shoot here, the recoilless system is going to break.' A little bit surprised, I asked him, "What are you waiting for? For the enemy to fix it for you if you don't fire?' The back-and-forth continued and then he aimed the mortar and fired. I was anxious to hear the sound of it over there, because you can hear it more than four kilometers away. But I didn't hear anything. About a minute and a half went by, which is about how much time it takes a mortar shell to fly. And nothing. 'Ok, fire again!' I ordered him. And again, I heard nothing. So I said to him, 'Where are you firing?' And he said, 'You can't hear it when it falls into the ocean, but I'm telling you, you can hear it.' And he said, 'I'm an artilleryman.' Then I got pissed off and said, 'Listen, when you were still a little snot-nosed kid, I was working my ass off firing these buckets.' And I realized that the man was firing the rockets without attaching the fuses. Just imagine: there we are at war, firing without fuses. The most harm it could do is crush the head of whomever it fell on. But would you believe it: two days after I got to Girón, I saw the same lieutenant with a mortar, and he said to me proudly —I'll never forget— 'I only have one left, but I'm firing, and with fuses!'"[39]

On the afternoon of April 17, the 326th Battalion —made up of workers, students, and local farmers— was traveling along the coast toward Cienfuegos and Playa Girón as discreetly as a combat unit could. Captain Orlando Pupo was in command. Fidel had given him the mission of getting to within a few kilometers of Girón and halting.

"The battalion was made up of about 400 men. We didn't have any mortars or bazookas. Our convoy of more than ten trucks headed toward Cienfuegos until we reached the Abreu crossroads. From

[39] Testimony of José Ramón Fernández.

314

there, we went down to the Constancia Sugar Mill, getting there at nightfall. We kept going south along the coast. We passed Las Charcas, Encrucijada and Juraguá. From there, making our way on strips of dog's tooth rock, we slowly approached Girón from the east; they were not expecting us to come from that side."[40]

By the evening of April 17, the revolutionary forces north of Playa Larga and at Playa Girón were able —without artillery, heavy weapons, or air cover— to flush out the paratroopers from their forward positions, push them south, and reduce the size of the beachhead.

In the area around the Covadonga Sugar Mill, two companies from the militia's 111th Battalion, backed by volunteer soldiers and civilians, drove out the paratrooper battalion from its positions along the Jocuma curve. The paratroopers retreated to a point called Canal de Muñoz, where they became more confident after reinforcements arrived. From then on, the militia troops could only advance by traveling down six kilometers of access road surrounded by swamps, which meant they could not leave the narrow road. At dawn, Filiberto Olivera Moya sent out an exploration party; at night, he harassed the enemy with mortar fire.

On the Yaguaramas front northeast of Covadonga, the paratroopers had retreated at noon. Captain Víctor Dreke of the revolutionary forces had gone to the disembarkation area in a car early in the morning, and was now marching in the vanguard of two companies from the 117th Battalion that were traveling down that road to San Blas. At nightfall, he halted the troops. A little while later, they received important reinforcements: the 113th Battalion. The arrival of those troops made it possible for the first time since dawn for Commander René de los Santos, who was leading the revolutionary forces on that front, to be able to continue forward in those difficult circumstances.

In the west, in the direction of the Australia Sugar Mill/Pálpite/ Playa Larga, a dramatic battle took place early that morning.

[40] Testimony of Col. Orlando Pupo. Miguel Ángel Sánchez. *Girón no fue solo en abril*, p.189.

At the Australia Sugar Mill, Fidel was informed before dawn of another landing northwest of Havana province. He doubted it was true, but after assurances that it was, he decided to return to the capital. He was no doubt upset at leaving the battlefront but he was determined to confront the enemy at the other landing point. Since his initiation in revolutionary struggle, Fidel Castro had demonstrated impressive energy and extraordinary personal valor. Charles de Gaulle, a statesman from a place very distant from where Fidel Castro had shown his leadership abilities, had once been informed after an uprising by a group of generals in Algeria opposed to negotiating with the Algerian FLN that the main conspirator, General Challé, would be in Paris at any moment with his paratroopers. De Gaulle said, "Yes, if it were Fidel Castro, he would be here by now, but not Challé."[41]

Actually, there was no second landing. It was a diversionary operation by the CIA. They had placed ships near the coast and used sophisticated sound and lighting equipment to simulate a full-fledged landing, including explosions from guns of varying caliber. However, they did not manage to divert any of the Cuban forces engaged in battle at the Zapata Swamp. Perhaps their most significant success was to get the leader of the Revolution to physically leave the battleground.

At midnight, the Militia Leadership School battalion formed ranks on the Pálpite highway. They planned to march on the enemy in the first stage, followed by Rebel Army Column 1.

"The first to advance was Company 3, led by Professor Díaz. Captain Fernández himself said to the troops in Pálpite: 'Left, left, face front until you meet the enemy, march!' We began marching on the left side of the access road. They had told us that Playa Larga and the enemy were four kilometers away. After a while, the word was passed on quietly, 'Leave behind anything that makes any light or noise.' The mortar shells were flying overhead toward enemy positions. Later we found out that almost all of them had fallen into the ocean."[42]

[41] Nicolai Molchánov: *General De Gaulle.* Editorial de Ciencias Sociales, 1990, p. 346.
[42] Testimony of Emérito Hernández, militia member, 1990. Author's archives.

Brigade 2506's 2nd Battalion was in an exceptionally advantageous situation. They were holding their positions in an upside down V-shape, with the aim of opening fire once the militia column came near. Oliva ordered a group of five bazooka artillerymen to the left flank. From their angle, they had a broad advantage over any armored vehicle that might appear. The road leading up to them was clear. They had placed their 77-mm. recoilless guns on a small hill with one of their tanks nearby, well-camouflaged. They had mortars and heavy machine guns and had situated their infantrymen in firing position.

On the other side, the road from Pálpite to Playa Larga was so straight that the fire from the brigade's artillery would batter the revolutionary forces as they came marching down the road, even if they were one or two kilometers back, because their advance was a frontal one. Therefore, even if the fire didn't hit the column's vanguard, it would hit the center or rearguard. And that is exactly what happened.

Captain Fernández had ordered the artillery to cease fire. Four tanks emerged from the undergrowth and began advancing with their lights off. On the curve, Oliva gave the order to open fire.

"When they opened fire, we dove into the ditch on the side of the road. They had set up their 50-mm. machine guns five inches off the ground. That's why a lot of comrades were hit in the back and buttocks. Others died from the low-flying shots."[43]

"Benito Garay had said to me that afternoon, 'Hector, do you think I'll be able to see my daughter?' His wife was nine months pregnant. That night, while we were marching to Playa Girón, he was hit with bazooka fire and killed. When we got back to the school some days later, I saw a telegram saying his wife had had a little girl."[44]

When the tanks got to the forward point, Professor Díaz ordered his men behind them and started the march again. They had already entered the narrow strip of land that led directly to the enemy's trenches. They left behind dozens of wounded and dead.

Oliva ordered the 77-mm. gun artillerymen to open fire on the tanks that were approaching. The tank group's commander, who

[43] Testimony of Emérito Hernández. Author's archives.
[44] Testimony of Héctor Argilés. Author's archives.

was riding in the first tank, had seen the red lights of the shells from far off. Lieutenant Néstor López Cuba was in the exact same place where the militia members of the 339th Battalion had battled Company E twenty-four hours earlier.

"We were heading toward an area without vegetation when the tank began to veer right. I thought it was the sandy edge of the ditch and I told the driver to give it more power so that we could get off the slope, but the harder we tried to turn the other way, the harder we kept going to the right. I finally realized that they had hit one of our treads. I ordered a fragmentation shell to be loaded. We also had armor-piercing projectiles, but I couldn't see any of their tanks, so I asked for a fragmentation shell to fire on their infantry. We tried to load one into the cannon's chamber, but it wouldn't go in."[45]

Not only had one of the tank's treads been hit, but a bazooka shell had pierced its main gun. If the cartridge had been loaded into the chamber, the tank would have blown up.

"Lieutenant Díaz was marching behind a tank, and when it became disabled, he continued to encourage his men, yelling, 'Forward! I've never commanded gutsier troops!' A little while later, he was killed."[46]

"In the midst of the darkness and surrounded by firing, the men got confused. They lost track of the forward detachment, their platoons, everything. The commanding officers lost contact with their men. Each one of us marched with a small group around us, but they weren't our units. In that difficult situation, the worst thing I remember about that battle was when they started bombing us with napalm. The little fires that sprung up on the mountain lit up our positions and made us easy targets for the snipers lying hidden."[47]

Shortly after that, two more tanks fired on them, and they were ordered to halt their offensive. The men began retreating to Pálpite.

Captain Fernández sent an urgent message informing the commander in chief that the offensive had been halted and an

[45] Testimony of Major General Néstor López Cuba. Miguel Ángel Sánchez. *Girón no fue solo en abril,* p.185.

[46] Testimony of Emérito Hernández. Author's archives.

[47] Testimony of Brigade General Harold Ferrer. Miguel Ángel Sánchez. *Girón no fue solo en abril,* p.186.

undetermined number of men had been killed or wounded. Immediately, Fidel issued new orders, sending them through Commander Augusto Martínez Sánchez at the Australia Sugar Mill command post. Sánchez maintained telephone contact with Fidel, who was at Point One at dawn on April 18.

4:40 am.

From Augusto to Fernández
Fidel received your message and he informs me that I should give you the following orders:
1. You should position all the antiaircraft artillery to protect our people.
2. The tanks should keep attacking and you should reposition the units (122-mm. mortars).
3. You should deploy every single piece of antiaircraft artillery.
4. He recommends you send troops from either from the 180th or 144th Battalion, to march through Soplillar and come out in Caleta del Rosario to cut off the road to the enemy and cut them in two.
5. If necessary, they can send you the ten tanks that are about to arrive from Jovellanos.
6. You can divide those ten tanks into two groups: by highway and through Buenaventura.
7. If it is necessary to move the tanks during the day, he can send you heavy AA protection.
8. Lastly, Fidel says Playa Larga must be taken. No excuses.

—Augusto.[48]

Several aspects of this order are striking. Fidel Castro had just been informed that the offensive had been repelled on that front. Immediately, he ordered it to be renewed, this time with new elements: a circling maneuver by several tanks driven through the mountains to the village of Buenaventura, later turning around and attacking enemy positions from the left flank while simultaneously attacking again over the access road.

[48] Archives of the Ministry of the Revolutionary Armed Forces. Girón Collection.

Another significant aspect demonstrating Fidel's confidence that the invaders would be defeated was his order to send a battalion to cut off their retreat to Girón. This mission was carried out by the 144th Battalion, but when it arrived at its destination —Caleta del Rosario, a point near Playa Larga on the road to Girón— the 2nd Battalion and other reinforcements had already gone by. Actually, the 144th Battalion was delayed in leaving Pálpite because the guide had become frightened.

"Fidel always criticized us for letting those people escape, and it's true, but the battalion that was supposed to carry out this mission was waiting in their trucks for about an hour for the guide, who disappeared. So they left for Caleta del Rosario without the guide and they made it."[49]

The militia members and soldiers in Pálpite thought that the retreat signified defeat, but they were wrong. They had shown such courage in their advance that the invaders could not relax, despite the excellent positions they held.

"One of their tanks came back with wounded and dead. The wounded had to be taken to Girón because there weren't any doctors. The ones who fought and were relieved spoke badly about their officers. In the middle of all that, they brought in one of our tank operators who was taken prisoner. He was steaming mad. One of the mercenary officers asked him in front of us, 'Were you driving a tank?'

'Yes, sir.'

'And were there more tanks behind you?'

'Behind me there was a battalion of one hundred tanks and about 10,000 militia members.'"[50]

The tank operator's information was false, but it added to Oliva's worries. At 5 a.m., he told the brigade's commander that his situation was desperate. An hour later, a messenger brought the response: "Resist until death." Despite the reinforcements and their strong positions, Oliva thought their chances were slim. He contacted the head of the 5th Battalion, Montero Duque, who had managed to get to the coast and regroup almost his entire battalion after their ship was attacked with rockets. They were on the coast

[49] Testimony of José Ramón Fernández, ídem.
[50] Testimony of José Ramón Suco, militia member.

about four kilometers from Playa Larga, and would have to go through the village of Buenaventura, which was not being defended by military forces; there were just a few dozen militia members from the 339th Battalion who had become separated from the rest of the troops and a few local charcoal makers. A Cuban Navy launch was tied to Buenaventura's small dock a few hundred meters from Playa Larga. Its crew had dismounted a .50-caliber machine gun and set it up on dry land. But early on the morning of the landing, they had used up the little ammunition they had, and the gun was now silent. There was nothing to keep this battalion from heading back to Playa Larga once it was reorganized. "He told me that his battalion had had an attack, which was a lie, that it was disorganized, and that was the reason they could not arrive to help us in the fighting."[51]

Years later, one of the members of the 5th Battalion wrote an article asserting that, despite the difficulties, they had marched to Playa Larga but a militia troop had taken over Buenaventura, preventing the mercenaries from completing their mission.

"At about midday, we had gotten very close to the town of Buenaventura, and immediately Montero ordered us to halt and demanded absolute silence. He organized a patrol of five men under the command of Portuondo, a courageous and determined black man, a veteran on Trax Base. The rest of the men took their positions, mostly those who were armed, ready to battle the militias that were probably entrenched up *on the hill*[52]...because we were on a lower level of that same hill, with the ocean to our right and the swamps to the left. However, we couldn't wait any longer; we had to cross at all costs..."[53]

Lalondry is quite often inaccurate and rewrites history to the point of changing the geographic features of an area. What he doesn't realize is that landscapes don't change at the same speed as the

---

[51] Haynes Johnson: *The Bay of Pigs*, p. 138. Testimony of Erneido Oliva Norton. New York, 1964.

[52] Author's emphasis.

[53] Julio González Lalondry: *Sangre en Bahía de Cochinos*. Vanguardia Publishing Corporation. New York. 1965.

discourse of pseudo-historians. The village of Buenaventura and all of its surroundings are located above sea level. Apparently, Lalondry forgot he was talking about Zapata Swamp, or maybe, far off in the distance from the *Houston*—which he most likely never left—he imagined he saw a legion of militia members on top of a non-existent hill.

In Playa Larga, Oliva didn't think twice. His men would not be able to withstand another attack like the one early that morning. The night before, despite all of their advantages, his forces had suffered "forty to fifty wounded, ten to twenty dead."[54]

One incident illustrates the morale of the invaders at Playa Larga. After being captured by militia troops several days later, one invader told his interrogator that "…the Brigade's second-in-command, the mercenary Oliva, was interrogating a militia member who was wounded and had been taken prisoner. He was trying to obtain information about how many Cuban forces were fighting, and when the interrogation was over and Oliva was leaving, his assistant Pedro González came up to him —he (González) has no prior record, but we've learned that he belonged to the police investigation bureau of the Batista dictatorship— and asked for permission to finish off the wounded prisoner, claiming that he would be a nuisance. Oliva did not object, allowing Pedro González to decide for himself, and González immediately went back to the prisoner and shot him with his pistol, killing him. Eric Fernández states that all of the above occurred in his presence and that he was upset by such proceedings and complained to Oliva, who tried to pacify him… This upset Pedro González, who threatened to kill Eric with his machine gun."[55]

This criminal attitude, which was not generalized among the mercenaries, contrasted with how the revolutionary forces treated the defeated invaders.

During the academic conference "Playa Girón: 40 Years Later," Fidel Castro told those present:

"We arrived with our tanks and positioned them on the shore. It did not occur to us to fire or anything, but we had the tanks set up

---

[54] According to what Oliva told Peter Wyden in *Bay of Pigs*.
[55] Eric Fernández del Valle eventually held the rank of lieutenant colonel in the U.S. Army. Pedro González Fernández, for his part, has been mentioned by U.S. investigators as being linked to the plot against President Kennedy.

on the shore. All of the tanks were arriving there, facing the U.S. ships. A small light blinked once; a small light was seen and nothing more. And then, a sad story—humane and also sad. I began searching the area to see if anyone was there and I got to one place, almost one of the last houses. It was not one of the ones for tourists. When I went inside, I saw a man moaning and saying, 'Kill me, kill me.' He was lying on a hard old bed. The only light was from our flashlight. I said, 'We're not killing anybody. What's the matter?' He had a bleeding ulcer, so he was asking to be killed. I said to him, 'We don't kill prisoners. What's the matter?' When we saw that, we hurried to look for a car. Our hospital was in Cayo Ramona."

"*Fidel Castro*: Who was there [at the hospital]? Anybody here?

"*Abraham Maciques*: I was there.

"*Fidel Castro:* And who took you there?

"*Abraham Maciques:* You gave instructions. It was a little cabin next to the main house, and while we were making the rounds, you were checking everything. We heard the moaning and we didn't know who the wounded person was, and then you entered the cabin. He was lying on a cot with his hands on his stomach and kept saying over and over, 'Kill me, kill me.' You looked at him, you even touched him, and you said what was wrong with him: 'If this man does not get an operation, he'll die, because he has a perforated ulcer.' And right there, you gave orders. There was a lieutenant, and you said to him, 'I want you to be responsible for making sure this man gets to a hospital.' And that man was taken away and his life was saved. They operated on him; in fact, after his operation he was sent to a center…"

"*Fidel Castro:* I'm going to tell the rest of the story. The man was taken there. There were a lot of wounded men there and he was just one more. I didn't hear anything else about him at the time. Afterwards, I met with many of the prisoners. I had met with them previously at the Sports Palace, then in the prisons, and one day when I went to speak with one of the leaders, I'm not sure if it was San Román or Oliva, looking for information there at the Príncipe [prison], I went in there and saw a rosy young man, who came up to me and said, 'Thank you, thank you.' I said, 'Thank you for what?' He said, 'I'm the guy who was in that cabin, the one you sent to the hospital.' I said, 'How about that! How are you feeling? Are you better?' That must have been two or three weeks after the events—maybe four, I couldn't say exactly.

"So I started thinking. That man came up to me with a nice expression, apparently grateful, and the truth is, he probably was. Near Matanzas, there was a prestigious mineral spring center, San Miguel de los Baños, and I decided to do a test, telling myself that he seemed like a decent kid. So I arranged things with the people at the prison, the compañeros from the Ministry [of the Interior] and I said, 'Why don't we do a test with this guy? Why don't we send him to the San Miguel resort, to be free there?' He was freed. I thought that because of what had happened and the attitude the guy should have had, he would behave correctly.

"Afterwards, they told me what happened. I found out about twenty days later that he had been given asylum at an embassy. That is the only criticism I want to make, the only complaint I have, because I was very disappointed. Those things had happened and it was sheer coincidence that I ran into him.

"I don't remember his name now, but it should be recorded at the prisons and at San Miguel de los Baños.

"—*Luis Tornés*: We know about what you're saying, and we criticized the attitude of going to the embassy. We know who he is; they call him 'Azuquita'.

"—*Fidel Castro*: He was given asylum. I did not place the slightest condition on him.

"—*Luis Tornés*: But all of us prisoners criticized his attitude, because we knew all about it.

"—*Fidel Castro*: If that guy had behaved correctly, it would have been a factor… there could have been amnesty, reprieve, anything; there wouldn't have been any problem. But I decided to do a test, because you have an idea about your adversary; that he acts in such-and-such way, and when he appeared with that gesture, that face, he looked really young, healthy, rosy, compared to the image of when he had said, 'Kill me, kill me.' That is the human side of the story… But he should be criticized. You did? But it's a sad memory, that. He acted completely incorrectly."[56]

"At about 6 a.m. there was movement. The trucks full of mercenaries left, skidding in the sand. You could see they were in a hurry to

---

[56] Taken from Council of State transcriptions.

leave. Then we heard airplanes; we didn't know whose they were, and people brought out a white sheet and laid it out on the ground. With that same sheet, we left a little while later for the crossroads. There were a lot of bodies there."[57]

At close to 7 a.m., a scouting party from the militia's 180th Battalion led by Lt. Jacinto Vázquez de la Garza from the first graduating class of the Militia Leadership School in Matanzas, approached the crossroads where a fierce battle had been fought early in the morning of the previous day:

"I found a Dantesque scene. The dead and wounded on our side—the mercenaries had everything for holding out; a narrow, empty well-barricaded road on a slight curve in a hollow; burned-down *bohíos*; a truck, also burned, and next to it, several dead people, including a woman. Seeing that dead woman made everyone even more outraged… There was a hole with a [.50-caliber machine gun] with several dead mercenaries behind it. A few meters from the barricade, Lt. Díaz, a professor from the [Militia Leadership] school in Matanzas, was also dead, and on top of the barricade itself, several *compañeros* from the school… Despite the narrowness of the road and the .50, they'd made it this far! Since then, I've often thought that the war was decided in the minds of the mercenaries there at Playa Larga because of the heroism of the combatants from the second graduating class of the Militia Leadership School and their teachers."[58]

In the United States, one justification for the retreat of the mercenaries' 2nd Battalion and the invasion's defeat is that they ran out of ammunition. Evidently, the brigade faced difficulties with its war materiél, mostly because the ships *Caribe* and *Atlantic* took off and the *Rio Escondido* sunk. The *Houston*, for its part, had been left out of the battle. But that did not incapacitate the brigade. The 2nd Battalion in particular was supplied and reinforced at Playa Larga on Monday, April 17.

"Captain Hugo Sueiro, leader of the battalion, which eventually had a maximum of 370 men after receiving reinforcements from Capt. Bacallao's 4th Battalion, destroyed attack after counterattack

---

[57] Testimony of José Ramón González Suco, militia member. Author's archives.
[58] Testimony of Jacinto Vázquez de la Garza, leader of the 180th Battalion in Quintín Pino. *La batalla de Girón.* P.118.

by the enemy. These forces, backed by one tank at first and later by three, plus 60-mm. and 81-mm. mortars, annihilated Castro's 339th Battalion… Two of the brigade's B-26s engaged in battle to support Sueiro and his brave troops, and after inflicting innumerable casualties, they were shot down in combat."[59]

Let's leave aside exaggerations of the brigade's commander, José Pérez San Román, such as "destroyed attack after counterattack by the enemy." Actually, the revolutionary troops had retreated after the nighttime offensive and it wasn't until they advanced again hours later, at dawn, that they discovered Oliva and his forces had retreated from the beach. Let's also leave aside the claim that the enemy "annihilated Castro's 339th Battalion." The reality was very different. A single company from this battalion—and within that, its forward unit—engaged in battle and stopped the brigade's advance, preventing the mercenaries from taking Pálpite and securing the beachhead.

What is true is that Oliva retreated, and not exactly because he had run out of ammunition. During the few hours that he was at Playa Larga, at no time did he ask for more ammunition or complain to the brigade's command that he had run out.

"At about 0730 the 2d Battalion at Red Beach [code for Playa Larga] reported for first time in message traffic, saying that its position could not be maintained without air support for more than 30 minutes."[60] As we can see, it was the first time that Oliva had spoken with any urgency since their disembarkation thirty hours earlier, and he was asking for air support, not ammunition or even reinforcements, because these had been sent. Some people say that San Román ordered him to hold their position and he disobeyed. He retreated, taking considerable forces with him, as San Román himself says. And as he did so, he didn't even put up any resistance along the thirty-nine kilometers between Playa Larga and Playa Girón. This stands in contrast to Alejandro del Valle, leader of the paratroop battalion on the northeast front from the outskirts of Covadonga to Girón. Presumably, Oliva was afraid the early-morning offensive would

---

[59] José Pérez San Román. *La verdad sobre Girón*. P. 24.
[60] Document "Sequence of Events (D2 to D+2)," declassified by the CIA. In *Foreign Relations of the United States 1961-1963*, vol. 10, p. 436.

be repeated and he wouldn't be able to resist it. A tank operator who had been taken prisoner had told him that Fidel and Capt. José Ramón Fernández were in Pálpite. That was enough to make him sleepless. He may have even thought he was encircled. If he did, he was right. If he had waited a couple of hours longer before ordering their retreat, the 144th Battalion, carrying out an order from Fidel, would have arrived at Caleta del Rosario, halfway between Playa Larga and Playa Girón, but closer to the first, and cut off their retreat. Without the troop reinforcements from the 2nd Battalion, Girón most likely would have fallen that same afternoon.

Brigade 2506 was supplied by air during all three days of combat, helping them with their provisions. "In the afternoon, three C-54 transports were prepared to carry urgently needed supplies to the beaches at Girón... Approaching Girón Airport, we began the drop as scheduled. We later learned that half of the weapons had fallen into the sea. Fortunately, some had been recovered by members of the Brigade. The rest did land in the vicinity of the airfield.... Captain Manuel Navarro took off in a C-46 immediately after Goodwin and Herrera.... They were to land at Girón and deliver 8,5000 pounds of ammunition. Just before sunrise, Navarro had completed his mission. After unloading the plane, he picked up the injured Matías Farías, who had been shot down two days earlier."[61]

Three days after the battle was over, the G-2's Department of Information office in Las Villas drafted a report on the weapons and ammunition seized from the invaders at Playa Girón. Some of these figures are eloquent testimony: 672 rounds of ammunition for 75-mm. guns; 413 fragmentation hand grenades; 464 bazooka rockets; 416 60-mm. mortar rounds and 130,005 .30-caliber bullets.[62]

Therefore, it was not a shortage of war materiél that caused the mercenaries to abandon their positions at Playa Larga.

After Cuba's troops took over the beach, Capt. Fernández sent an urgent note to the Australia Sugar Mill.

---

[61] Eduardo Ferrer. *Operation Puma.* Pp. 209-214. Ferrer's summary does not include the fact that two more C-54s took off with the exact same mission.
[62] Archives of the FAR. Girón Collection.

Commander Augusto:

1. The enemy retreated from Playa Larga, which is being occupied by our troops. The enemy has moved to Girón.
2. I am transferring antiaircraft artillery and field artillery to Playa Larga to prepare for attacking Girón.
3. I hope to be able to attack during the daytime...

On the Covadonga-San Blas-Girón front in the north, the Cuban troops began marching to San Blas as soon as it was daylight. It was the most dangerous stretch, because there was nothing but swamp on either side of the access road. That gave a further advantage to the invaders' paratroop battalion, which had been reinforced with field artillery. They began to bomb the road with mortar fire. "Arteaga, a militia member, recalls, 'I was carrying a bazooka, my American bazooka, and an M-3 that I had picked up on the way... I was carrying all of that gear: backpack, bazooka, M-3. I looked like a one-man circus marching down the road... and then I felt a mortar shell go whistling by on my left. The damn thing whistled on my left, and then another on my right. I turned around and saw the spectacle. The mortar shells had fallen in the middle of a group of militia members. There were three on the ground. I knew all three. One of them was Enrique. From the waist down he was completely torn apart, and when I saw him like that, I said, 'Enrique, what happened to you?' 'They've messed me up, goddamn it. The other two are even worse.'"[63]

Their march did not stop, and fire from the mortars, howitzers and guns of the revolutionary troops also battered the paratroop battalion's lines of defense. Néstor Pino, second-in-command of the mercenaries' A Company, who was on the leading edge, radioed his commanding officer, Alejandro del Valle, to ask for more heavy weapons to stop the Cuban troops' advance. At about 11 a.m., San Román received the report. Soon after that, the 3rd Battalion, which was on the Brigade's right flank (east of Girón), received the order to march on San Blas and place themselves under the orders of the paratroopers' leader. This unit's positions were occupied by several

[63] Quintín Pino Machado. *La Batalla de Girón*. pp. 119-120.

smaller units of the 4th Battalion and a tank, which remained in the reserve.

On the way out of Girón, in the direction of Playa Larga, troops from the 6th Battalion were positioned, backed by several armored vehicles. The 2nd Battalion became part of the reserve.

Despite the calm that reigned over Playa Girón, where there was no battle taking place—there were no troops anywhere on the road to Playa Larga, either, because at that early hour of the morning, the troops under José Ramón Fernández had occupied it—San Román lied again. He sent a dramatic message to Quarters Eye: "0824—Brigade Commander reported Blue Beach under attack by 12 tanks and 4 jet aircraft. Ammunition and supplies requested."[64]

At that time of the morning, the closest tank was thirty-four kilometers away, entering Playa Larga. Shortly after that, San Román radioed in another alarmist report: "1200—Blue Beach reported under attack by MIG-15's and T-33's, and out of tank ammunition, and almost all out of small arms ammunition also."[65]

At that time, the first MIG-15 that Cuba ever received was sitting on an airbase in the Soviet Union and its Cuban pilot was either sitting in a classroom or training in the field, learning how to use that kind of fighter plane.

As he was leaving Playa Larga in a truck, José Ramón Pérez Peña saw a group of farmers walking and carrying a white flag, looking for the militia. That was why he asked if there were any farmers when he arrived in Girón. He was told they had been released the previous afternoon and ordered to return at 6 a.m. the following day.

"And where are they?"

"None of them showed up," was the answer. "All we have are five communist teachers in a cabin."

Ana María Hernández, the head of the literacy campaign volunteers at Girón, and literacy instructors Valerio Rodríguez, Patria Silva, Yoyi

---

[64] Document "Sequence of Events (D2 to D+2)," declassified by the CIA. In *Foreign Relations of the United States 1961-1963* vol. 10 p. 436.
[65] Document "Sequence of Events (D2 to D+2)," declassified by the CIA. In *Foreign Relations of the United States 1961-1963* vol. 10 p. 436.

and Gerardo were all inside the cabin. They were being guarded by Antonio Blanco, the son of a bar owner in Girón; father and son had joined the invaders. Tony was wearing a camouflage uniform. Looking out the window, the literacy teachers had recognized him, which may have been the reason he avoided talking to them.

"There were a lot of mercenaries around the cabin. You could hear gunfire in the distance and they seemed nervous. They put a tank in front of our cabin, and that scared us. 'Let's write down our names and where we're from, so they can identify us if we're killed,' Patria Silva proposed. Each one of them wrote on a piece of paper and put it in a pocket. I did, too."[66]

East of Girón, near Caleta Buena, charcoal maker Manuel Alvariño and one of his children heard voices. They looked around the area and then they saw them; it was the militia. "I explained to Capt. Pupo about the weapons I had seen in Girón while I was a prisoner of the mercenaries. But I didn't know what they were called. So I said, 'Well, there was a bulldozer with five wheels on each side without tires, with treads like tractors, with a long, fat tube with a club on the end.' He told me, 'Those are tanks.' 'Some of them were wearing backpacks with really long tails.' 'Those are for communications. I wish I had one,' the captain said. 'There are tubes that are in two parts that come together and they put them on their shoulders.' 'Those are bazookas.' Then we went to my house. That's where my family was."[67]

"When Pupo came to my house, he said to me, 'Make this pound of coffee for the troops. And instead of putting in sugar, I put in detergent. That thing foamed. When the captain saw it, he asked me, 'What've you done?' I started to cry. He hugged me, and I kept crying. Then he said to me, 'Don't cry. You're doing just fine, considering your age and everything you've gone through. We're going to strain it and when all the foam is gone, we'll drink it."[68]

Soon after that, the 326th Battalion continued on its way to Girón. Captain Pupo had orders from Fidel to remain about four kilometers

[66] Testimony of Ana María Hernández Bravo. Author's archives.
[67] Testimony of Manuel Alvariño. Author's archives.
[68] Testimony of Xiomara Alvariño, charcoal maker, 1990. Author's archives.

from Girón and to occupy it without making any noise. Fidel was sure that once the invaders were defeated they would try to retreat in that direction, thinking there wouldn't be any troops to stop them.

At the Brigade 2506 command post on Tuesday morning, some of the commanding officers were able to meet, including Manuel Artime, Erneido Oliva and Ramón J. Ferrer, head of their general staff. San Román chaired the meeting. After discussing the situation on the different battlefronts and hearing a report from Oliva on the Cuban forces that would probably come from Playa Larga, San Román proposed concentrating their forces in Girón and opening up a path to the east, along the coastal road, in the direction of the Cienfuegos area, and from there they could reach the Escambray.

"I told Oliva that it was too far away; that I was expecting an enemy attack along that road because Cienfuegos is a very big and important city, and I thought that there must be some enemy concentration there... I was sure they were coming today with help. I was sure of that...[69]

"Two weeks later, as we sat on the floor of my cell, Fidel Castro and I discussed this tactical point. Smiling, he told me that my decision had been correct, and he used the extremely Cuban expression, 'Te estaba esperando con todos los hierros' [I was more than prepared for you]."[70]

On the other side, on the way to Playa Larga, the invaders occupying the barricades understood that if something didn't happen soon, they would have to engage in battle. In the early morning hours, vehicles had passed with dead and wounded invaders, and at dawn, they had seen the arrival of a caravan with about 400 men, tanks, mortars, artillery and armored trucks that had retreated from that beach. That is why they were on alert all day; they didn't take their eyes off the road.

[69] Haynes Johnson. *The Bay of Pigs.* (Testimony of José Pérez San Román), p. 142.
[70] José Pérez San Román: *La verdad sobre Girón*, P. 51.

Twenty kilometers further, a dozen Leyland-make city buses were speeding toward Girón. The commanding officers, under the orders of Capt. Fernández, knew there were no enemy troops along the stretch of highway they were traveling. They had confirmed that themselves an hour earlier. The order they had been given was to go twenty kilometers, approximately the length of road that had been recently explored, and then stop the buses and continue on foot until they met the enemy.

These troop movements were detected by U.S. Navy jets that were monitoring the beachhead. They immediately informed the *Essex* aircraft carrier, a U.S. ship, that a long caravan of tanks and trucks was approaching Blue Beach from the west.[71]

Inside the buses, the members of the militia's 123rd Battalion held their FAL rifles in their hands and looked out at the woods and the ocean. The battalion was made up of non-military men from all walks of life and all ages: bricklayers, carpenters, schoolteachers, salesclerks, shopkeepers, dock workers, bank and office workers, telephone workers, musicians, artists and writers, Santería priests, surveyors, doctors, architects, painters and others. They were workers from the capital. Very few of them liked military life. They were carrying weapons and wearing uniforms for the same reason as 600,000 other Cubans who were members of the National Revolutionary Militias.

Maybe it was because of their lack of combat experience that they didn't pay much attention to the three airplanes painted with the colors of the Cuban flag and bearing down on them. All of a sudden, rockets and .50-caliber bullets began raining down on them. The bus drivers slammed on their brakes, and watched in horror as their windshields shattered and their vehicles were riddled with holes. The militia members trapped inside struggled to get out.

"I had been told that our planes were going to attack the mercenaries at Girón and that we would assault Girón. I decided to send the buses so our infantry could get there faster. On foot it was impossible; it's thirty-four kilometers from Playa Larga to Girón. It would have taken them at least eight or nine hours of

[71] Document "Sequence of Events (D2 to D+2)," declassified by the CIA.

walking, and that's at a good pace and without running into the enemy... They were so sure that the planes were ours that when my officers leading the caravan saw the planes, they ordered the bus drivers to continue, because they knew that at three o'clock, our planes were going to attack Girón and they thought those were the planes."[72]

Once again, that grotesque violation of the rules of war devastated the ranks of Cuban combatants. "We got out of the buses as best we could, and headed for the coast, some for the mountain... They surprised us in the middle of the road, with nothing to fire back. The artillery was behind us."[73] After their second pass, the B-26s began dropping napalm. "I didn't know what napalm was... We thought it was an expanding bomb, and because of what we thought and what we'd read, the idea was to get as close as possible so that it would have the least effect. But it was a napalm bomb and it covered us in fire. I covered my face with my rifle and my hands... Napalm doesn't go out. The people who were burning up threw themselves into the water or rolled around on the ground, but the napalm doesn't go out. When the wind blows a little bit, it revives the fire."[74]

The B-26 squadron that attacked the buses had taken off at 2 p.m. from Happy Valley and was made up of six planes. As they approached the Bay of Pigs, three of them headed for San Blas north of Girón to support the forces engaged in battle there. The other three, after learning about the Essex, turned left to Playa Larga. Two of the pilots were Americans, Billy Goodwing and Doug, another of the trainers. Each plane had taken off with a full load of rockets and ammunition for their machine guns and 6,000 pounds of napalm bombs. When the American pilots returned to base, they described their successful missions. They were euphoric. Some of them thought they were reliving the Korean War. The next morning, four more American pilots flew toward the Bay of Pigs. None of them returned.

[72] Testimony of José Ramón Fernández. Author's archives.
[73] Testimony of Humberto Valdés, militia member. Author's archives.
[74] Testimony of Humberto Valdés, militia member. Author's archives.

There was a commotion in the town of Jagüey Grande. The 123rd Battalion had suffered almost one hundred casualties including dead, wounded and those in shock from the napalm attack. "It was very hard. They didn't want to lie in bed because of the burns. We applied lotion to their wounds. Afterward they were transferred to Colón, Jovellanos, and Matanzas. The *compañeras* went with them because they had IVs and transfusions."[75]

"I cried because I thought they were losing and that the mercenaries were about to enter Jagüey".[76]

"They brought in a mercenary with a hand wound. He was the son of García Serra. He was wearing a medal of the Virgin of Caridad del Cobre. I brought him juice. 'How is it possible for you, a man who believes in a saint, to come here and kill your brothers?' I asked him. 'If they had only told me it would be like this... I came because of this saint.' 'No, you came to kill.' That man embraced me. If he is still alive and is honest, he will remember that day."[77]

Actually, that particular invader could not believe what he was seeing. Nobody in that town wanted him there, but they were treating his wounds. The town of Jagüey Grande did not have the conditions for taking care of so many wounded or evacuees. Nevertheless, its people began doing so starting at dawn on the day of the invasion.

At 6:30 [a.m.] on April 17, a truck with a loudspeaker drove through the town asking for blood donors, because the first wounded had already arrived. They also asked for provisions to set up improvised hospitals, because the only one in town had just ten beds—not enough.

The people's response left no doubt about their massive support for the Revolution. They went out to meet the truck and offered mattresses, sheets, pillow cases, and beds. The whole process was repeated several times during the first day of battle, and by the next

[75] Testimony of Caridad González, Jagüey Grande.
[76] Testimony of Carmen Cavadilla, Jagüey Grande.
[77] Testimony of Bambi Martínez Díaz, Jagüey Grande, 1990. Author's archives.

morning, the people of Jagüey Grande had set up eight hospitals with approximately 400 beds.

When the blood-soaked sheets began to pile up, a woman took a bundle of them home. "I called my neighbors," María Carmen Cavadilla recalls. "We took two rolls of clothesline, six big barrels, and organized the washtubs. Since we needed firewood for boiling the bedclothes, my youngest son, José Luis, who was eight, and a bunch of his little friends went to find some. We were boiling, washing, and ironing bedclothes for five days without stopping, but the injured people never went without clean bedclothes."

About 1,000 Zapata Swamp residents who had been evacuated from the combat zone or who had been hurt by the fighting, the death of a relative or friend, or the loss of their homes or belongings began gathering at the town hall. Someone from the town said, "I'll take a family to my house." That was enough for others to follow. Of an estimated 1,000 evacuees, about 800 were invited to stay at private homes. The rest were housed in communal spaces and the church, which opened its doors.

Eleven community kitchens were spontaneously organized. Almost every single family donated food for the combatants and the wounded.

"After the attack by enemy aircraft, the 123rd Battalion was reorganized personally by me on the spot, and the order was given to march. The next morning, the battalion got to within about five kilometers from Girón. It was then ordered to turn north, enter the forest and form columns of platoons. There were about thirty platoons for containing the mercenaries, who I was sure would flee; I had no doubt about it. This battalion was really able to recover very quickly from the air attack. After the attack, we continued marching and arrived at Punta Perdices —eleven kilometers from Playa Girón— without coming into contact with the enemy... The police battalion arrived... The offensive was organized for the next day."[78]

[78] Testimony of José Ramón Fernández, 1990. Author's archives.

21:00 hours

Commander Augusto
1. - We plan to march until we meet the enemy in Girón. We believe we can bring our lines to within two to three kilometers from Girón.
2. - We are positioning the 122s and the mortars. I request that you send me two more batteries of 120[-mm.] mortars now to be able to use them. With all of that, I'm going to fire on the enemy during the night.
3. - We plan to attack Girón at dawn with artillery, infantry, and tanks and an infantry advance.
4. - In view of experience, we believe we need a crane for removing damaged tanks. Urgently request tank tracks from Managua.

—Fernández

That afternoon, April 18, in the direction of Covadonga-San Blas-Girón, Néstor Pino, a former officer in the pre-revolutionary Cuban army and now a leader of one of the mercenary paratroop companies, asked battalion leader Alejandro del Valle for heavy weapons support to stop the advance of the revolutionary forces. Heavy machine guns and 81-mm. mortars were sent as reinforcements to La Ceiba, a point near the village of San Blas that was still being held by the invaders. The combat there was very intense.

"On a curve in the road that we identified as La Ceiba, we found a cluster of resistance. They had much more firepower than the [invaders at] Canal de Muñoz [...] That is where we suffered our heaviest casualties up until that point... We actually tried three times to take San Blas, failing the first two times."[79]

At noon on April 18, Commander Pedro Miret arrived at the Covadonga Sugar Mill leading several 122-mm. gun batteries. "He asked me, 'Is there any aspirin around here?' They gave him aspirin and made him some tea. 'Hey, where is there a room around here

[79] Testimony of Félix Duque in Elio Carré. *Girón, una estocada a fondo.* P.134.

where we can lay out some maps?' ...Then one of the men who had come with Miret took off his shoes and climbed onto a desk with a measuring triangle, and started measuring and drawing lines and talking to the other guy who was with him. 'Pedrito, what are those guys doing?' 'Look, they're taking those points of reference for positioning a weapon that has never been fired here, which are the 122-mm. guns.' Then Commander Filiberto Olivera arrived and Pedrito told him, 'Hey, Filiberto, you can withdraw the infantry for me at what time?' I said to myself, 'Shit, they're going to withdraw!' When Filiberto left, I asked Pedrito, 'Pedrito, what's this about withdrawing the troops?' 'Look, you're a militia member, but you've never trained in warfare. We have our infantry extremely close to the enemy, and we're going to fire at the enemy with a powerful weapon, which is the 122-mm. gun, and our firing could hurt our troops.' 'Oh, now I understand!'"[80]

That night, the gun batteries fired on the mercenaries' positions in Bermeja, Helechal, Cayo Ramona, and San Blas.

By the end of the second day of battle, Tuesday April 18, the beachhead held by Brigade 2506 had been significantly reduced. After occupying Playa Larga in the west, the revolutionary troops had advanced despite being attacked from the air and were at Punta Perdices, eleven kilometers from Girón. The mercenaries' 5th Battalion had become completely separated from the rest of the brigade and was hiding in Punta Cazones, in front of where the *Houston* had run aground. Almost all of that battalion's troops surrendered without resistance. In the north, the paratroop battalion had retreated to San Blas, where it was attacked with 122-mm. guns. The revolutionary forces had crossed the swamp, both through Yaguaramas and Covadonga, and were preparing to attack San Blas, fifteen kilometers from Girón. Along the coastal road in the west, on the brigade's right flank, a militia battalion was waiting for the mercenaries to retreat or scatter.

Everything was prepared to end the battle the next day, less than seventy-two hours after the mercenaries had disembarked. For the first time, the militias and soldiers of the Rebel Army on both main

[80] Testimony of Gonzalo "Chele" Rodríguez Mantilla. Author's archives.

battlefront —Playa Larga/Playa Girón and Covadonga/Yaguaramas/ San Blas/Girón— would have equipment that matched what the invaders had: tanks, mortars, heavy-caliber guns, heavy machine guns, and antiaircraft artillery. But they still did not have something very important in a war: communications equipment. All alerts, orders, reports and requests were being sent by messenger in any vehicle available.

The first combat on the last day of battle happened in the air. Back at the Happy Valley base, the decision was to send five B-26s to attack the forces that had the mercenaries practically encircled in the north and west. What the brigade's leaders did not know was that in the east, a militia battalion was within four kilometers of Girón, quietly waiting for the final outcome. Fidel had told them to be prepared "to go all out," because that was where the invaders would try to flee. The brigade's pilots were promised that a group of [Navy] jets would give them protection in the air for a little over an hour. The mission of these jets was to place themselves between the B-26s and the planes of the Cuban air force, and to attack if fired on. An error in coordination between the operation chief in Happy Valley and the naval forces resulted in the jets being in the designated area an hour too late, after everything was over.

Colonel Gar Teegan, chief of operations for the brigade's tactical air force, gathered the pilots together to tell them about their mission and the air coverage. Some of the Cubans seemed pessimistic.

"I said No, if I didn't have the air support promised. The American chief of operations told me that he would give me his word of honor that we would have air support, that they were just waiting for the word from Washington. I said we would go, but said that if we did not have fighter cover by the time we flew over Grand Cayman we would return to Nicaragua, and he said 'O.K.'"[81]

As he flew over Grand Cayman Island, [pilot Oscar] Vega did not see any Navy jets, so he turned around and returned to the base in Nicaragua.

[81] Haynes Jonson. *The Bay of Pigs*. Testimony of Oscar Vega. P.154.

Five more planes flying in a V-shape formation approached Cuba's coasts. The first was piloted by adviser Thomas Willard Ray, with Leo Francis Berliss as the navigator. Their mission was to bomb the Australia Sugar Mill, the headquarters of the Cuban forces. When the two B-26s that closed the formation were flying over the ocean near Cienfuegos, they were spotted by the Cuban air force T-33s piloted by Álvaro Prendes and Enrique Carreras. Without losing a second, the Cubans followed in pursuit. Shortly after that, the B-26 piloted by Riley Shamburger and Wade Gray fell into the sea in a ball of fire. The other B-26 flown by Joe Shannon and Nick Sedano, made a hard left turn. The pilot pushed his throttle controls all the way forward, desperately trying to gain altitude. That plane made it back to base. In another plane, Billy Goodwin and Gonzalo Herrera were approaching the San Blas zone when they began to receive heavy antiaircraft fire and were hit. They dumped their load of bombs and napalm over the mountains, spun around and accelerated in the direction of the ocean. A few minutes earlier, they had heard a radio call of "Mayday! Mayday!" It was Shamburger. Two hours later, Billy Goodwin landed with a rocket hanging from one of his wings, nose down. The rocket dragged along the ground sparking but did not explode.

"We were under attack from a B-26," Commander Augusto Martínez recalls telling Fidel by telephone at the time, as the B-26 piloted by Thomas Willard Ray and Leo Francis Berliss was making its first pass over the Australia Sugar Mill. "And the antiaircraft artillery?" Fidel asked. "Are they firing?" "Yes, Commander." "Are the antiaircraft guns well-positioned?" Six four-barreled antiaircraft guns were positioned on the ground and on truck beds in the sugarcane fields and firing at the enemy planes. The telephone conversation continued as the B-26 made its second pass. Fidel kept asking if the antiaircraft guns were firing. At one point in the conversation, he assured Augusto that they could shoot down the planes. He was right. The plane, riddled with bullets, lost altitude and slid over a canefield. An explosion tore the right engine off and it rolled away, killing an ox near a *bohío*.

The two pilots abandoned their plane without major injuries and ran in different directions into the cane fields. A group of militia members surrounded the area and began searching for them. The militia group's leader repeatedly told his men not to open fire on the pilots as they pursued them. It was Commander Oscar Fernández Mell. He knew how important it was to take the two men alive. The battle was about to end and none of the pilots who had been shot down had been captured. The pilots who were able to eject before their planes fell into the ocean had been rescued by ships from the U.S. fleet that remained near the beaches where the battle was taking place. But when the militia troops found the B-26 pilots and urged them to surrender, the pilots opened fire. The outcome was fatal. Perhaps, aware of the seriousness of their actions —neither Eisenhower nor Kennedy had authorized U.S. forces to participate directly in battle— they had decided to escape any way they could or die trying. That is the only explanation for why they fired on their captors. That is how the first combat ended on the morning of the last day of battle, but the battle itself was decided on the ground in the following hours after fierce fighting.

At dawn on the 19th, the revolutionary forces began their march. Near Covadonga, Commander Félix Duque placed himself at the head of his troops. Mortar shells soon began raining down on the troops. "They were really punishing us. I was lying on the ground near 'Gallego,' a guy I knew from the Civic Plaza. We were together and they were hitting us hard. They were hitting us hard. We couldn't even raise our heads. Mortars were whistling overhead."[82]

The mercenaries' 3rd Battalion, supported by two armored vehicles, began a counteroffensive against the militias and held them back momentarily. After a brief attack using their 122-mm. guns, the militias continued their advance and the mercenaries' 3rd Battalion began a chaotic retreat. Alejandro del Valle dismissed the leader of this battalion, Noelio Montero, and replaced him with Roberto San Román.

"We began an offensive that was stopped in its tracks."[83]

"We advanced on San Blas under the mortar fire. One company went in and then another. We occupied Kilometer 14 and kept marching on San Blas."[84]

[82] Víctor Casaus. *Girón en la memoria*, Editorial Letras Cubanas, 1982, p.149.
[83] Statements by Julio Mario Alonso Fernández, invader. MININT archives.
[84] Testimony of Rebel Army Commander Filiberto Olivera Moya, 1990. Author's archives.

East of Covadonga, on the road to Yaguaramas —which also led to the village of San Blas— a heavy offensive was prepared with eight tanks, one company riding in trucks and the infantry behind. That force, led by Captain Emilio Aragonés, was three kilometers from San Blas. The invaders were not expecting that kind of attack there. The offensive was set for 9 a.m.

It was on the coastal road that the first and only combat between the two forces took place. Protected by a tank, a company from the brigade's 3rd Battalion came into contact with an advance of twenty of Pupo's men. The revolutionaries fired on the tank with a bazooka, hitting its tread. The company that was marching behind the tank stopped and after an exchange of fire, they retreated.

"I was going to order them to fire again with the bazooka. It was going to be an easy job, because we could surround it once the infantry's protection was gone. But no, the tank was there, immobilized, without giving any signs of life... Our comrades ran from the left side, by the shore, and climbed onto the tank. They opened its hatches and aimed inside, yelling, 'Surrender! Surrender! It's over for you!' Nobody responded. No, it wasn't a tank with a phantom crew. They had a hatch in the floor, and the crew got away without us realizing it."[85]

Also at dawn that day, the advance had begun on the road from Playa Larga to Playa Girón. Commander Samuel Rodiles placed the light combat company from the 116th Battalion in the first echelon. That battalion had arrived the night before at Punta Perdices as part of the National Revolutionary Police battalion. The company's mission was to explore Girón's western side and find the invaders who were defending that position. The company was divided into two groups. On the left, on the forest side, was a group headed by Sandino, a police captain; on the right, on the shore side, another group was led by Capt. Carbó, also from the police battalion.

[85] Testimony of Orlando Pupo. In Miguel A. Sánchez. *Girón no fue solo en abril.* P. 225.

Captain Fernández had positioned the field artillery and was firing over Girón. "So we transferred everything to the artillery positions about four kilometers from Girón. We had four batteries of 122[-mm. howitzers], an incomplete battery of 120[-mm.] mortars, a battery of 85-mm. [guns] and another that was added later.

"We ordered spotters to be placed on the front lines as we finished setting up the artillery on rocky, uneven ground. Despite all the resources we used, the spotters could not pinpoint the enemy's positions because of the uneven ground and thick vegetation.

"So we ordered the 120[-mm.] mortars to begin firing, keeping in mind that the enemy was 4.2 kilometers away. The artillery was a little further back. The guns were spaced about forty meters apart. In view of the lack of information and the need for saturation fire to batter the entire area, we ordered the four batteries to be placed at the height of 3.8 km and to begin firing, with three salvos at the same height, followed by 100-meter increases. This resulted in eighteen shots from the first salvo falling on the first position, but immediately, the gun behind fired eighteen shots at that position, and so on successively every 100 meters, until reaching 4,800 meters.

"That was how all of the batteries changed their direction, firing 300 meters to the right and pulling back the line of fire the same way they had pushed it forward. When they returned to the shortest position, about 3,800 meters, they changed their direction again, firing 600 meters to the left, moving the line of fire forward again until reaching the maximum distance.

"We think that all of the enemy's weapons and all of their positions were inside the rectangle that we formed and saturated with our fire.

"It had effective results, and after the enemy had been destroyed, we seized numerous heavy weapons, mortars, and recoilless guns that had been directly hit by our artillery. Some of the mercenaries we took prisoner wanted to know the procedure we had used for adjusting our fire and making it fall on them continuously."[86]

Shortly after the artillery attack began at 9:14 a.m., José San Román, the commander of Brigade 2506, radioed the *Blagar*: "Blue Beach under attack by two T-33s and artillery."

---

[86] Report on the operations at Playa Girón by Commander José Ramón Fernández, September 18, 1961. Document declassified by the Cuban government during the academic conference Playa Girón: 40 Years After.

The chances were not at all good for the police and militia members who were marching to Girón, forced to spread out along the reefs between the access road and the shore in a space about twenty to forty meters wide, and on the edge of the access road bordering the mountain. There was little they could do to protect themselves. And the march had its price.

"When we were already on the left flank of the access road, compañero Sandino began marching along the opposite flank. During the march we got bad news: our compañeros in the militia, who had little combat experience, did not realize as they were marching along the right flank that they were walking over a trench made of rocks that the mercenaries had built between the access road and the ocean. They killed several of our militia compañeros there; they let them come close and then fired at them practically at point-blank range... Afterward, we were able to confirm why we took so many casualties on that curve in the road: it was because they had a tank and artillery pieces positioned there. On a stretch about 500 or 600 meters long, they inflicted a lot of casualties on us, because we couldn't dig any trenches. We didn't have anywhere to take shelter. In total, I believe we had about thirty-two deaths and one hundred wounded."[87]

That excruciating situation lasted for a number of hours, but the light combat company of the 116th Battalion and the forward units of the police battalion did not retreat or halt their offensive. "I stopped the trucks next to the tanks and we advanced on foot. We walked right into the middle of a hail of bullets. We took cover in the ditch. We advanced; there was another tank close to us. We saw gunfire coming from the coast and more fire coming from the left side of the road, where all you could see was the forest. It is undeniable that they had prepared a good defense, going from the coast, over the two roads to Girón, which fork at that point and circle, skirting around Girón and meeting up with the road that goes to San Blas. The coastal road is the one that goes into town. That's where Commander Samuel was engaged in battle, next to the ocean."[88]

[87] Testimony of Major General Samuel Rodiles. In Elio Carré. *Girón, una estocada a fondo.* P. 177.
[88] Testimony of Brigade General Efigenio Ameijeiras. *Bohemia* magazine, July 1989.

Brigade 2506 commander José San Román had sent Erneido Oliva to take command of that area, with the 2nd Battalion and another tank as reinforcements.

That is why the revolutionary squads commanded by Captain Carbó and advancing along the shoreline received such deadly fire when they got to the crossroads. They were hit from the middle and from the left flank. To make things worse, only the group in the vanguard could fire back at the enemy, while the rest remained behind in the area hidden by the curve.

The invaders, realizing that another group of troops was marching through the mountain, turned part of their flank in that direction. A tank was placed at the edge of the brush. At that moment, several T-34 tanks appeared. Fierce fighting broke out. When he saw the tanks, Captain Carbó ordered his people to get behind them and march.

A barrage of lead was fired squarely at the men marching behind the tanks. "Carbó was a few meters behind me, and gave the order to the compañeros. He began urging them on, encouraging them and going from one side to the other on foot, constantly exposing himself to the fire. Some of the compañeros who were there told us that they said to him several times to be more careful, not to get so excited, because he could be wounded, and besides, he was the only captain there at that moment. And sure enough, a few minutes after crossing the access road from the tanks to the sea grape trees on a little hill there, he was hit in the left shoulder. But he kept encouraging his comrades and firing his FAL. He was so unlucky, that a few minutes after that, he got hit in the face; he fell, mortally wounded. And in all honesty, without trying to make this sound dramatic, he wouldn't let go of his FAL. He died facing the enemy and clutching his FAL in his right hand. He was the most outstanding of our comrades, the most determined, just like in the Sierra Maestra."[89]

A perforating projectile pierced the tank that was protecting the troops from the 116th and police battalions. Three crew members climbed out, their overalls in flames. The driver had driven the tank from

[89] Testimony of Major General Samuel Rodiles Plana. Elio Carré. *Girón, una estocada a fondo* P.182.

344

Managua, almost 300 kilometers away, because they had not been able to obtain any appropriate transport for the tanks. When they got to the battlefield, another tank driver realized how tired his comrade was and proposed relieving him. "If I've made it this far, I'm in for the fight," was the answer. He died soon after that, as they entered Girón.

The second T-34 that reached the curve also was bombarded. "It was as if a rocket had blown up in our heads. I was thrown back and slammed really hard against the dividing compartment. A red ball was spinning around inside. One of my comrades ended up with his guts hanging out, disfigured."[90]

Under enemy fire, the forces under Commander Samuel Rodiles continued their march, inch by inch. One crucial moment in the "battle of the crossroads" came when the crew of a Sau-100 self-propelled gun began firing directly on the mercenaries' positions. It hit an M-41 tank manned by the second-in-command of the brigade's tank company. Alemán and his crew were killed, and the tank was out of the battle. Then the militia members and police concentrated their rifle fire on the defensive triangle of the brigade's 2nd Battalion. The casualties they inflicted included two machine-gunners who had been sweeping Giron's defense perimeter from the turrets of their multipurpose trucks.

Erneido Oliva ordered six of the invaders' bazooka operators to concentrate their fire on the curve, where the crossroads opened up that gave access to Girón. He also positioned three trucks there with heavy multipurpose machine guns, and ordered the leader of the mortar battery, Julio Díaz, to maintain sustained fire on the coastal access road. "The barrage of mortar fire came, hitting a boulder. The explosion was so big that it killed five of the police compañeros who were there with me, shoulder to shoulder with me. I stayed really still; I felt like I was exploding. I could taste dust and blood... Then I saw another police compañero with a very big wound behind his arm."[91]

Oliva followed that procedure because he knew that if didn't stop the advance of the revolutionary forces, they would break through

---

[90] Testimony of Roldán Anglada. Tank driver. Miguel A. Sánchez. *Girón no fue solo en abril*, p. 227
[91] Testimony of Jorge Travieso. Miguel A. Sánchez. *Girón no fue solo en abril*, p. 228.

the front and enter the tourist area, the last position held by the mercenaries. According to Peter Wyden, Oliva "massed seven of the tubular weapons [bazookas] along a curve, together with the men of the Sixth Battalion. The Second Battalion arrived from the beach. Oliva placed it in reserve. Then came three Brigade tanks. He stationed them pointing at the curve... One Brigade 81-millimeter mortar squad fired so fast that its weapons started to melt."[92]

Oliva also ordered the leader of the 2nd Battalion's Company G to advance and push back the police and militia members who were marching along the shoreline. The company was supported by a tank. "The tank was positioned and it began coming toward us. At that moment, the only comrade who had an anti-tank grenade was Lt. Sosa. You could say that we were out in the open. The tank moved forward and stopped about thirty meters away from us, between the uvas caleta trees and the little hill. They couldn't see us, but we could see the upper part of the tank's turret and its antenna. That's when the order was given to Lt. Sosa."[93]

The explosion didn't hit the tank, but it shook the ground and sufficiently scared the crew members, who must have thought that more accurate throws were coming. They turned the tank around and began to retreat. Actually, the police did not have any more grenades. Their best support was the fire from the 122-mm. howitzers.

Erneido Oliva watched the tank retreating along with the second company of the battalion he was commanding. He ordered Ruiz Williams from the heavy weapons battalion to go to headquarters for more ammunition. But Williams couldn't get there because of the fire from the artillery units under Lt. Milián and Capt. Fernández.

"I was coming back in the middle of the road there in Girón when the *guajiro* told me, 'look at the blasting.' I heard the blasting two or three times and then it stopped so he said, 'This is very close, very close, Williams.' and I said, 'Which one?' As Williams

---

[92] In the opinion of José Ramón Fernández, this claim about the melting mortar barrels was exaggerated.

[93] Testimony of Major General Samuel Rodiles Plana in Elio Carré. *Girón, una estocada a fondo.* P. 184.

turned to look, a shell exploded next to him 'and I was blown up in the air and there was a truck there. I was so high in the air I saw the .50 caliber machine gun on the truck below me. So I landed. When I came down I started looking for Vila, and he was almost dead, but I saw some movement in him. I could not move one side because I was hit in the neck.' He called out to ask if his men were all right, and the *guajiro,* although badly wounded, said he was 'O.K.'" [94]

"Milián had guided the jeep to within a few meters of the battle line. His vehicle hit by numerous bullets and it was a miracle none of us were injured, because the enemy saw the jeep and tried to put it out of commission. Milián climbed a tree and from there watched the fire from the artillery that he had been leading since dawn under Capt. Fernández. After each shot, he climbed down the tree and used the jeep's radio to call in and adjust their fire." [95]

The decision to keep marching, which was made after the tank and Company G retreated, was what determined the final outcome of the battle in favor of the revolutionary forces. "A little while later, we occupied another of the enemy's trenches. We found some dead militia members there, some of them inside the rock trench and others on the access road, right next to the trenches." [96]

At close to midday, Capt. Fernández got a message from the command post at the Australia Sugar Mill:

Fernández:
Ast: I am sending you a battery of 120[-mm.] mortars under the command of Lt. Eduardo Rodríguez, to be placed under your orders. I am sending two copies of communications from the General Staff:
They sent a company from the 120th Battalion to Buenaventura, where they say they've taken two prisoners and there are about thirty more.
We've taken San Blas.

[94] Haynes Johnson. *The Bay of Pigs.* P. 167.
[95] Testimony of Orlando Pérez Díaz in *Playa Girón: derrota del imperialismo.* Ediciones Revolución, Havana, 1962, Volume 1, p.224.
[96] Testimony of Major General Samuel Rodiles Plana. Elio Carré. *Girón, una estocada a fondo.* P. 184.

The other compañeros are going to take Girón if you don't hurry up.

One of our helicopters is going to Australia and Yaguaramas at top speed.

Note: I don't have the 122-mm. howitzer ammunition. I've asked for it.

It was true. At about 11 a.m., San Blas had fallen to the revolutionary troops who had marched from Covadonga. Soon afterward, they were joined by the forces who had marched down the Yaguaramas road.

The mercenaries' 3rd battalion was retreating toward Girón, and Alejandro del Valle was positioning his defense when something completely unexpected happened before his very eyes.

A jeep with a Rebel Army commander pulled up in front of them. The commander was serene. "As they were forming their position, the paratroopers were astonished to see a jeep driven by a captain in Castro's militia come racing straight into their lines. Sitting beside the captain was Major Félix Duque, one of the top enemy commanders.... In the mistaken belief that the forces coming from Covadonga already had taken San Blas and moved south, he took a short cut—straight into the lap of the Brigade... "Let's hang these communists."... Duque answered: "You don't know what's coming toward you. I have five thousand men and fourteen tanks. You'd better surrender." [97]

Commander Duque's gesture left no doubt about the high morale and determination of the forces battling the invaders.

Actually, the forward troops under Duque's command were marching from San Blas under Capt. Víctor Dreke. "Our forward detachment had been ordered not to stop. When we got to a large curve in the road, I ordered a halt. I did not observe any strange movements and gave the order to continue marching. We had advanced about twenty steps when they opened extremely heavy fire on us." [98]

Dreke was hit and removed to the rear as the militia troops fired back. Two of the militia's tanks advanced over the road and a third

[97] Haynes Johnson. *The Bay of Pigs.* P. 158.
[98] Testimony of Capt. Víctor Dreke. Miguel A. Sánchez. *Girón no fue solo en abril,* p. 235.

over a field nearby. One of the tanks was disabled after it was fired on by a recoilless gun, and another was hit while a drama was unfolding inside it. The driver was asking the artilleryman over the intercom to fire, but the artilleryman couldn't hear him. They had confused the system's switches, and the driver's voice could be heard very clearly outside, as if he were speaking over a loudspeaker. "It was therefore impossible for the artilleryman to hear him, and then I heard him again from my tank when he said to the artilleryman, 'You see, goddamn it! They hit me because you didn't fire...'" The reality was, at that time we had almost no experience in handling tanks. We had just recently received them, and in fact we were taking classes when the attack happened."[99]

The militia columns continued their march on both flanks under enemy fire. Down in a ditch, a [militia] combatant threw a grenade into a machine-gun nest on the other side, blowing it up, and a few minutes later, one of the artillery trucks used by the 3rd Battalion to defend that point exploded.

"Step by step, the paratroopers, the Third Battalion and the two Brigade tanks were beaten back. Their ammunition was nearly expanded. By two o'clock Castro's tanks had formed a solid line and were firing straight into the Brigade position."[100]

Roberto Pérez San Román, the heavy weapons battalion leader who had replaced the leader of the 3rd Battalion dismissed by Alejandro del Valle, remembered that battle years later. "They hit so many men we knew we had to leave. Some men had already left and we only had about forty men left. So we decided to retreat."[101]

At about 5 p.m., the militia and Rebel Army troops and tanks took over a small settlement called Helechal just six kilometers from Girón. It was afternoon, and midnight that night would mark seventy-two hours since the landing of Brigade 2506. Completely defeating them within that time period was a challenge for the Cuban government.

---

[99] Testimony of Ramón Martínez, tank driver. Elio Carré. *Girón, una estocada a fondo*. P. 190.
[100] Haynes Johnson. *The Bay of Pigs*. P.159.
[101] Haynes Johnson. *The Bay of Pigs*. P.159.

And it was at that point so close to Playa Girón, right before nightfall, that Commander Fidel Castro arrived.

After talking to the officers who were there and getting detailed information about the troops, Fidel climbed onto a tank and addressed everyone. According to Captain Ángel Fernández Vila, his words were: "The enemy is trying to re-embark and make the world think that our attack was pathetic. We will not allow a single one of them to escape! Forward! We will not stop until we reach the beach! If the first one falls, the second one steps up; if the second one falls, the third steps up, but we are getting to that beach now. We will not stop our tanks until their treads are wet from the waves, because every minute those mercenaries are on our soil is an affront to our homeland."

A combatant from the Sierra Maestra's Column 1 remembers that moment. "He said the first tank would go full speed ahead, firing, and behind it would come the second, and then the third, and so on, all firing. If the first one broke down, the second would keep advancing and firing, and keep going like that to Girón. And referring to us, the infantry, he said 'You all have to go in behind the last tank, forming a line of fire.' He assigned a commander to each tank, I think to set an example, and then he went to climb into the third tank. People shot after him.

'Not you, Fidel, you're not going.'

'I am going, I'm in charge here!'

'Not you, Fidel, not you!'

As they argued, Lt. Joel Pardo, who was in his tank and had been doing battle since dawn, said to him, "Okay, commander, I'm going." [Pardo recalls,] "I said that with the purpose of gaining time; in case he decided to go, I would have gained quite a lot of ground, arrived at the beach or made contact with the enemy."

Maciques remembers the end of that argument between Fidel and the troops:

"And Fidel's answer was an answer that left us all stunned. The way Fidel told us energetically that he was the leader of the Revolution, and as leader of the Revolution, he had the right; he had the right to fight and to enter Playa Girón just like the rest of the compañeros… And people got quiet; everybody got quiet there."

And Fidel left in the tank.

He did not know that a few hours earlier, the brigade's commander, José Pérez San Román, had destroyed [their] radio and headed east to the mountain with forty more invaders. They were moving along the shore, toward a cordon formed by the 336th and 329th battalions under the orders of Captain Orlando Pupo and Commander Raúl Menéndez Tomassevich. They had reinforced that front a few hours earlier to prevent the invaders from fleeing.

In the west, the police and militia troops burst into Girón after an attack by the Cuban air force: two B-26s, two Sea Furies and two T-33s. It was the culmination of three days of non-stop battle for Cuba's aircraft. They had shot down eight B-26s; sunk two ships and three landing crafts, and flown many missions to give air coverage to the movements of the revolutionary troops.

"At 5:30 p.m. we all entered Playa Girón. On the second curve, in a ditch behind a mound of sand, we could see a destroyed tank and a dead mercenary on top of it. Further on, there was another destroyed tank, and then a commando truck with a destroyed .50-caliber [machine gun] on its platform. A severed leg is lying in a ditch. Its body might be nearby, still alive. Everywhere you looked there were abandoned weapons on the beach and in the little village, especially large-caliber guns, mortars and bazookas. There were three tanks and several artillery trucks with .50-caliber machine guns. There was an explosion of joy, of immense joy on the faces in that sea of people who were entering Girón: police, civilians, militia members, Rebel Army soldiers..."[102]

Captain Fernández also entered Girón on top of a tank. Far out on the ocean, the silhouettes of two U.S. destroyers had vanished. But two hours earlier, they had been within firing range of the artillery under his command.

"Hit the ships, Captain! Hit the ships, Captain!" Fernández looked out at the ocean and saw two warships inside of Cuba's territorial waters —at that time, just three miles— coming dangerously close to the coast off Playa Girón. Sixty-two hours had passed since he was woken up at the Managua base by the students telling him Fidel was calling over the radio. Like the men accompanying him, he

---

[102] Testimony of Brigade General Efigenio Ameijeiras. *Bohemia* magazine, July 1989.

was hungry, thirsty, and exhausted. But up until a few seconds earlier, he had felt euphoric; victory would come in a matter of hours, perhaps just two. The large pocket of his olive-green shirt was stuffed with dozens of messages. He remembered the last one, which he had received at midday and which said provocatively, "The other compañeros are going to take Girón if you don't hurry up."

As he looked through his Zeiss binoculars, the U.S. destroyer *Eaton* seemed to have its guns out, ready to open fire. On the back of his neck, Fernández could feel heat from the eyes of all of his men as they passionately demanded, "Hit the ships, Captain! Hit the ships!"

All of a sudden, he found himself at a dramatic crossroads, like something out of a Greek tragedy. "Why me?" he might have wondered. The Revolution to which he had given himself body and soul had sped up his heart rate, and like the entire Cuban nation, he had been experiencing one tachycardia after another.

But now as he stood on the cliff looking through the binoculars, he felt himself stiffening with an enormous weight on his shoulder like something he had never felt before, and he wished other top leaders were there so he could consult them.

But he was alone, completely alone. There was no communications equipment; during the battle he had used messengers who had to travel long distances. And he didn't have time. He had to make an immediate decision.

To make things even more complicated, small boats could be seen moving between the coast and the ships. Apparently, some were coming ashore and others were leaving. If he gave the order his artillerymen were clamoring for, he would surely hit the destroyers, inflicting casualties on the U.S. Navy. He did not know that was precisely the pretext sought by the hawks of the Pentagon and CIA to prevent the invasion from being a total failure.

Admiral Burke, General Lyman Lemnitzer, Dulles, Bissell and others held a late-night meeting full of reproaches and heated looks at the White House Oval Office. They had demanded authorization from the president for an escalation that would lead inevitably to direct intervention, but he had categorically refused. If a large number of officers and sailors were killed and wounded and the media covered it with sensationalist articles, Kennedy would have no choice but to give a green light to the military. The Cuban people would be immersed in a merciless war, defending their homeland inch by inch, city by city, house by house, mountain by mountain, at the cost of thousands or even millions of lives, until death or until the last of the invaders was driven into the sea.

Fernández ordered the 85-mm. guns and tanks to be lined up at the water's edge. To their left, he lined up the ten SAU-100 self-propelled heavy guns. "Not the ships, the boats," he ordered.

He was not willing to create a pretext for reprisals and an escalation of the war. Moreover, he reasoned that it would be illogical for the destroyers to engage in battle and attack without air cover.

Fernández was an imposing officer, a professor of officers and cadets. Nobody would dare question his orders. The artillerymen began firing at the boats, very close to the U.S. warships. So close, in fact, that some of those shots may have caused officers aboard the *USS Eaton* to believe they were being fired at.

"Captain Perkins, also on the bridge, thought they had been bracketed.[103] The ship's gunners were ready. They asked for permission to return the fire.

"Cruchfield refused. He did seriously consider returning the fire. If the shells had landed 'any closer,' he would have…Now was the time to stay cool…

"He told Pete Perkins to get under way. Followed by the *Murray*, they moved east, away from the beach and enemy fire."[104]

"It is true that the ships retreated. At that moment, I had the impression that the war was over, and I felt an enormous silence in my head, as if I was floating on air —that was how intense the decompression was for me."[105]

During the academic conference "Playa Girón: 40 Years Later," Commander in Chief Fidel Castro, who is accustomed to making

---

[103] This is one long shot and one short, which in artillery slang means they had pinpointed the target and the next shot would hit it.
[104] Peter Wyden. *Bay of Pigs*. P. 282.
[105] Testimony of José Ramón Fernández.

decisions of great importance, reaffirmed his approval of Fernández' decision, asking him in a joking tone, "Who did you consult?"

Fernández spread his arms wide in a supplicating gesture and with a hint of a smile answered, "I was alone. Who was I going to consult, the gods?"

The militia members, police, and Rebel Army soldiers began searching the tourist cabins and took about twenty men prisoner. Those who were wounded were sent immediately to medical posts. Suddenly they found a group of kids.

"At dawn on Wednesday the 19th, it seemed like the world was ending. At about 10 a.m., they took us out of the cabin and led us down to the breakwater. Two mercenaries kept guard over us. In the afternoon, we found ourselves in the middle of fire from both sides and bombs from our aircraft. We went into the water, into a rocky little hole, and at about 5 p.m., the two mercenaries said they were going to see what was going on. They dropped their weapons and ran off. It had become extremely quiet. We left too. We saw Mariano Mustelier and he told us they had gone. So we got a white sheet from a cabin and went out in front of the club. One of my eyes was very inflamed and I could hardly see. Right then, some police came, and we told them who we were, but they asked us for identification. That was when Patria Silva began to cry. 'How can you ask us for identification?' she said to the police. Then the police took us away. They carried me, because I felt really ill. Valerio, the fourteen-year-old literacy volunteer, was psychotic. He was yelling that the planes were coming. He was in very bad shape. And Patria was crying because the police had confused her. She never cried for the three days we were held prisoner."[106]

Days later, U.S. President John F. Kennedy admitted to the world that his administration had been behind the invasion and he assumed all responsibility. One of his final comments was, "Victory has a thousand fathers; defeat is an orphan."

[106] Testimony of Ana María Hernández Bravo, 1990. Author's archives.

About 1,200 of the defeated invaders were hiding in the mountains and trying to escape. They changed into the clothing of peasants at nearby homes to try to break through the encirclement.

"Our house was riddled with shrapnel. We found pistols under the mattresses. The closet was almost empty. They had taken all our clothing. They broke our lantern. I watched as my dad hid a portrait of Fidel. 'Dad, are you scared?' I asked him. 'No, honey, I'm not scared. I just don't want those people to break this.'"[107]

[107] Testimony of Bernarda Hernández Rodríguez, charcoal maker, 1990. Author's archives.

Epilogue

I am absolutely sure —and I say this in all frankness— that it was very fortunate that the invasion failed. It was very fortunate for us, and for the United States too, because Vietnam would have come about in Cuba instead of Vietnam.

They anticipated the success of the expedition and the taking of that piece of land, and they had the members of a new government aboard a plane with their bags ready to land on an airfield that the Revolution itself had built a few months earlier as part of developing the poorest part of the country. (This is why I knew the area like the back of my hand, because I had been there often, enthusiastic over its development.) Considering all this, I believe that had such a government established itself, the OAS no doubt would have recognized it immediately and the United States would have intervened militarily. In the case of certain platoons or battalions, the OAS would have called the shots and the United States would have provided the troops, just like what happened later in Santo Domingo and elsewhere.

I am convinced of that, because I remember very well the mood of our country and I know our people very well—that's why I said it was as if we had come out of an effort that seemed impossible, very difficult. Hundreds of thousands of armed men and women would have put up resistance and millions of citizens would have battled the U.S. troops, because our troops there would have had behind them determination and honor.

Our country had had the experience of a ten-year struggle, from 1868 to 1878, where there were no airplanes or anything else, but it

357

was heroic. Battle was waged for thirty years, our people were imbued with that tradition, and those of us who were leading at Girón were imbued with it and proved capable of transmitting it to our people.

It was not a question of socialism or communism that determined the attitude of the people at the time. It was hatred of the blood-soaked Batista regime, the thousands of people murdered, the immorality and the plunder; it was admiration for a group of young people, none of whom were known very much at all. I was a little more well-known because I had been a leader at the university. It was the people's admiration for those who had achieved the impossible feat of overthrowing that well-armed regime—80,000 men, including soldiers, sailors, and police—and for the laws passed by the Revolution, above all those giving dignity to citizens.

When ordinary citizens became the power, the power was identified by its weapons, and they had the weapons in their hands...

We were able to bring whole battalions to their knees, hundreds of men, and afterward we took thousands of men as prisoners. They were our weapons suppliers, because nobody else supplied us. We had not been a Vietnam in the sense of anyone being able to get a single bullet to us; rather, our entire mentality and our entire consciousness and experience were to have armed ourselves with the weapons that we captured from the enemy's soldiers.

That is, someone might ask, "You were able to resist?" Yes, we were able to resist; we were absolutely confident, and we still believe it, which is the most important thing. Who knows how long, who knows the cost of how many hundreds of thousands of Cuban lives and—without a doubt, without a doubt!—you could talk about tens of thousands of U.S. lives. I am convinced, moreover, that it would have produced an extraordinary complication in the world. But we weren't counting on complications in the world; we were counting on ourselves, exclusively. We knew that if there were a war, there would be no way to help us, no matter how strong the desire and will of another international power.

It would have created a very great danger of war, some have said. The Soviets no doubt would have reacted; in Berlin, no doubt, the situation would have become extraordinarily complicated. It could have been a danger similar to the October [Missile] Crisis, which somebody said was the most serious danger ever of a nuclear war.

But for Cuba, and without missiles here, a tremendous complication could have been created—I say this placing myself in that exact moment—if the invasion had been successful, if they had been able to install a government, which would have led inexorably to a U.S. invasion.

So we should be glad. Here there is talk of some being victorious or successful and others not being successful or being defeated. And really, if we're going to be consistent, I think that both you and we should be glad that it was a failure. And I hold a very deep conviction: if it had been Nixon instead of Kennedy, then the U.S. forces, the U.S. military forces, would have intervened in that conflict and what I am talking about here would have happened.[1]

---

[1] Excerpts from a speech by Commander in Chief Fidel Castro during the conference "Playa Girón: 40 Years Later," held in Havana March 22-23, 2001.